FREDERICK COUNTY
M A R Y L A N D
BACKGROUNDS

Steve Gilland

HERITAGE BOOKS
2012

HERITAGE BOOKS
AN IMPRINT OF HERITAGE BOOKS, INC.

Books, CDs, and more—Worldwide

For our listing of thousands of titles see our website at
www.HeritageBooks.com

Published 2012 by
HERITAGE BOOKS, INC.
Publishing Division
100 Railroad Ave. #104
Westminster, Maryland 21157

Copyright © 1995 Steve Gilland

Other Heritage Books by the author:
Early Families of Frederick County, Maryland, and Adams County, Pennsylvania
Early Families of Frederick County, Maryland, and South Central Pennsylvania

All rights reserved. No part of this book may be reproduced or transmitted in any form or by any means, electronic or mechanical, including photocopying, recording or by any information storage and retrieval system without written permission from the author, except for the inclusion of brief quotations in a review.

International Standard Book Numbers
Paperbound: 978-1-58549-374-6
Clothbound: 978-0-7884-9354-6

"FREDERICK COUNTY BACKGROUNDS" were written by B.F.M. MacPherson, of Gettysburg, PA., under the pseudonym of Samuel Carrick, her ancestor. These articles were published in the Chronicle Newspaper, Emmitsburg, Frederick County, Maryland, in the late 1930's and early 1940's. This compilation was transcribed from carbon copies of the original manuscript. Unfortunately some of the copy was missing and therefore this is an incomplete record. These articles were researched by B.F.M MacPherson, along with research from other historians and family tradition from members of these families. It must be taken into consideration that family tradition is not always accurate and that there may be error in some of these studies.
- Steve Gilland, Gettysburg, PA.

ABBREVIATIONS

```
b  - born                  12/24/1866 - month/day/year
d  - died                  76/12/15 - age  yrs/mos/ds
m  - married               yrs - years
e  - emigrated             mos - months
bp - baptised              ds - days
dy - died young            d/o - daughter of
bd - buried                s/o - son of
nr - near                  w/o - wife of
ca - circa - about
```

ADELSPERGER

John F. Adelsperger & Ellie M. Duphorne, m 4/18/1878, (Elias Records) (Note: Ellie M. Duphorne was the daughter of Samuel and Maria Duphorne.) John was a schoolmaster, b1/12/1853, d 3/22/1914, bd Elias Lutheran, Ella (Ellie) M. Duphorne Aldelsperger, b 6/4/1853, d 11/18/1923, bd Elias Luth.
children:-
1. Alice Duphorne Adelperger, b 6/15/1883, d 2/29/1916, bd Elias.
2. Barbara Lucy Adelsperger, b 2/19/1886
3. Ruth Maria Adelsperger, b 6/14/1888
4. Esther Adelsperger, b 9/5/1895, d 8/17/1946, bd Elias.
5. Annie Mary Adelsperger, b 6/19/1874(?).
6. Hugh Harold Adelsperger, b 2/21/1881
7. Joshua A. Adelsperger, 1/10/1892 - 1/13/1892, bd Elias.

ADELSPERGER BURIALS ELIAS

Barbara S., wife of J.J. Adelsperger, d 3/1/1896, 46/4/16.

AGNEW

James Agnew - "In memory of / James Agnew / Died December 13, 1798 / Aged 65 years." - Tom's Creek Cemetery Inscription.

Mary Jane Agnew, wife of David Agnew, d 12/14/1886, 65/5/21. bd Tom's Creek Presbyterian.

ANNAN

Dr. Andrew Annan, b 4/29/1805, d 7/8/1896, bd old Tom's Creek Presbyterian, m 4/27/1830, by the Rev. J. Bossler to Elizabeth Motter, b 11/19/1810, d/o Lewis and Mary Martin Motter. d 6/5/1884, bd old Tom's Creek Presbyterian.
Children:-
1. Lt. John M. Annan, United States Army, d Nov 14, 1861, 20/7/28. Enlisted in Army shortly after the outbreak of the Civil War. He was killed, while in camp, when the gun of a comrade went off accidently. At the time he enlisted he was studing for the Presbyterian ministry. bd Tom's Creek Presbyterian.
2. David Landales Annan, 6/23/1851 - 5/22/1862, bd Tom's Creek Presbyterian.
3. Mary Jane Annan, d 8/25/1838, 3/5/24, bd Tom's Creek Presb.
4. William M. Annan, d 12/29/1847, 14/5/22, bd Tom's Creek Presb.
5. Charles E. Annan, d 1/3/1848, 12/8/11, bd Tom's Creek Presb.
6. Helen Francis Annan, d 6/4/1851, 1/11/8, bd Tom's Creek Presb.

Lt. John Motter Annan was the son of Dr. Andrew and Elizabeth Motter Annan, was born in Emmitsburg, Maryland on March 17, 1841. He made a profession of religion in early life. With a view to prepare for the ministry, he entered LaFayette College on September 7, 1859. By the time he had passed through the Junior Class, the rebellion had broken out, and the call for volunteers had been sounded throughout the land. To this patriotic appeal his loyal heart responded. He entered in Company "C", the First Brigade of the Potomac Home Brigade, Maryland Calvary, Captain John Horner, and was made First Lieutenant of the Company. He was an efficient officer and took a great interest in the moral and spiritual welfare of the soldiers. He organized a prayer meeting in one of the tents of the Company and by personal effort sought to lead his comrades to the Saviour, as the best preparation they could make for battle.

While at Camp Thomas, Frederick County, Maryland, and before the Company had been called into active service, Lt. Annan was suddenly cut down by a distressing casualty. This occurred on November 13, 1861, by the accidental discharge of a carbine in the hands of a private soldier with whom he was conversing. He died from the effects of the wound on the following day." - Emmitsburg Chronicle. The marker at Lt. Annan's grave is somewhat unusual. A beautiful carved American Eagle is depicted thereon.

- Robert(1) Annan, was b & d in Scotland. He married into the Landales family. He was the father of the Rev. Robert(2) Annan, the first of the family to emigrate to America.

- Rev. Robert(2) Annan was b in the town of Capar, Fife, Scotland, in 1742, studied theology at the University of Saint Andrew's under Alexander Moncrieff, licensed by the Presbytery of Perth. The young minister arrived in New York in 1761. In 1765 he was minister over the Associate Congregation at Neelytown, NY and remainded there for fourteen years. In 1783 he removed from Neelytown to Boston and in 1786 moved to Philadelphia, Pennsylvania. In 1801 or 1802 he removed to Baltimore, Maryland, to a pastoral of a newly found congregation. Eleven years later he retired to his home in York County, Pennsylvania. He died December 10, 1810 as a result of an accident. He was 'thrown with great violence from his carriage'. He was interred in the burial ground of Octorara Church. He married twice. In 1764 he m Margaret, the daughter of William Cochran, of Carrollsburg (Carroll's Tract) now Adams County, Pennsylvania. She d 10/13/1793. He m 2 Elizabeth Hawthorne, d/o Samuel & Elizabeth Hawthorne. Elizabeth d 7/23/1813, Lancaster Co., PA.

The Rev Robert and Margaret Cochran Annan were the parents of three children:-
1. Dr. Robert(3) Landales Annan 1765-1827, m Mary Cochran 1765-1826.
2. William(3) Annan, 1767-1797, m Jennett Schuyler.
3. Margaret(3) Annan 1789-1826, m1 John Curtis Clay, m2 Simmons Edey.

The Rev Robert and his second wife, Elizabeth Hawthorne Annan were the parents of one known son:-
1. Dr. Samuel(3) Annan, 1797 - 1868, m1 Mary Jane McKaleb, m2 Ann Buchanan.

- Dr. Robert Landales(3) Annan, s/o Rev Robert(2) & Margaret Cochran Annan, b 1765, d July 12, 1827, age 62, m Mary Cochran, b 1765, d Feb 7, 1828, age 57. The Dr. Robert Landales Annan, physician and surgeon, practiced his profession 'on both sides of the Mason and Dixon Line'. He was a graduate of Brown University, Providence, Rhode Island, and a pupil of Dr. Rush of Philadelphia, PA.

According to family history Dr. & Mrs. Robert Annan were first interred in the Tract graveyard, but were later removed to Tom's Creek Presbyterian churchyard. They were the parents of nine children, two of which were listed:-
1. Sally(4) Annan, 1792-1796.
2. Robert(4) Annan, 1793-1866, m Mary J. Moore 1809-1885, both bd Tom's Creek Presbyterian.

-Robert(4) Annan s/o Dr. Robert Landales(3) Annan & Mary Cochran Annan, b 1793 Oct 27, d 1866 Apr 7, age 72 yrs, bd Tom's Creek Presbyterian, m Mary J. Moore, b May 4, 1809, d 1885 (Aug 13, 1883/5), age 74 yrs., bd Tom's Creek Presbyterian. children:-
1. Margaret(5) Annan, 1836-1854, bd Annan plot Tom's Creek Presb.
2. Mary (Martha Jane) Annan, d 1834, 4/9/18, bd "   "   "
3. Robert Landales(5) Annan, 1832-1844, 11/11/8, "   "   "
4. James Moore(5) Annan, d 1835, 0/9/6, bd   "   "   "
5. Henry Clay(5) Annan,1843-1914, m Elizabeth McCandless
6. Mary Jane(5) Annan, d 1835, 4/5/24, bd Annan plot Tom's Creek.
7. Ann Eliza(5) Annan Galt, m Henry Galt.

- Dr. Robert Lewis Annan, b 2/22/1831, d 1/14/1907. bd Tom's Creek Presbyterian, ml Alice C. Motter, d/o Lewis Martin Motter, 1843-1878, children:-
1. Gertrude Annan, 3/11/1870 - 2/28/1943, bd Tom's Creek Presb.
2. Elizabeth Annan, d 8/21/1872, bd Tom's Creek Presbyterian.
3. Ann Annan, d Jan 1971, bd Tom's Creek Presbyterian.

- Dr. Samuel Annan, s/o Rev. Robert Annan and Elizabeth Hawthorne Annan, b 1797, d 1868. Samuel studied medicine and in due time received his degree of MD. After the death of his first wife he became a resident of Baltimore, MD.
m 1 Mary Jane McKaleb, d/o Major John and Mary Ann Clingan McKaleb, d 7/23/1825, 21/11/0, bd Piney Creek Presbyterian, Harney, MD. children:-
1. Emily Annan
2. William Howard Annan
Samuel's second wife, Ann Buchanan, 1816-1864.

"ANTRIM" - Ege - McKaleb - Clabaugh - Lamberton

"Antrim", Taneytown, Carroll Co., MD., built in 1844, by Col. Andew Ege, 17 room manor house. It was built by Col. Andrew Ege, for his bride, Margaret Ann McKaleb, d/o Major John McKaleb. Major McKaleb gave the land for the manor and the tract alone contained 2600 acres. It is said that Col. Ege 'went broke' in the process of construction and shortly after the completion it was sold to the Piper family of Carroll Co., MD. George Washington Clabaugh, a farmer bought 'Antrim' in 1860. Col. Ege's wife died in 1851 so even had the estate remained in the possesion of her husband she would not have lived to long to enjoy it.

The estate came down through a succession of owners to George W. Clabaugh sometime in 1860. On the death of Mr. Clabaugh's widow the property came into the possession of their eldest son, Harry W. Clabaugh, Chief Justice in the District of Columbia Supreme Court and Maryland Attorney General ... Judge Clabaugh died in 1908 and left the property to his wife, Katherine Swope Clabaugh. In 1938 it became the property of the Lamberton family.

Legend has it that looking from the observation tower of Antrim a Union observer in the Army of General Meade signalled the advances of on coming Confederates during the Battle of Gettysburg. Some say the observer was General Meade himself.

ASHBAUGH

William H. Ashbaugh, Soldier of the Civil War, b 3/29/1837, d 4/24/1912, bd Mountainview Emmitsburg.
M.F. Shuff Burial Records - William H. Ashbaugh, d 4/24/1912, 75 yrs., Soldier.
Mrs. William H. Ashbaugh, d 6/31/1905, 70 yrs.

BARLOW

Col. Stephen Barlow, m Hester McNaughton(4) BIRNIE, d/o Clotworthy(3) and Harriet Worthington Birnie. Their children:-
1. Alice Worthington Barlow, b 1875
2. Helen M. Barlow, 1865-1953.
3. Maxwell Barlow
4. Stephen Barlow, 1874-1926.

BARTON

- Isaac D. Barton & Sophia Gaugh, both of Frederick County, Maryland, m 1/11/1846, at St. James Lutheran Gettysburg, PA., by Rev. Benjamin Keller.

- Thomas H. and Harriet Barton, children;-
1. Emma Catherine Barton, b 5/8/1858
2. Harriet Rebecca Barton, b 3/3/1869
3. William Henry Barton, b 12/13/1861.

BAUGHER - BAGER

- The Rev. John George Baugher (Bager) was born 3/19/1746(?), at Niederlingweiter in Nassau, Saarbrucken. He was ordained at Simmern in December 1749. He was pastor at Simmern in the Palatinate before he came to America and while there he married Anna Elizabeth Schwal. Their infant son, Carl Theodore Bager died in Holland while on their way to America. They arrived in Philadelphia on the ship "Bowley" on Oct 23, 1752. The Rev. John Casper Stover met the Rev. and Mrs. Bager when they landed and and took them to Lebanon, Pennsylvania. In the same year Rev. Bager took charge of the congregation at Hanover, Pa. In 1763 he was called to St. John's Lutheran Church in New York City and remained their until 1767, at which time he returned to Pennsylvania and took charge of the Lutheran congregation at York. By 1768 he was back at his home "Poplar Springs" in the Pigeon Hills.

As a traveling minister he rode horseback to Chambersburg and south to Baltimore. The hardships he must have endured - how discouraged he must have been at times - but he carried his service on. He was pastor again at Hanover from 1777 to 1785.

The Rev. John George Baugher (Bager) died June 9th 1791. His wife Anna Elizabeth died Dec 7, 1790. Both were buried at the Lutheran churchyard at Abbottstown. This plot was sometimes called the 'old Winebrenner Graveyard' and the 'old Dutch Cemetery'.

- Frederick Baugher, of Abbottstown, s/o the Rev. John George Baugher, had 2 sons, Joseph Baugher and Isaac Baugher.

- John Christian Frederick Baugher, known as "Frederick" was the son of the Rev. John George Bager (Baugher) and his wife Anna Elizabeth Schwal. He lived in Abbottstown and had a tannery. He married Catherine Motter, the sister of Lewis Motter of Emmitsburg, Maryland. He was born 1764 and died 1831. His wife, Catherine was born 1761 and died 1862. She lived to be 101 years. They were the parents of 14 children. Two of their sons were:-
1. Isaac Baugher, an early merchant of Emmitsburg, married Anna E. (?), both bd Mt. Olivet Cemetery, Frederick, MD.
2. Joseph Baugher, was a large land owner in the vicinity of Fairfield, which included the present day Fountaindale. He established a tannery in a meadow along a creek, and built a somewhat 'elaborate' house with a fountain in the front yard, Gradually a settlement came into being and was known as "Baugher's Dale". When a post office was established here in 1837 the name was changed to "Fountain Dale" because of the fountain in the Baugher yard. Mr. Joseph Baugher was also chosen the first postmaster. He married Louisa, the daughter of Christopher and Catherine Hager, of Lancaster County, Pennsylvania. She was born 1791 and died 1828 at Fountain Dale. Joseph and his wife are buried at Elias Lutheran Churchyard, Emmitsburg.

BEAM

The Beam family were natives of Westminister, Carroll County, Maryland. George (P. or F.) Beam married Jane Guthrie and went into partnership with her father, Adam Guthrie, in the livery stable business, and became a resident of of Emmistburg.
- George Beam, 4/19/1835 - 11/21/1917, operated 'Guthrie and Beam's Livery Stable' of Emmitsburg, m Jane, d/o Adam and Margaret Wagner Guthrie, of Emmitsburg. They had one known son;
1. Harry Beam, m Lucy Hundly, of St. Louis, Missouri, both died at the home of their son and are buried at Waynesboro, PA.

Beam cemetery inscriptions at Tom's Creek Presbyterian Cemetery, near Emmitsburg:-
1. Geo. P. Beam   4/19/1835 - 11/21/1917
2. Jane Guthrie Beam   2/15/1836 - 8/28/1911
3. Susan G. Beam, d/o Robert & Elizabeth Beam, 3/10/1917 - 4/8/1920.

BEARD

- Frederick Beard, carpenter, Soldier of the American Revolution, pioneer settler at Tom's Creek Hundred, one of the first inhabitants of the town of Emmitsburg, is buried at Elias Lutheran churchyard. The inscriptions follows:- "In memory of / Frederick Beard / Died March 9, 1842 / Aged 83 years, 5 months, / and 9 days." "In memory of / Magdalena Beard / wife of Frederick Beard / Died August 19, 1849 / Aged 86 years, 3 months, / and 10 days."
Frederick Beard - "Died, March 8, 1842, Mr. Frederick Beard, of Liberty Twp., Adams County, PA., aged 84 years. A Patriot of the Revolution." (Gettysburg 'Adams Centinal') Frederick Beard, his wife, and several of their children are interred in Elias Lutheran Churchyard, Emmitsburg.
Frederick died without a will and his estate was administered by the Orphan's Court of Adams County. According to the records his heirs consisted of the following;- " Monday February 27, 1843 - Heirs and Legal Representatives of Frederick Beard, late of Liberty Twp., Adams County, Pennsylvania, Deceased - Mary Magdalena Beard, the widow of Frederick Beard, and issue as follows:- Jacob Beard, John Beard, Frederick Beard, George Beard, Samuel Beard, Polly Beard intermarried with Robert Linn, Catherine Beard intermarried with Henry Reese, Margaret Beard intermarried with John Kerr, Elizabeth Beard intermarried with Christopher Seitz and who both died before the death of said intestate, leaving issue:- Joshua Seitz, Erastus Seitz, Jeremiah Seitz and Hetty Maria Seitz intermarried with Barney Devine, Margaret Beard intermarried with John McIntire, Joshua Beard, who also died before intestate, leaving issue:- Obed Beard, Napoleon A. Beard, Athabiad Beard, and Melinde Beard; all of whom are still in their minority, David Beard, who also died before Intestate, leaving issue:- Adeline Beard, Louisa Beard, Mary Jane Beard, and John Beard, all of whom are still in their minority."
- Beard Family Burials at Elias Lutheran Churchyard:-
1. Frederick Beard, d 9 Mar 1842, 83/5/9
2. Magdalena w/o Frederick Beard, d 19 Aug 1849, 86/3/10
3. George Beard, d 18 Nov 1843, 49/0/16
4. Lydia Sylvia Beard, d/o Samuel & Elizabeth Beard, d 10 Jan 1845, 4/6/10
5. Sarah Beard, d 7 July 1838, 64/6/1

BECK
- Rev. Ludwick Beck - According to the Hagerstown Lutheran Records he died at "Thomas Creek" in 1766 and was interred in that Churchyard.

BENSILL
- William Bensill, d 9/24/1906, 33 yrs. - MF Shuff Burial Records.

BIGHAM
- The Bighams were early settlers of the Marsh Creek Settlement in what is now Adams County, Pennsylvania. They have an old gravestone in the Upper Marsh Creek Presbyterian Cemetery with the family coat - of - arms cut thereon. They were Scots from the North of Ireland and came to America in the early part of the eighteenth century.

- Bigham Family plot at Tom's Creek Presbyterian, near Emmitsburg, Maryland.
1. Margaret Bigham, d 10/13/1739, 70 yrs.
2. Robert Bigham, d 11/25/1798, 88 yrs.
3. James Snodgrass, d 5/6/1794, 30 yrs.
4. William Bigham, d 5/9/1829, 72 yrs.

BIRNIE
- Clotworthy(1) Birnie, 1717-1768, a Native of Ireland. Many of his descendants are interred at Piney Creek Presbyterian Churchyard near Harney, Maryland.

- Clotworthy(1) Birnie, born 1717 in Ireland, died 1768. He married Margaret Scott in 1740. They were the ancestors of the Maryland Birnies. They came to America about 1763. Margaret Scott Birnie was born in Ireland in 1717, the daughter of Francis Scott (d 1766) and Margaret Craig Scott (d 1741). [Note: Francis Scott Key, lawyer and poet, churchman and the author of the national anthem of the United States, was a descendant of Francis Scott and Margaret Craig Scott.]
Clotworthy(1) and Margaret Scott Birnie were the parents of the following children:-
1. Henry(2) Birnie, 1741-1745
2. Margaret(2) Birnie, 1742-1745
3. Hugh(2) Birnie, 1746-1822, came to America in 1763. He is buried at Piney Creek Presbyterian. "In memory of / Hugh Birnie / A Native of Ireland / Died August 21, 1822 / Aged 76 years."
4. Dr. John(2) Birnie, 1749-1779, d at Annapolis, MD.
5. Francis(2) Birnie, d infancy
6. Margaret(2) Birnie, 1753-1784

7. Clotworthy(2) Birnie, d infancy
8. Upton(2) Birnie, d infancy
9. Francis Upton(2) Birnie, d at sea, 1763.
10. Clotworthy(2) Birnie, 1765-1845, m Hester McNaughton, on 11/23/1793 at Glenaran, Ireland. Clotworthy built Thorndale, the family estate in Carroll County, Maryland. His land grant, at one time, consisted of 3000 acres. Here at Thorndale, the school for young ladies was established.

Clotworthy(2) Birnie, 1765-1845, m Hester McNaughton, They emigrated from Ireland in 1810. Their seven older children were born in Ireland. They were the parents of 11 children:-
1. Rogers(3) Birnie, 1811-1891, born at Glen Burn, now Carroll Co. MD, and died at Thorndale. m Amelia Harry d/o George & Amelia Knod Harry, both buried at Piney Creek Presbyterian, Harney, MD.
2. Margaret(3) Birnie, 1794-1878, born at Bellyean, Ireland, one of the teachers at Thorndale School. She never married and was buried at Pineycreek Presbyterian.
3. Hester(3) Birnie, 1796-1855, born at Belfast, Ireland, schoolmastress at Thorndale School, never married, and buried at Pineycreek Presbyterian.
4. Rose(3) Birnie, 1798-1893, born at Belfast, Ireland, teacher at Thorndale School, never married, bd Piney Creek Presbyterian.
5. Clotworthy Birnie, 1799-1882, m Harriet Worthington
6. Upton(3) Birnie, 1801-1838, born Chichester Quay, Belfast, Ireland. bd Piney Creek Presbyterian.
7. Ellen(3) Birnie, 1805-1890, born Bouers Hill, Belfast, Ireland, teacher at Thorndale School, bd Piney Creek Presbyterian. She was the twin sister to Ann.
8. Ann(3) Birnie, twin, 1805-1893
9. Frances(3) Birnie, b & d 1807.
10. Frances(3) Birnie, 1809-1904, born Belfast, Ireland, d at Taneytown, teacher at Thorndale School, and bd Piney Creek Presbyterian.
[NOTE: According to this research Clotworthy(2) Birnie was born 1765 in Ireland, two years after his parents emigration to America in 1763.]

- Clotworthy(3) Birnie, s/o Clotworthy(2) and Hester McNaughton Birnie. He married Harriet Worthington and had issue:-
1. Clotworthy Upton(4) Birnie, b 1831
2. Robert Emmit(4) Birnie, b 1835
3. Edward(4) Birnie, m Jenny (?)
4. Harriet E.(4) Birnie Noble, b 1841, m Capt. Noble
5. Hester 'Hessy' McNaughton Birnie Barlow, b 1843, m Col. Stephen Barlow
6. William(4) Birnie
7. Mary Worthington(4) Birnie.

- Rogers(3) Birnie, s/o Clotworthy(2) and Hester McNaughton Birnie was born 1811. He married Amelia Harry d/o George and Amelia Knod Harry of Washington Co., Md. Both Rogers and Amelia are buried at Harney Piney Creek Presbyterian. Their children:-
1. Margaret(4) Birnie, 1840-1903, m Rev. Wm. Scarborough
2. Dr. Clotworthy(4) Birnie, 1843-1917, practiced medicine in Taneytown, Md., bd Harney Presbyterian, Piney Creek.
3. George Harry(4) Birnie, 1845-1925, m Elizabeth Zollickoffer, 1851-1937, both bd Harney Piney Creek Presbyterian, Their children:-
    1. Eliza Roberts(5) Birnie, 1884-1954, bd Piney Creek
    2. Eleanor(5) Birnie, b 1887, bd Piney Creek
    3. Clotworthy(5) Birnie, b 1889, m Dorothy Chapman Biggs, 1898-1950, both bd Piney Creek.
4. Upton(4) Birnie, 1848-1909, m Susan Galt, 1849-1937, both bd Piney Creek Presbyterian. Susan Galt was the d/o Matthew and Mary Galt. Their children:-
    1. Samuel Galt(5) Birnie, 1875-1938, bd Piney Creek.
    2. Upton(5) Birnie, b 1877, m Sue Schench, 1878-1956.
5. Colonel Rogers(4) Birnie, 1851-1939, m Helen Gunn, b 1855, both bd West Point Military Academy Cemetery.
6. Hester McNaughton(4) Birnie, 1854-1938, m Dr. Robert L. Annan, 1831-1907, both bd Tom's Creek Presbyterian.
7. Amelia(4) Birnie, 1856-1934, unmarried, bd Piney Creek
8. Ann M.(4) Birnie, 1860-1916, m George Clabaugh, 1864-1926, both bd Piney Creek.

BLAIR

- William G. Blair, d 5/4/1900, 54 yrs. - M.F. Shuff Burial Records. William G. Blair, 1844 - 1900, m Mary A., d 7/5/1915, both bd Emmitsburg Mountain View.

BOLLINGER

- Mrs. Jacob Bollinger, d 6/21/1894, 74 yrs. - M.F. Shuff Burial Records. Note: Christina Overholtzer Bollinger, the wife of Jacob Bollinger, both bd Emmitsburg Mountain View. Jacob Bollinger 1808-1883, Christina Bollinger 1819-1894.

BRECKENRIDGE

- Rev. James Grier Breckenridge, grandson of Rev. James Grier, was a member of Piney Creek Church and entered the Presbyterian ministry in 1833. Both he and his wife died comparatively young and are buried in Piney Creek churchyard near Harney, MD.

- Rev. James Breckenridge - "The Rev. James Breckenridge, son of Robert and Mary Grier Breckenridge, was born in Carroll Co., Md., on May 30, 1808. His parents were members of the Piney Creek Presbyterian Church. He received his educatiion at Dickinson College, Carlise, PA., and Princeton Theological Seminary. He was a minister at Bedford, PA. and Schellsburg, PA., While visiting family in Carroll County, Md., the young minister and his wife were 'prostrated' by typhoid fever, from which neither recovered. The Rev. Breckenridge died Nov. 1, 1833 and his wife Mary died Nov. 19, 1833. They were buried in the family plot at Piney Creek Presbyterian churchyard.

- Rebecca McKinney Breckenridge - "Sacred / to the memory of / Rebecca McKinney Breckenridge / daughter of William Breckenridge / Died April 16, 1821 / Aged 37 years." - Harney Presbyterian Cemetery Inscription.

- Robert Breckenridge - "Buried in the 'old section' of of Piney Creek churchyard are members of the Breckenridge family. The inscriptions as follows;- "In memory of / Robert Breckenridge / Died June 29, 1821 / Age 30 (?) years / Also / Mary Breckenridge / consort of Robert Breckenridge / Died August 9, 1838 / aged 53 years." Note:- Robert Breckenridge was a member of the Piney Creek church. He was married to Mary Grier, the d/o the Rev. James Grier, pastor of the Deep Run Church, Bucks Co., Pa., Robert and Mary Grier Breckenridge were the parents of the Rev. James Grier Breckenridge and Mitilda Breckenridge Allison, of Emmitsburg, MD. The Rev. James Grier Breckenridge and his wife are interred in the family plot at Piney Creek churchyard. The inscriptions as follows:- "Sacred / to the memory of / the Rev. James G. Breckenridge / Died October 31, 1833 / Aged 26 years./ Also / Sarah M. Breckenridge / consort of / the Rev. James G. Breckenridge / Died November 19, 1833 / Aged 30 years."

- William Breckenridge - "Sacred / to the memory of / William Breckenridge / Died April 10, 1844 / Aged 89 years." - Piney Creek Presbyterian Cemetery inscriptions.

BROWN

- David H. Brown, 1/19/1847 - 6/17/1905, m Malinda, 1/23/1848 - 11/15/1907, 59 yrs., both bd Emmitsburg Mountain View.

- Enoch Brown - see Susan King Cunningham, and Eleanor Cochran Junkin.

- Mrs. Isaac Brown, Jr., d 12/8/1905, 42 yrs. - M.F. Shuff Burial Records.

- Colonel Ridgely Brown, C.S.A. - "Colonel Ridgely Brown, C.S.A. On May 15, 1862, with seventeen young Marylanders, organized the Company A First Maryland Cavalry. He served consistently and gallantly, rising from private to the rank of Lieutenant - Colonel. He was killed at Dabney's Ferry, South Anne River, Virginia, on June 1, 1864. His body was returned to his home farm, one mile north of the village of Unity, Montgomery County, Maryland and interred in the family burial ground, located not far from the old mansion house known as "Elton" (stone manor house). "Elton / The Birthplace of Ridgely Brown, C.S.A. / 1833-1864". There is a Confederate States Army marker at Col. Brown's grave.

Brown Family Burial Ground

1. Alice B. Brown, d 28 May 1816, 17/0/0
2. Mary E. Brown, d 21 May 1836, 35/0/11
3. Annie Brown, 10 Oct 1811 - 29 April 1892, 80/6/19
4. Sally R. Brown, d 16 Jan 1899, 20/0/0
5. Ridgely Brown, d 1 June 1864, 30/9/19, C.S.A., Confederate States Army Marker.
6. Louise M. Brown, d 19 Feb 1857, 40/0/18
7. Elizabeth Ridgely Brown, d 15 Jan 1882, 86/0/0
8. Sarah Ridgely Brown, d 31 Mar 1866, 73/6/12.

- Sarah Ridgely Griffith Brown, the daughter of Nicholas and Ann Ridgely Griffith, the wife of Amos Brown and the mother of Colonel Ridgely Brown, was born in 1792. She married Amos Brown of Philadelphia, PA., in 1808. After their marriage they came to live at Elton. Amos Brown died about 1845.

BRUCE

General Normand Bruce was the founder of Bruceville, Frederick County, Maryland. The Bruce and Flemings families were intermarried.

BUFFINGTON

Ephraim Buffington, b 8/11/1832, d 3/31/1895, m. Louisa Ohler, d/o John and Catherine Ohler (5/12/1830-8/4/1922), both bd Middleburg Methodist.

BYERS

- BYERS FAMILY - by Edward McPherson, historian.
"The first German settler in the western part of what is now Adams County, Pennsylvania, was Samuel Byers, who in 1769, established himself on the farm since owned by Christian Byers - on the road leading from Gettysburg to Fairfield, in Highland Twp. The tract was known as Clearfield (embracing at the time what have since become the Byers and Wintrode farms. 1889). This tract was bought by the said Samuel Byers for forty pounds.

David Byers, a son of Samuel Byers and a brother Christian Byers, bought land in the Knoxlyn neighborhood and there is a family burial ground on this property.

Samuel Byers, of Clearfield was probably a son of David Byers, of Donegal, Lancaster Co., PA.

David Byers, according to the historian William Henry Egle, came from the North of Ireland into Donegal, Lancaster Co., PA., in 1730. He died May 20, 1743. In his will he mentions the following members of his family:-
1. son, David (apparently emigrated to what is now Adams County)
2. son, John, m Rebecca Galbraith, widow of Robert Galbraith, and moved to Cumberland Co., PA., in 1754/5

3. son, Samuel (apparently emigrated to what is now Adams County, PA.)
4. wife, Mary Byers.

- David Byers - "The Byers family were of Scotch descent. There is a tradition in the family that one of David Byers' son emigrated into Maryland.
    Located near Knoxlyn, in what is now Adams County, PA., on what is known as the John Bream Farm, is the Byers family burial ground. Here is interred David Byers, the Revolutionary ancestor of the fammily. In his will, which was written in 1828 and entered to probate in 1831, David Byers, mentions the following members of his family:- Sons:- John Byers, David Byers; Micheal Byers; George Byers; and Christian Byers. Daughters:- Fanny Byers intermarried with Joel Brayble, Children of my daughter, Mary Byers, now deceased, formerly intermarried with Samuel Carpenter, Elizabeth Byers intermarried with Micheal Stoner. David Byers was a Soldier of the American Revolution and pioneer settler in the Manor of the Masque.

- Joseph Byers, of 'Pleasant Level', married Eleanor Gilbert, of Carroll County, MD. They may have resided in Carroll County before moving to the Emmitsburg District. One of their sons, George Gambell Byers was born 26 Sept 1861, m 15 April 1890 to Nellie G. Patterson of Adams County, PA. Other children of Joseph Byers were:- Jacob Krise Byers, M. Janette Byers, Gilbert G. Byers, Carrie J. Byers, and Maggie Byers Black.
- Joseph Byers d April 11, 1898 - aged 74 years & 22 days. Eleanor Gilbert Byers, wife of Joseph Byers, d Feb 5, 1912. Both are bd Emmitsburg Elias Lutheran churchyard. The inscription follows:- "In memory of Joseph Byers / Born March 19, 1824 / Died April 11, 1898." "In memory of / Eleanor Byers / wife of Joseph Byers / Born Jan 7, 1828 / Died Feb 5, 1912."
- Joseph Byers, b 3/19/1824, d 4/11/1898, m Eleanor Gilbert, (1/7/1828-2/5/1912), d/o Adam & Catherine Diffenderfer Gilbert.
- Joseph Byers and Eleanor Gilbert Byers, Children:-
1. Gilbert G. Byers, d 10/8/1869, 2/10/8, bd Emmitsburg Elias.
2. Carrie J. Byers, 7/1/1863 - 11/16/1951, bd Emmitsburg Elias.
3. Maggie Byers Black, m 1888, at Gettysburg, PA., to Guy Black, of Mechanicstown (Thurmont), MD.
4. M. Janette Byers, d 2/4/1944, 72/11/25, bd Arlington National Cemetery, nurse, served at one time in Panama and Havana, Cuba. In both countries she served as a superintendant of hospital.
5. Blanche G. Byers Rhodes, m 7/4/1907, at the First English Church, Balt., MD., to J. Lewis Rhodes.
6. Jacob Krise Byers, 1864-1951, m1 Emma J. Bollinger, m2 1905 Ada G. Fitez.
7. George Gambell Byers, m 1890 to Nellie Patterson d/o Milliard Patterson, of Freedom Twp.

- Jacob Krise Byers, 1864 - 1951, bd Emmitsburg Mountain View Cemetery, s/o Joseph and Eleanor Gilbert Byers. m1 Emma J. Bollinger (1869-1900), bd Mt. View. Children:-
1. Maud Elizabeth Byers.
2. Harry Bryan Byers.
3. Luther Gilbert Byers.
4. Charles Robert Byers, d 3/30/1906, 3/6/0, bd Mt. View.
Jacob m2 1905, Ada G. Fitez, 1870-1957, bd Mt. View. Children:-
1. Ethel Grace Byers, b 7/10/1906
2. Hazel Marguerite Byers, b 4/14/1908
3. Merle Glenn Byers, b 3/16/1915.
4. Jacob Krise Byers, Jr., b 2/27/1918.

CALDWELL

- Francis T. "Frank" Caldwell, 4/22/1828 - 9/30/1905, bd Emmitsburg Mt. View, - Frank Caldwell, d 9/30/1905, age 77 yrs - M.F. Shuff Burial Records.

- John Caldwell, d 6/1/1907, 34 yrs., - M.F. Shuff Burial Records, bd Emmitsburg Mt. View - John W. Caldwell, b 6/9/1873, d 5/31/1907.

CHURCHES AND CEMETERIES

CLOSE FAMILY CEMETERY - SEE WHITMORE FAMILY CEMETERY.

CONCORDIA - "THE UNION CHURCH OF CONCORDIA - One country church, which has long since disappeared, was the one known as the 'Union Church of Concordia'. It stood on what was known as Chapel Road, in Mount Joy Township, Adams County, Pennsylvania. However, due to the fact that it was located not far from the Mason and Dixon Line it included some Frederick County, Maryland families among its membership.

Concordia was a 'union church' and served both the Lutheran and Reformed congregations. It was a small frame structure, erected on an embankment with large sandstone steps which were still in place in the 1930's and then were removed when the road was repaired.

Concordia as a parish had practically ceased to exist by the formation of Mount Joy Lutheran Church. The Concordia Church records became a part of Mount Joy Records. The records contained a list of 28 baptisms, no marriage or burial records although it is known that 'a dozen or more' burials took place in the ground to the east and rear of the church.

The data pertaining to Concordia parish follows - as given in the record:- On Nov 10, 1824 the cornerstone of the present church was layed ... after this church building was erected, the dedication ceremony was held on Nov 5 and 6, 1825 ... Pastor Uhlhorn and Pastor Leidy preached ... On Nov 6 Pastor Uhlman gave his dedicatory sermon and the Church received the name. The Union Church of Concordia.

CHURCHES AND CEMETERIES

In the list of baptisms, the following family names are to be found:- Bauer, Linn, Sadler, Eichelberger, Senss, Wolf, Kober, Stier, Jungling, Orendorf, Hoover, Mehring, Zahn, Merckle, Feaser, Bowers, Bentzel, Snider and Konig.

ELDER FAMILY CEMETERY - a half mile from Mount Saint Mary's College, near Emmitsburg, MD.
The old burial ground of the Elder family, laid out and set aside by William Elder remains to this day - a memorial to that Roman Catholic pioneer. The burial ground laid out on his farm, 'Pleasant Level', half a mile from Mount Saint Marys' College. Here he built a permanent home with a house - chapel attached, which stood until 1862 and was known as "Elder's Station". Inscriptions from this cemetery:-

1. 'In memory of / William ELder, Sr. / Born 1707 / Died / April 22, 1775.'
2. 'In memory of / Ann Elder / wife of William Elder, Sr. / Died August 11, 1739 / Aged 30 Years.' Note: Ann Wheeler Elder, the first wife of William Elder.
3. 'In memory of / Jacoba Clementina Livers / Elder / Wife of William Elder / Senior / Died September 19, 1807 / Aged 90 Years.' Note: Jacoba Clementina Livers Elder was the daughter of Arnold Livers and the second wife of William Elder.
4. 'In memory of / Sarah Delozier / Born October 4, 1754 / Died March 1, 1780.' Note: Sarah Delozier was probably related to Phebe Delozier who was the wife of Richard Elder, s/o William Elder.
5. 'In memory of / Aloysius Elder / Died August 11, 1827 / Aged 70 years.' Note: Aloysius Elder was the son of William and Jacoba Clementine Livers Elder.
6. 'In memory of / Mary Elder / wife of Aloysius Elder/ Born March 27, 1774 / Died March 18, 1842.' Note: Mary, the wife of Aloysius Elder, who may have been the last burial made in this plot.
7. 'In memory of Henry Thompson / Born November 2, 1777, / Died September 7, 1800.' Note: Nothing is known pertaining to this man.
8. In memory of / Arnold Elder / Born February 15, 1745 / Died February 22, 1812.' Note: Arnold was the son of William and Jacoba Clementina Livers Elder. It was from this member of the Elder family that the title for the farm upon which stands Mount Saint Mary's College was obtained.

- There is a tradition that an infant, born to a family living at "Clairvoux", was interred, early in the Twentieth century, in this burial ground. If so the grave is unmarked.

CHURCHES AND CEMETERIES

ELIAS LUTHERAN CHURCH, EMMITSBURG, MARYLAND - References:-
Helman's "HISTORY OF EMMITSBURG"
Scharf's "HISTORY OF WESTERN MARYLAND"
William's "HISTORY OF FREDERICK COUNTY"

Elias Lutheran and Reformed Churchyard - Located back and to the west of Elias church, in all there are over nine hundred and forty marked graves. At least one hundred and fifty unmarked burial sites and twenty-three graves designated by fieldstones without inscriptions. These grounds were first put to use as a 'place of sepulchre' in 1797. The name of the first person interred therein cannot be determined at this late date - but - the earliest graves are located immediately back of the church. The majority in this section are unmarked.

A copy of the inscriptions, from Elias churchyard, made in 1956, has been placed in the parish archives. In 1906 James A. Helman in his "History of Emmitsburg, Maryland", wrote of Elias Lutheran and Reformed churchyard:- "The Lutheran Cemetery in town holds embosomed many of the early settlers and their children to the fifth generation ... Many graves of the early settlers are not marked ... yet they sleep on, undisturbed, visitors of an immortality bequeathed to all the sons of men."

- EMMITSBURG MOUNTAIN VIEW CEMETERY - Emmitsburg Chronicle - Dec 9, 1882 - "... Mt. View Cemetery ... was incorporated in May 1881, since which time quite a number of lots have been sold and interments made ..."

- FOUNTAINDALE LUTHERAN CHURCH, FOUNTAINDALE, HAMILTONBAN TWP., ADAMS COUNTY, PENNSYLVANIA. - This burial ground of the Lutheran church at Fountaindale was the 'daughter' of Elias Church, Emmitsburg, Maryland.

The stone church ediface was erected in 1842 on a plot of ground on the south side of the tract owned, at that time, by Joseph and Isaac Baugher. As an active force it lasted about sixteen years and today only the remains of the old graveyard mark the spot.

During the first quarter of the twentieth century there were 'at least 25 or 30 tombstone' markers in the churchyard. This is the testimony of a man who well remembers the place for he lived on the land adjoining. The churchyard was enclosed by a stonewall. The foundation walls of the church could still be seen at that time - it stood in the upper or western end of the enclosure.

During the Confederate retreat, after the Battle of Gettysburg, a wounded Confederate soldier was left at the John Musselman farm, now the Elevation Orchards. He died and was buried in the eastern end of this churchyard. His grave was marked but the white marble stone has long since disappeared. Even his name has been lost.

In the Records of Trinity Lutheran Church, Taneytown, Md., are listed the Communions at Fountaindale. Those who took the Sacrament on December 9, 1842, are as follows:- Henry Arbaugh, Rebecca Arbaugh, Matilda Arbaugh, Joseph Baugher, Elizabeth Baugher, Levi Baird, Miram (Hiram) Baird, Margaret Baird, Catherine Baird, widow, Rachel Ann Baird, Sarah Baird, Magdelene Baird, James Cochran, Susan C chran, Margaret Donaldson, Margaret Dentler, Amelia Ann Eyler, Sarah Eyler, Margaret Lucinda Eyler, Susanna Eyler, Eliza Eyler, John Eyler, Samuel Flohr, Ann Eliza Flohr, Catherine Ann Flohr, Mary Ann Geiger, Elizabeth Gordon, Jacob Hafleigh, Susan Hafleigh, Mary Ann Hafleigh, Mary Ann Hoover, Eliza Hoke, Eliza Hutchison, Eli Jones, Catherine Jones, Catherine McDonnel, Catherine Reese, Violetta Reese, William Sprenkle, Jeremiah Sites, Louisa Seitz, Louise Seitz, Mary Sprenkle, Elizabeth Sprenkle, William Steel, Isaac Weagley, Lydia Ann Weagley, William Wolf, Catherine Weagley, Malinda Weagley, Elizabeth Werts, Lucinda Werts and Louis Wartenbacker.

There are thirteen graves marked by native stones without inscriptions and a number of unmarked graves in this burial ground. In 1943 the following gravestones were still to be found in the plot:-

1. DODENDORF - 'Anna Maria Dodendorf / Died October 6, 1861 / Aged 48 years, 6 months / and 22 days."
2. HARDMAN - ' Micheal Hardman / Died July 17, 1850 / Aged 64 years, 4 months, and / 13 days.'
3. HARDMAN - 'Eliza Ruth Hardman / wife of / Micheal Hardman / Died ? / Aged ? / (Stone broken - remainder of inscription lost.)
4. DENTLER - 'Eve Margaret Dentler / wife of George Dentler, Sr. / Died December 9, 1852 / Aged 78 years and / 26 days.'
5. DETRICK - 'Jacob Detrick / June 13, 1896(?) / Died September 25, 1842.'
6. RIFFLE - 'Lydia Ann C. Riffle / daughter of G. and M. Riffle / Died November 17, 1851 / Aged 11 years / and 29 days.'
7. STOVER - Jacob Stover and his wife were interred here but their stones disappeared before this set of inscriptions was completed.
8. RIFFLE - James Bishop Riffle / son of G. and M. Riffle / Died October 31, 1861 / Aged 3 years / 6 months / and 2 days.'
9. RIFFLE - 'George C. Riffle / son of / G. and M. Riffle / Died September 22, 1860 / Aged 5 months and 22 days.'
10. RIFFLE - 'Maria Riffle / daughter of Nathan Boyd / and wife of / George Riffle / Died April 28, 1866 / Aged 31 years and / 18 days.
11. RIFFLE - 'Laura J. Riffle / daughter of G. and M. Riffle / Died June 23, 1851 / Aged 1 year, 2 months / and 2 days.'
12. SPRENKLE - Also buried here was Daniel Sprenkle, who died Nov. 6, 1821, and his wife Christine Sprenkle.

CHURCHES AND CEMETERIES

- ST. ANTHONY"S CATHOLIC CECMETERY, near Emmitsburg, MD., also known as; 'the Mountain cemetery'; 'College cemetery'; 'Mt. St. Mary's churchyard'; 'old churchyard on the hill'; 'Mt. St. Mary's "old churchyard on the hill".

- SHIELDS FAMILY CEMETERY - "On an overgrown hillside, at the foot of Carrick's Knob, in the Hampton Valley, near Emmitsburg, Maryland, just off the Crystal Fountain Road, are the remains of the Shields Family burial ground. Today only two markers, enclosed by a pipe fence, remain to mark the site of what was once a fairly large plot - set aside for the last resting place of the pioneer William(1) Shields, his immediate family, and their descendants. When founded this plot was located on the 'home place' - not too far from the house - on lands 'taken up' originally by William Shields.
William and Jane Bentley Williams Shields are buried here. According to one Shields family history 'originally there must have been from 20 to 30 graves' in the family ground. As late as the mid-nineteen-fifties' as many as six gravestones could be found in the area.
Inscriptions from the two tombstones at the cemetery:-
1. "In memory of / William Shields / Born in County Armagh, Ireland / July 14, 1728 / Arrived New Castle, Delaware / August 1, 1737 / Settled in Frederick County, Maryland / Emmitsburg District, 1748 / Surveyor, Patriot / Officer in the Revolutionary War." Next to the tombstone of William Shields is a smaller monument, a fieldstone bearing a bronze tablet, inscribed:- "Revolutionary Soldier / Major William Shields / 1728 - 1797 / Placed by the Eugenia Washington / Chapter N.S. D.A.R."
2. "In memory of / Ebenezer Shields / Eighth son of / William Shields / Died July 1, 1837 / Aged 58 years, 6 months / and 8 days."

TOM'S CREEK LUTHERAN AND REFORMED CHURCH AND CEMETERY
"In 1757 the early Lutherans at Tom's Creek purchased one given acre of ground on which to build their church and lay their dead to rest. The historian Helman writes that the dead were 'buried three and four deep', for this was the only grave-yard within a large radius. This was one of the oldest burial grounds located in the vicinity of Emmitsburg.
In 1782 the Lutheran and Reformed Congregations of Tom's Creek united and built a new church on the site of the first. Here they worshipped until 1797 when the present stone church (Elias) was built in Emmitsburg. The Methodist of Tom's Creek who hither to had held services in the schoolhouse and homes of the members, took over the old log church, standing in the midst of the graveyard, and thereafter it was known as Tom's Creek Methodist church. The churchyard for this congregation is just across the road from the Lutheran and Reformed plot. In due course of time the Methodist congregation built a new church. The old church stood until 1904 and was torn down and materials sold.

CHURCHES AND CEMETERIES

At old Tom's Creek Lutheran Churchyard the following names are still to be found on the tombstones:- Oyster, Traxel(Troxel), Munshower, Forney, Ocker, Ohler, Row(Rowe), Sluss, Smith, Crabbs, Crebs, Gaugh, Hockensmith, Hoover, Danner, Waddle and Davis.

TOM'S CREEK PRESBYTERIAN

In January of the year 1824 there was a list of the Communicants of Tom's Creek Presbyterian Church made. It reads as follows:- "James Crocket, John Witherow, William Long, and William Bigham, Ruling Elders. William Grayson, Agnes Grayson, David Morrison, Harriet Morrison, Patrick Reid, Fielding Donaldson, Kitty Donaldson, William Ferguson, Miss Ferguson, Charles Bigham, Margaret Bigham, William Long, Elder, Mary Long, Hugh Patterson, Nathaniel Grayson, Eliza Ann Grayson, Mary Emmitt, Sarah Emmitt, Margaret Long, Marton Hill, Jane Williams, Margaret Holmes, Abigail Emmitt, Elizabeth M. Hays, Margaret Gilliland, Margaret Agnew, Jane Eichelberger, Jane, McKeehan, Jane Faries, Sarah Hoover, Betsy Hunter, Nancy Armstrong, Miss Danner, Margaret Witherow, Mary Danner, James Paxton, Cassandra Paxton, James Crocket (Elder), Margaret Ferguson, Margaret Knox, Mary Knox, Margaret Annan, Hannah Robinson, Martha McKeehan, Susan Little, Mina Armstrong, Molley Patterson, Jane Patterson.

John Stewart, Rosanna Stewart, James Moore, John Witherow (Elder), Jane Witherow, Sarah Witherow, Eleanor Ross, William Curren, Jane Curren, Lavinia Curren, Robert McGuigan, Barbary McGuigan, Peggy Nolton, William Bigham (Elder), Phebe Bigham, Phebe Bigham, Jun., Kitty Bigham, Hannah Law, Esther Clark, Sarah Crockett, Hannah Morrison, Melcher Sheaner, Elizabeth Sheaner, Elizabeth Jordon, Polly Day (colored), Nancy Boens (colored), Ellen Boens (colored), Jane Armstrong, Sally Breckenridge, Polly Breckenridge, William Breckenridge, Samuel Witherow, Polly Witherow, Betsy Shriver, Nancy Linn, Joseph Kerr, David Kerr, Sally McKinley, Barnabas McSherry, Senior, Peggy McKee, Nancy McKee, Nathaniel Randolph, Eliza Randolph, Joseph Randolph, Sally Randolph, Peggy Caldwell, Peggy Caldwell, Jun., John Myers, Martha Myers, Nancy McCreary, Elizabeth Grier, Joseph Clark, Betty Hasslet, Sophia Dumfee, John Gezelman and John McKee.

The above should prove of great historical and genealogical value to all interested in old Tom's Creek Presbyterian church and its graveyard. Many of the men and women listed found a last resting place within the bounds of the ancient burial ground and probably still others rest in graves that are now unmarked.

A pastor of Old Tom's Creek, the Rev. Robert Smith Grier, is buried in the old graveyard, who as his tombstone states, was Pastor for fifty two years of the United Churches of Tom's and Piney Creek.

CHURCHES AND CEMETERIES

- WHITMORE FAMILY CEMETERY - The Whitmore family cemetery was until the 1960's, located in a circuit of trees on the 'Carrie Dern Farm' - just a short distance from the Tom's Creek Lutheran and Reformed Cemetery. In 1961 nine stones, with legible inscriptions, remained in this plot and they were copied by J. M. Holdcraft ("NAMES IN STONE"). Seven sandstones with somewhat 'primitive lettering' were removed by the late George Martin to the Whitmore family plot in Mountainview Cemetery in the mid 1960's. Was the Whitmore family Cemetery also known as the 'Close Cemetery'?

According to Mrs. Rosanna Fuss Long - "the Close farm later became the property of the Whitmores". According to Mrs. Margaret Rupp the cemetery was about 60 feet square with at least 20 to 30 graves therein. Some of the graves were marked with white marble stones. Six graves were marked by small marble headstones, ten by rough fieldstones and three of the latter bore crude inscriptions. The inscriptions:-
1. "In memory of / Barbara Whitmore / Died May 14, 1863 / Aged 59 years and 7 / months."
2. "In memory of / Fred. Whitmore / Died May 6, 1848 / Aged 45 years, 4 months / and 12 days."
3. "In memory of / Elizabeth Whitmore / Died March 1, 1846 / 70 years, 6 months, and / 28 days."
4. "In memory of / Christian Whitmore / Died May 26, 1862 / Aged 86 years, 9 months, / and 6 days."
5. "In memory of / Benjamin Whitmore, Sr. / Died March 11, 1818 / Aged 89 years."
6. "In memory of / Mary Whitmore / Died April 4, 1820 / Aged 67 years and / 11 months."
7. Fieldstone - "G.W. / Mo 172(8?) / May 22, 17--(?)"
8. Fieldstone - "F.H. / Mil 1793 / a 23"

A man named Martin, a suicide, was buried in the Whitmore Cemetery.

- ZACHARIAS FAMILY GRAVEYARD - The Zacharias family burial ground, at Stoney Branch, located on the lands now included in the Castle Farms Dairy, near Motter Station.
- Mathias(1) Zacharias, the pioneer ancestor of the family, set aside land for a family burial ground on his plantation, on "Stoney Branch", known as "Mon Dollar", near present day Motters Station The first burial in the Zacharias family burial ground of which there is record was Mathias Zacharias, himself. He died October 7, 1773 and two days later was interred 'on his farm'. His remains, along with others buried there were removed to Mountain View Cemetery, near Emmitsburg, in the early part of the twentieth century. His grave was probably marked with a native stone, as were so many others for no regular markers exists at the present time for the pioneer.
- "Died September 11, 1885, at her home in Shippensburg, PA., of apoplexy, Mrs. Sarah Zacharias, widow of the late Christian Zacharias, of Stoney Branch, near Emmitsburg, MD., aged 73 years, 4 months, and 11 days. Mrs. Zacharias passed all but the last few years of her life near the place of her birth, and on the

CHURCHES AND CEMETERIES

farm of her husband at the Stoney Branch, where she reared 4 sons and 3 daughters. Two sons and her husband preceded her to the grave. The remains of Mrs. Zacharias were followed to the family burial ground, on the old homestead property, by a large number of relatives and friends.' - Emmitsburg Chronicle September 14, 1885.

Zacharias family cemetery burials and inscriptions:-
1. Catherine Louise Groft 1821-1829. "In memory of / Caroline Louisa Groff / Born February 11, 1821 / Died September 29, 1823." Footstone with the initials "CLG".
2. Footstone with the intials "J.Z.T." (Note:- Probably a child of Mary Elizabeth Zacharias who married John W. Troxell.
3. Mathias(1) Zacharias, the ancestor of the family in America.
4. Elizabeth Margaret Kuhn, the wife of Mathias(1) Zacharias.
5. Mary Zacharias 1794-1846.
6. Anna Z. Zacharias 1796-1850.
7. John Zacharias 1788-1832.
8. Mathias Zacharias 1790-1849.
9. Anna Zacharias 1790-1840.
10. Mathias S. Zacharias 1759-1825.
11. Mathias P. Zacharias 1838-1882. "Beautiful Monument - We noticed a few days ago, in the yard of William H. Hoke, a white Bronze Monument to the memory of Mathias P. Zacharias. It is four feet, six inches high and six inches thick. Mr. Zacharias died August 1, 1882, aged 44 yr 10 months and 16 days. Mr. Hoke expects to erect the monument next week in the family burial ground at the late homestead of the deceased." - Emmitsburg Chronicle - June 9, 1883.
12. Christian Zacharias 1802-1885.
13. Sarah Picking Zacharias 1812-1886.

   Eleven of the above list were removed to Mountain View Cemetery in about 1900. Undoubtedly there were others interred in this plot - but their identity has been lost.

CLABAUGH

- William C. Clabaugh, died at his daughter's home in Baltimore, MD., bd Friendscreek Cemetery, beside his wife - grave unmarked. m "8/31/1881, in Liberty Twp., by J.E. Baker, Esq., William Clabaugh to Angeline A. Shriner, both of this county." - Chronicle Sept. 3, 1881.
Angeline A. Shriner Clabaugh, d 3/7/1892, bd Friends Creek Winebrennarian Cemetery. Children:- 1. Amy E. Clabaugh, d 7/1/1887, 1/9/4, bd Friendscreek.
- "Lost - On the Mountain
   The beginning of this chronicle - a tragic story - contained in the files of the 'Emmitsburg Chronicle', the story of the Clabaugh family tragedy is best told in the original account - as published in the Emmitsburg paper.

Saturday, July 9, 1887 - On Friday, July 1, 1887, a little child of William Clabaugh, who lives on the mountain several miles from Emmitsburg, was lost in a manner altogether inexplicable, and no trace of it has yet been found.

The child, less than two years old, followed its father on his leaving home, accompanied by an older sister, and the mother not perceiving its absence, knew nothing of the matter until the father returned and inquired for the child. As it was less than two years old, and in its bare feet, it seemed quite impossible that it could have gone very far over the rough, stony ground, but when search in the immediate vicinity of the house failed to trace the little one, an alarm was sounded in the neighborhood, and a band of forty or fifty mountaineers started to scour the woods, whilst the frantic mother left to the care of the sympathizing women, refused to be comforted. All night long the unavailing search went on, and in the morning one of the men was sent to Gettysburg to conult an old colored woman who, it seems, is believed by the mountaineers and a good many sensible, intelligent people besides, to possess the mysterious power of seeing and knowing things hidden from mortal eyes, unless assisted by the devil or some other evil spirit.

The old woman reported that the child was living and in the possession of a neighbor, whose person and dwelling she described. When this information was carried to the excited hunters they immediately surrounded the house and demanded it (the child). The inmates declared that they knew nothing of it, and though a thorough search was made and failed to reveal any trace of the lost child's presence, they continued to keep guard around the premises, threatening to shoot or hang the inmates, and of course growing more and more excited as the hours went by. Another deputation was sent to the Gettysburg Witch, who insisted that her first statement was correct, but that the old woman who had the child was also a Witch, and made use of some charm to prevent their finding it. She then gave them a counter charm, which they were to manipulate in a certain way till the child's stealer's charm was broken, then they would get possession of it. The opposing charms are still working against one another, nothing has transpired, and the poor little innocent is still missing." In the next two paragraphs the editor gives his opinion of the belief and in the use of witchcraft. Needless to say his dissertation is not complimentary.

Saturday, July 23, 1887 - "The Body Found - An Inquest - The Verdict - Story of the lost Child - On Saturday morning, July 16, 1887, information was lodged before Henry Stokes, Esq., Justice of the Peace, that the body of the child of William Clabaugh, that mysteriously disappeared on July 1, 1887, had been found near the top of the mountain, near what is called Sheeps Rock. The Squire thereupon commissioned Constable W.H. Ashbaugh to summon a jury of inquest. The jury was composed as follows:- Henry Stokes, coroner, Francis A. Maxell, J. Henry Stokes, Micheal Hoke, Joshua S. Motter, George P. Beam, Daniel Lawrence, Albert Smith, William H. Hoke, James M. Kerrigan,

Walter D. Willson, Singleton Dorsey, Jacob L. Topper, and Dr. Robert L. Annan, physician. The jury repaired to the place where the remains were found, and having viewed them and their surroundings, carefully removed them to the home of William Clabaugh, where the inquisition was held. Thirteen witnesses were closely examined, and the following verdict was rendered:- 'That on the first day of July, in the year 1887, at the home of her parents, the said Emma Clabaugh, wandered away from home and perished from exposure or some other cause unknown to the jury.'

The facts of the case may be summed up as follows - that about ten o'clock in the morning of July 1, 1887, William Clabaugh went to a neighbor's to get some butter. His oldest child, a daughter about four years of age, and Amey E. (known as Emma in the family), aged about 22 months, about half an hour afterwards started to follow him, and their mother very soon missed them, after they left the house. The other child met the father at Bensell's, wither he had gone, but all she could tell him of her sister was 'she went up the road'. On his return home his wife inquired about the child, Emma, and he knew nothing regarding her whereabouts. Shortly after William Clabaugh and his wife started to search for the child and returning to the house he (William Clabaugh) went forth and secured the aid of some neighbors. In the course of time others volunteered their services, until large bodies were on the search through the night, and for days succeeding without finding any trace of the missing one. About one and one half miles from the Clabaugh home, near the top of the mountain, is a very rough region and not far from some heavy rocks overhanging, the body of the child was discovered on Saturday last. About ten paces from it - at the roots of a tree - the skull, destitute of any integuments without or within and yet perfect in form - was found. It had evidently rolled down the declivity on being detached from the body. The feet and parts of the legs were the only discernable members. One arm was missing and a couple of ribs; the most of the skin remained in a dried state. The child's clothing, greatly soiled and torn, was the only basis of identification. The verdict of the jury leads to the conclusion that the child, hearty and vigorous for her age, must have wondered to the place where the remains were found, and dying of exposure and starvation, became the prey of the buzzards, whose breeding grounds are in the vicinity. The remains of Amey Emma Clabaugh were interred in the Winebrenarian churchyard, in Friends Creek Valley, on Saturday afternoon."
- Some five years later - the following obituary appeared in the 'Chronicle' under the date of Friday, March 11, 1892 - "Died, March 7, 1892, near this place, Mrs. Angeline J. Clabaugh, wife of William C. Clabaugh, aged 26 years, 1 month, and 27 days. Burial in the Friends Creek Cemetery with the Rev. Mr. Engler of the Winebrennarian Church officiating."
- Angeline Shriner Clabaugh was buried beside her daughter. According to neighborhood tradition she never recovered from that effects of the tragedy. William Clabaugh, the husband and father, never married. He died, some years later, at the home of his daughter, in Baltimore, MD. His body was returned to the Friends Creek Valley and the little churchyard. His grave is not marked. Friends Creek Cemetery Inscriptions:- "Angeline J. Clabaugh / wife of William C. Clabaugh / Died March 7, 1892 / Aged 26

years, 1 month / and 26 days." "In memory of / Amy E. Clabaugh / daughter of W.C. and A.J. Clabaugh / Died July 1, 1887 / Aged 1 year, 9 months, and / 4 days."

CLAIRVOUX

- Clairvoux - an old mansion house, also known as the William Elder farm, located on the property of Mount Saint Mary's College, near Emmitsburg, MD.
- see Cretin - Mrs. Emmeline Dielman Cretin (obituary). d/o Dr. Henry Dielman, wife of John T. Cretin.

CLARK

- Analize Clark, d 4/13/1838, 6/1/12, and Vincent W. Clark, children of John & Eliza Clark, bd Tom's Creek Presbyterian.

COCHRAN

- William Cochran, 1699-1785, the emigrant ancestor of the Cochran family settled in what is Delaware County, Pennsylvania, but in 1732 bought a tract of land in the 'Manor of Carrollsburgh' ("Carroll's Delight") from Daniel Carroll of Dudington. When the hundred year border dispute between Pennsylvania and Maryland was finally settled by the Mason and Dixon Line, Cochran's tract was in Liberty Twp., Adams County, Pennsylvania. He built a stone house in 1768 and in times of unrest and danger, particularly from the Indians, this Cochran home was used by the settlers in this locality as a place of refuge and served as a blockhouse as well.
William Cochran married Sarah Cochran, 1702-1785. They were both buried at Tom's Creek Presbyterian Cemetery near Emmitsburg. The inscription from their tombstone reads:- "Here / Lyeth interred the bodies of / William Cochran / Who departed this life / December / The 18th 1775, in the 78th year of / His Age / Also / The body of Sarah Cochran / The Wife of the above named / Who departed this Life February / 6th in the Year of our Lord 1785 / In the 83rd year of her Age. / Time was like me, they life possessed. And time shall be, when I shall rest."
They were the parents of:-
1. Andrew Cochran
2. William Cochran, m Rebecca Morrow (? may be the son of James)
3. James Cochran, 1732-1810, m Jane Cochran, 1742-1815. This branch of the family remained at Carrollsburgh.
4. John Cochran settled on the site of present day Waynesboro, Pennsylvania.
- James Cochran, 1732-1810, s/o William & Sarah Cochran. He lived on the family plantation in Liberty Twp., and was known as 'James of Carrolsburgh'. He married Jane Cochran, 1742-1815. Children:-
1. William Cochran, b 1775, m 6/26/1805, Rebecca Morrow, 1779-1838, d/o John Morrow. They moved to Miami Co., Ohio.
2. Malinda Cochran
3. James Cochran.

- John Cochran, s/o William and Sarah Cochran, m Eleanor Baird. Eleanor died 2/28/1791, aged 74 years, and was buried at the Cochran Family burial ground at Waynesboro, PA. Children:-
1. John Cochran
2. Jean Cochran Clark, m James Clark.
3. Eleanor Cochran Junkin, m Joseph Junkin
4. Mary Cochran Findley, m William Findley.

John Cochran was a devout Covenanteer, the Straitest and strictest sect among the Presbyterians. Their home was a 'regular stop' for the Rev. John Cuthbertson on his missionary journeys. Rev. Cuthbertson's diary mentions John Cochran and his family many times during the period from 1751 to 1790. John Cochran was a pious and outstanding man - a pillar of the church. There is a story told of 'old John Cochran' and his strict observance of the Sabbath. It is said that the entire family often walked over the South Mountain on Sunday mornings to Marsh Creek (probably the Hill Church) for worship. The trip covered at least ten miles and the service lasted several hours. Doubtless they had to start early in the morning and would not reach home again until late in the evening. So strict was John in the observance of the Sabbath that his children were not permitted to pick huckleberries from the laden bushes as they passed.

According to family tradition it was the custom of 'old John Cochran' to sit under the shade of a large walnut tree that stood beside the little family graveyard and read his bible. He was often heard to say that he wished to be interred beneath this tree. As he requested his body was buried beneath the tree's spreading branches.

CORBIN

- Margaret Cochran Corbin, a descendant of William and Sarah Cochran, was a heroine of the American Revolution. She took part with her husband in the Battle of Fort Washington and was severely wounded at that time. The remains of this brave woman now rest in the burial ground of the West Point Academy.

CORRELL

- Christian Correll, m June 1818, to Betsy Gilland, d/o John Gilland (Gillelan) and Mary (Hays) Smith Gilland.
1850 Census Frederick County Maryland, Emmitsburg District
Correll, Christian, age 55, farmer, b in Fred. Co.
Elizabeth, age 51, b in Fred. Co.
Lydia E., age 23, b in Fred. Co.
John Q., age 21, farmer, b in Fred. Co.
- John Quincy Correll was born 1829 the son of Christian and Elizabeth 'Betsy' Gillelan Correll. His mother was a descendant of the Hays Smith and Gillelan families of Emmitsburg. He married Alice Jane Sluss, d/o John Sluss and were members of Elias Lutheran Church, Emmitsburg. The baptism records of their children can be found in the Elias Church Records. After 1868 they moved to Baltimore, MD. Their children:-

1. William McClellan Correll, b 1/27/1862, d 10/22/1863
2. Susan Elizabeth Correll, bp 10/24/1863, d 11/12/1863.
3. John Sluss Correll, 1864-1904, bd Tom's Creek
4. Harry Taylor Correll, 1866-1867, bd Toms Creek
5. Alice Virginia Correll, b 12/9/1867

Cemetery inscriptions of Tom's Creek:-
1. "In memory of William McClellan Correll son of John and A.J. Correll Died October 22, 1863, Aged 1 year 8 months and 25 days."
2. "Sacred to the memory of Susanna Elizabeth Correll daughter of John Q. and Alice Jane Correll Died November 11, 1863 / Aged 3 months and 6 days."
3. "In memory of J. S. Correll Born September 28, 1864 Died October 10, 1904."
4. "In memory of Harry Taylor Correll son of John Q. and A.J. Correll Died February 9, 1867 Aged 5 months and 18 days."
5. "In memory of S. O. Correll Born May 2, 1877 Died Nov. 9, 1900."

CRABBS

- John Crabbs - One of the early mills erected on Tom's Creek, in the Emmitsburg district, was built by one John Crabbs. This man was probably the pioneer ancestor of the family in this locality. John Crabbs attended the meeting held in 1770, at the schoolhouse on Tom's Creek, to add his voice to the protest against the Stamp Act.
James A. Helman writes that the mill built and operated by the Crabbs family until 1849, at which time it was sold to Samuel Maxell (Maxwell). "Crabbs built the mill also known as Maxell's, on Tom's Creek, below the pike."

CRAPSTER

- Ruliff Crapster, the pioneer ancestor, was buried on his own farm but some years later removed to the Reformed Church Cemetery at Taneytown, MD. The family estate was known as 'Locust Grove'. m Abigail.

- John Crapster, s/o Ruliff and Abigail Crapster. John and his wife Susannah (Klein) Little Crapster were interred at the family burial ground at 'Locust Grove' but later removed to Taneytown Reformed Cemetery.
John Crapster 1761-1824, m 1783 Susannah Little (or Klein), the d/o Peter Little (Klein), the founder of Littlestown, PA. Children:-
1. William Crapster; 2. Mary Crapster Hickson; 3. Eveline Crapster O'Neal, m Walter O'Neal; 4. Peter Crapster; 5. Sophia Crapster Jennings; 5. John Crapster; 7. Basil Crapster.
- John H. Crapster & Sarah A. Gramber, m 8/30/1852.
- Gustavas W. Crapster & Sophia Simpson, m 12/29/1843, by the Rev. Mr. Collier.

CRETIN

- James Cretin, d 2/17/1857, age 69 yrs., bd Mountain Cemetery (St. Anthony's Catholic, Mt. St. Mary's) m Mary Ann, 9/8/1802-2/21/1879, bd Mountain Cemetery.
Children:-
1. Mary Cretin Dielman, 12/21/1835-3/5/1892, bd Mt Cemetery, m Lawrence L. Dielman.
2. Ann E. Cretin Fuey, m Francis P. Fuey.
3. James P. Cretin
4. Joseph A. Cretin
5. Agnes C. Cretin, d 3/12/1860, age 19/3/5, unmarried, bd Mt. Cemetery.
6. Samon (Simon) G. Cretin.
- John H. Cretin and family moved from Hagerstown, Md., to "Andora", the late residence of Dr. Henry Dielman, near the college. - Emmitsburg Chronicle Feb 23, 1884.
- John Henry Cretin - "Died, March 17, 1906, at Andora, near Mount Saint Mary's College, John Henry Cretin, aged 80 years and 8 months. Burial took place in Mt. St. Mary's churchyard. Mr. Cretin was a son of Andrew Cretin. His mother was Ann Green, a descendant of General Nathaniel Green of Revolutionary fame." - Emmitsburg Chronicle March 23, 1906.
- Emmeline Dielman Cretin - "Died, February 27, 1914, Mrs. Emmeline Cretin, the widow of John T. Cretin and daughter of the late Dr. Henry C. Dielman, the great musician, also of Mt. St. Mary's, aged 80 years, 7 months, and 3 days. Mrs. Cretin died at her home at 'Clairvoux'. She is survived by one brother and one sister - Lawrence Dielman and Mrs. Rebecca Dielman Moore, both residing near this place. Burial took place in the 'Old Cemetery on the Hill". - Emmitsburg Chronicle March 6, 1914.

CULBERTSON

- The Culbertsons were early settlers of Cumberland Valley of Pennsylvania in what is now Franklin County. 'Culbertson's Row' is famous in the annals of provincial history and a member of that family was killed by the Indians at the Battle of Sideling Hill.
- Culbertson plot at Tom's Creek Presbyterian:-
1. Twin babies of Joseph and Sarah Culbertson, died 11/2/1834.
2. Elizabeth Gibson, d/o Joseph and Sarah Culbertson & wife of R.G. Gibson, d 1/30/1864, 27/0/17.
3. James F. Culbertson 6/13/1839-6/11/1917.
4. Catherine, wife of James Culbertson, 3/4/1844-4/15/1907.

CUNNINGHAM

- Susan King Cunningham - "The tale of this particular tragedy begins with the appearance of a band of Indians, who were seen near Fort Loudon, near the Concheque Settlement, in what is now Franklin County, Pennsylvania, on July 22, 1764. On July 25, 1764 Susan King Cunningham, sister of the Rev. John King, left her home located near the present site of Mercerburg, and started through the woods to call on a neighbor. When she did not return as expected a search was made and soon her body was found not far from her home. She had been murdered and scalped.

The next day, July 26, 1764, the murder of Enoch Brown, school master, and ten of his scholars took place. This tragedy was unique in frontier atrocities. - also see Eleanor Cochran Junkin.

CURREN

- William Curren - "In memory of Our / Parents / William and Jane Curren." - Tom's Creek Presbyterian Cemetery.
- Jane J. Curren - "In memory of / Jane J. Curren / Born August 4, 1826 / Died April 15, 1900." - Piney Creek Presbyterian Cemetery, Harney, MD.

DAVIDSON

- Margaret Davidson, wife of Jessie Davidson, d 4/10/1830, 30/5/0. - bd Tom's Creek Presbyterian Cemetery.

- The Rev. Patrick Davidson, 10/9/1775 - 10/9/1824, bd Frederick Presbyterian churchyard, later moved to Mt. Olivet Cemetery, Frederick, Maryland.
Graduated at Dickinson College, Carlise, PA.
1796 - candidate for holy orders by the Rev. Nathan Grier at the Presbytery of New Castle.
1799 - ordained and installed pastor at Fagg's Manor, PA.
1800 - pastorial relation was disolved at Fagg's Manor, accepted as pastor to Tom's Creek Presbyterian Church near Emmitsburg, Maryland.
1809 - elected Principal of the Frederick, Md., Academy
1814 - Presbytery of Baltimore, where he remained until his death in 1824.
Rev. Patrick Davidson, 10/9/1775 - 10/9/1824
Mary Davidson, wife of Rev. P. Davidson, d 10/13/1835.
Charlotte Davidson, d/o Rev. P. Davidson, d 8/23/1846, 46 yrs.
- Marriage Records of the United Churches of Tom's Creek and Piney Creek Presbyterian Churches, marriages by the Rev. Patrick Davidson:-
1. "March 27, 1806 - Robert Robertson to Polly McCallen."
2. "March 27, 1806, - Samuel Thompson to Peggy Clingan."
3. "April 29, 1806 - John McClonahan to Ann McCune."
4. "May 1, 1806 - William Stevenson to Peggy Wilson."
5. "May 1, 1806 - John McCune to Mary Leech."
6. "July 24, 1806 - Robert Breckenridge to Mary Grier."
7. "September 11, 1806 - Abraham Linner (Linah) to Ann Linn."
8. "October 20, 1806 - Archibald Clingan to Ann Ferguson."
9. "November 27, 1806 - James McGaughy, of Marsh Creek, to Nancy Grier, of Piney Creek."
10. "December 4, 1806 - Nathan Paxton, of Mr. Dobbin's congregation, to Mrs. ---(?) McNealy (widow), of Piney Creek."

11. "March 8, 1807 - Jonas Graham to Polly Thompson."
12. "October 6, 1807 - Philip Heagy to Rachel Black."
13. "October 8, 1807 - James Allen to Sally Musgrove."
14. "1807 -   ---(?) Snider to Peggy Thompson."
15. "February 28, 1808 - John Coulter, of Mr. Dobbin's congregation, to Sally Heagy, of Piney Creek."
16. "March 29, 1808 - Samuel Hutchison to Esther Balden."
17. "May 26, 1808 - Robert King, of the Hunterstown congregation, to Nancy McElhenny, of the Piney Creek congregation."
18. "November 24, 1808 - Richard Philip Miller to Rachel Balden."
19. "November 24, 1808 - James McCurdy to Martha Moore."
20. "March 21, 1809 - Robert Fleming, of Tom's Creek, to Polly Love, of Piney Creek."
21. "March 23, 1809 - William Alexander to Nancy Clingan."
22. "June 8, 1809 - Charles Donaldson to Sally Guinn."
23. "October 5, 1809 - James Wharlen to Isabel Alexander."
24. "October 26, 1809 - Thomas Donwody to Ann Wilson."
25. "November 22, 1809 - Robert Black to Sally Hosack."
26. "December 20, 1809 - Alexander Horner to Mrs. S. Marshall."
27. "January 9, 1810 - Mathew Longwell, of Gettysburg, PA., to Miss Jean Klinhoof."
28. "January 9, 1810 - Thomas Cornell to Mary Paxton."
29. "January 13, 1810 - Robert McCurdy to Polly Clingan."
30. "March 13, 1810 - John Adgy to Nancy Dunwoddy."
31. "March   20, 1810 - George Heagy to Eliza Black."
32. June 7, 1810 - William McCurdy to Nancy King."
33. "December 1810 - Andrew Walker to Ann Wilson."
34. "March 7, 1811 - John Horner to Sally Linn."
35. "May 1811 - John Ferguson, Jr. to Rebecca Slemons."
36. "June 1811 - Benjamin Cornell to Jean Paxton."
37. "May 1813 - John Hunter to Polly Kerr."

DEITRICK

- Jacob Deitrick, s/o Martin and Susan Deitrick, b 1790 d 1794 - bd Tom's Creek Lutheran and Reformed Cemetery.

DIELMAN

- Emily Dawson Dielman - "Died, Sunday August 3, 1879, at Andora, near Mt. St. Mary's College, Mrs. Emily Dielman, the wife of Dr. Henry Dielman and the daughter of Capt. Phileman Dawson. Mrs. Dielman was born July 22, 1815 in Baltimore, Maryland. ... Her funeral took place Monday and burial was in the 'Mountain Cemetery'. Dr. Dielman was absent on a visit and did not know of his wife's illness and death until his return home Sunday afternoon ..." - Emmitsburg Chronicle August 9, 1879.

- Dr. Henry Dielman - "Our good friend, Dr. Henry Dielman, is enjoying a pleasant vacation among his friends in Hagerstown, MD. We miss him at the organ on Sundays but wish him a pleasant and beneficial vacation." - Emmitsburg Chronicle August 2, 1879.

- Dr. John Casper "Henry" Dielman
b 4/26/1811, at Frankford-on-the-Main, Germany, eldest son of John Casper Dielman, emigrated 1826, became American citizen in 1834, m 9/9/1834, Emily Dawson, d/o Capt. Philemon Dawson, of the English Merchant Marines, at Saint Peter's Episcopal Church, Baltimore, MD. bd Mountain Cemetery (St. Anthony's Catholic).
- Professor of Music at Mount Saint Mary's College - 39 years.
- Dielman's "Christmas Carol".
- 1849 Doctor of Music from Georgetown University.
- Musician - Conductor of various orchestras in this country before coming to Baltimore, MD.
- organist at the "Church on the Mountain".
- The home of the Dielman's near Mount Saint Mary's College was known as "Andora". According to tradition this was the gathering place for the cultural groups of the neighborhood. Good fellowship and worthwhile conversation were the order 'of the day'.
- 1827 His first post in the New World - that of first violinist in the Chestnut Street Theatre in Philadelphia, lasted 2 years. 1829 - He left Philadelphia and went to Baltimore and Washington. He took part in the muscial life of these cities for 14 years. 1843 - accepted the post on the faculty of Mount Saint Mary's College near Emmitsburg, MD. Shortly after his arrival he organized an orchestra - The Saint Cecelia Society.
1863 - 1880 He also taught German at Mt. St. Mary's College.

- "Dr. John Casper Henry Dielman, Professor of Music at Mount Saint Mary's College for almost 40 years, died at his home near Emmitsburg, Maryland. He was a native of Germany, having been born at Frankford-on-the-Main, April 26, 1811. He was the Eldest son of John Casper Deilman, a musician of that place. His talent for music developed early, and his instruction in the violin began at the age of 11 years. Mr. Dielman emigrated to America in 1827 - to accept the post of First Violinist in the Phildelphia orchestra. In 1829 he came to Baltimore, Maryland, where he resided for some 14 years. Here, in addition to his other duties, he was organist at St. John's Episcopal church. In 1843 Dr. Dielman became professor of Music at Mount Saint Mary's College. He became a member of the Roman Catholic Church after coming to Mt. St. Mary's. Mrs. Dielman was a daughter of Captain Philemon Dawson. Her mother was of the family of Lowndes, who were of English descent and nobility. Professor Dielman was the first in this country who was distinguished by the title of Doctor of Music. This distinction came in 1849 from Georgetown University and he received his diploma from the hands of President Taylor, who presided at the commencement exercises that year. Mrs. Dielman died about 10 years ago. Burial was made at the Mount Saint Mary's churchyard."
- Emmitsburg Chronicle October 14, 1882."

- Dr. John Casper Henry Dielman - "On Sunday last, His Grace, Cardinal Gibbons, visited Dr. Deilman, who is very ill at present. He sat by the bed for a considerable time. He imparted his blessings." Emmitsburg Chronicle October 14, 1882.

- Children of Dr. John Casper Henry Dielman & Emily Dawson Dielman:-
1. Mary(2) Dielman Cretin, b Baltimore, MD., m John Henry Cretin, bd Mountain Cemetery "Mary C. Dielman Cretin, wife of John H. Cretin, d 3/11/1899, 64 yrs., 2 daughters; Mrs. Richard Bennett & Miss Josephine Cretin.
2. Rebecca(2) Dielman Quinn Moore, b 4/8/1838, Balt., MD. d 5/30/1915, bd Mt. Cemetery. m1 7/14/1858, Bernard Quinn, a student and later instructor at Mt. St. Mary's College. m2 Ignatius Moore. Children to both marriages; Josephine Mary Quinn, d 1864 2/2/0, bd Mt. Cem.; a son H.A.Quinn, who moved to the west; and Nina Quinn who married Harry F. Manning; Georgia Moore 1868-1940, bd Mt. Cem.; Emma Chase Moore 1887-1945, bd Mt. Cem.
3. Henry(2) Dielman, b 1839, Baltimore, MD. Attended Mt. St. Mary's College. He was the first of the Dielman children to die. His death took place at Alton, Illinois, Dec 25, 1863, 24 yrs.
4. Emily(2) Dielman Cretin, b 7/24/1843, Baltimore, MD., married a cousin of her sister's husband, John Thomas Cretin. Both bd Mt. Cemetery. "John T. Cretin 10/20/1831 - 12/6/1903, Emily Dielman Cretin 7/2/1843 - 2/27/1914."
5. Lawrence 'Larry'(2) Dielman, b 8/ 9/1847, Emmitsburg, MD. d 1923, m Mary Cretin.
6. Adelaide(2) Dielman Jourdan, b 7/24/1852, Emmitsburg, MD. m Charles H. Jourdan, professor of Mathematics and Chemistry at Mt. St. Mary's College from 1865 to 1913.

- Lawrence 'Larry' Dielman - "On Pleasant Level, near Hayland, there stands an old house, long used as a store now occupied by Mr. Lawrence Dielman. (1880). This ancient building was converted by Father Dubois, and used as a school and was the beginning of Mount Saint Mary's College." Emmitsburg Chronicle, Emmitsburg and Vicinity, by Samuel Motter and Mary Lowe Patterson.
- Lawrence 'Larry' Dielman
b 8/9/1847, Emmitsburg, MD., the son of Dr. John Casper Henry Dielman and Emily Dawson Dielman.
d 1923, bd Old Mountain Cemetery (St. Anthony's Catholic).
m Mary Cretin, d/o James & Mary Ann Cretin
b 12/21/1835, d 3/5/1892, bd Old Mountain Cemetery.

His father, John Casper Henry Dielman, desired that his son 'Larry' receive a classical education in music but that young man had other ideas. It is to his credit that the boy tried to do as his father wished but was "found to be a better dancer than musician". This explains his father's remark - "All of Larry's music is in his heels."

-Lawrence 'Larry' Dielman - "Larry Dielman will be on hand at 4:30 am, one hour before the first mass at Saint Anthony's church, on Christmas morning. For a number of years it has been his beautiful custom to proceed from his home to the Old Mountain church and while on the journey to play the Adeste Fidelis on his flute. Although this custom is an old one to us, and we have heard visitors who spend the Holidays with us say it was one of the most beautiful things they ever heard. No matter how rough the weather you can always depend on 'Larry' making this journey with his flute on Christmas morning." - Emmitsburg Chronicle December 13, 1908.

- "Larry Dielman, as usual made his trip to the old Mountain Cemetery and Church. His playing was greatly enjoyed by all. Larry also played on the hillside, in the churchyard at his father's grave before the midnight mass at the College on Christmas Eve." - Emmitsburg Chronicle - January 1, 1909.

- "Mrs. Lawrence Dielman, died 3/5/1892, aged 51 yrs. Burial at the College." - M.F. Shuff Burial Records. According to local tradition Mary Cretin Dielman died at Hagerstown, MD. She was buried with members of her family in the 'Mountain Cemetery'. It is known that Mrs. Dielman and her husband were separated at the death of the wife. It would appear that 'Larry' Dielman was not addicted to work and could not or would not support his wife. Larry kept a little store near St. Anthony's Catholic Church. Larry preferred to play the banjo or flute and refused to have a worry or a care.

- "Larry Dielman has played his last tune beside the grave of his father. The man, who far more than thirty years, had trodden from his lonely home, near Emmitsburg, to the spot where is buried the body of his beloved father, has fallen the victim of fate, a paralytic in the seventieth year of his age. It was Larry's custom to march off every Christmas to that lonely grave and play the "Adeste Fidelis" as a tribute to his devoted father. This year he was forced to abandoned the sacred custom because of illness. More than a year since the veteran musician, on the advice of his physician, gave up his home and store in the woods near Emmitsburg. In March he was paralized and taken to Mount Hope, where he partially recovered and was moved to a home near Thurmont, where he now lives with Mr. & Mrs. Frank Roddy."... undated clipping from the Emmitsburg Chronicle.

- "Larry Dielman is well remembered in the neighborhood for his traditional Christmas Eve visit to his father's grave to play on the flute his father's compositions of Dr. Dielman. Eye witnesses attest the beauty of this graveyard tryst as the eerie strains floated through the midnight stillness to the ears of the worshippers on their way to midnight mass. The legend of the ghost of Larry Dielman (who is still supposed to play the flute every Christmas Eve over his father's grave) is tradtional in the neighborhood. Many profess to have heard the music and there is no good reason why their testimony should be contradicted. All things are possible to those who believe.

DIELMAN

- Louis (Lewis) Dielman, son of John Casper Dielman, and half brother of John Casper Henry Dielman, like wise a musician, emigrated to America, became Professor of Music at Calvert College, New Windsor, Maryland.

- "Louis Deilman, one of the most widely known citizens of Carroll Co., MD., died at his home in New Windsor, December 31, 1910 ... from infirmities of old age. He was born in the free city of Frankford-on-the-Main, Germany. In 1843 he left his native country to seek his fortune in America. He landed in Philadelphia, where his older brother, Henry Deilman, was conductor of a theatre orchestra. In 1845 both brothers came to Mount Saint Mary's College, where Henry became professor of Music. Louis Deilman taught at Calvert College in New Windsor, Maryland. In July 1864, Mr. Deilman purchased the Hotel New Windsor. On October 15, 1895 Mr. Deilman's wife died and from that time his health declined ... Mr. Deilman was a member of St. Luke's Lutheran Church (better known as Winter's Church) and he was laid out to rest in the quaint old churchyard by the side of his wife. One sister, Mrs. Margaret Dieter, two daughters, the Misses Lena and Agnes Deilman, of New Windsor, are among the survivors. Two sons, Frederick and Louis H. Deilman, of Baltimore, MD., also survive." - Emmitsburg Chronicle - January 6, 1911

Children of Louis Deilman:-
1. Lena Deilman, New Windsor, MD.
2. Agnes Deilman, New Windsor, MD.
3. Frederick Deilman, b in Germany, became a successful artist in New York, lived in Baltimore, MD.
4. Louis H. Deilman, b at New Windsor, MD., in 1864 - was a librarian, Author, Editor and Historian. It was the later that he made 'his mark' in Maryland History. His records, particularly those of long forgotten, now obliterated burial grounds, are in the files of the Maryland Historical Society. He lived in Baltimore, Maryland.

DOTTERER

- Albert Dotterer, d 6/11/1912, 68 yrs. - Soldier. - M.F. Shuff Burial Records. Albert Dotterer, 12/25/1844 - 6/11/1912, bd Mountain View Cemetery, Emmitsburg, MD. - Soldier of Civil War.

DUPHORNE

- The Duphorne - Duphorn family of French Huguenot descent.

- Annie Duphorne - "Miss Annie Duphorne - Public Schools - Our public schools will open this year on Monday Sept 2nd and continue until the last day of May. The teachers appointed for the school year in Emmitsburg are Miss Annie Suphorne, principal, and Miss Fannie Frailey, assistant". - Emmitsburg Chronicle August 31, 1889. (NOTE: Miss Annie Duphorne was the d/o Samuel and Maria Duphorne.)

Duphorne burials at Emmitsburg Elias Lutheran Churchyard:-
1. Hannah Duphorn, d 5/2/1882 74/2/16
2. Samuel Duphorn, d 2/24/1884 (church record)
   8/4/1798-2/18/1883 (cemetery inscription)
3. Maria Duphorn, wife of Samuel, 12/21/1815-2/6/1888
4. Emma Barbara Duphorn, d/o Samuel & Maria, d 3/18/1852 0/4/10
5. Barbara, wife of Simon Duphorne, b 1770 d 10/1853 83 yrs
6. John H. Duphorne, d 7/23/1867 31/1/21 (church records)
   7/2/1836-7/23/1867 (cemetery records)
7. Sarah Duphorne, d 8/15/1853 5 yrs (church records)
8. Hannah Duphorn 1811-1882
9. Emma R. Duphorn d/o John & Rosanna Duphorn, d 1845
10. Robert s/o John & Rosanna Duphorne b & d 1842
11. Annie E. Duphorn 1841 - 1921

- John Duphorn of Emmitsburg, m 5/6/1840 Rosanna (Rose Anna) Dinwiddie of Gettysburg, PA. Children:-
1. Franklin Dinwiddie Duphorn b 1/28/1841
2. Robert John Duphorn b 2/27/1842, d 11/1842, bd Elias
3. Sarah Jane Duphorn b 9/19/1843
4. Emma H. Duphorn d 1845

- Miss Mary Hagen Duphorne was a teacher in both public and private schools. She died at her home 10/5/1906, near Emmitsburg, in her 73rd year. Miss Duphorne was a lady of strong personality, education, and refinement. Her life work was dedicated to the cause of education. - Emmitsburg Chronicle.

- Miss Mary Heagen Duphorn, 1833 - 1906, d/o Samuel & Maria Duphorn. She was a teacher at Hagerstown Female Seminary and taught at Dayton, Ohio, Hagerstown, MD., Birkettsville and Lutherville Seminaries, MD. She also taught a private school at Emmitsburg and district schools in Pennsylvania.

- Samuel Duphorne - Duphorn 1798 - 1884, bd Elias m Maria 1815 - 1888. "The renerable Samuel Duphorne celebrated his golden wedding on October 4, 1882. In addition he was 84 years of age on that day." - Emmitsburg Chronicle - October 7, 1882. "Died February 24, 1884, at his home near Emmitsburg, MD., after a protracted illness, Samuel Duphorn, aged 85 yrs, 6 mos & 16 ds." - Gettysburg Compiler Feb 28, 1884.
Children:-
1. Mary Heagen Duphorne, teacher at Hagerstown Female Seminary, 1833-1906, bd Elias
2. Annie Eliza (Eliza Ann) Duphorne, 8/2/1841-6/14/1924, bd Elias, teacher at Emmitsburg.
3. Calvin F. Duphorne, b 10/2/1843, of Sharon Springs, Kansas
4. Robert Samuel Duphorne, b 4/4/1846, of Harper, Kansas
5. Sarah Louisa Duphorne, 11/24/1848-8/15/1853, bd Elias
6. Ellie M. Duphorne, m 4/18/1878, John F. Adelsperger, Emmitsburg
7. Emma Barbara Duphorn b & d 1852 bd Elias
8. Thomas W. Duphorn 1839-1862
9. John H. Duphorn 1836-1867, 31/1/21, d in Phila., PA. bd Elias

EHREHART

- Rev. Prof. Charles J. Ehrehart, b 1/22/1827, Adams Co., PA., s/o Thomas & Margaret Ehrehart, d 11/26/1870, bd Evergreen Cemetery, Gettysburg, PA. m 1 5/21/1855, Martha Hill (d 11/8/1867), bd Evergreen - 4 children. m 2 8/5/1869 at Emmitsburg, to Mary Elizabeth Eichelberger, d/o Dr. James W. Eichelberger. The Rev. Ehrehart was a graduate of Pennsylvania College and the Lutheran Theological Seminary of Gettysburg. He was head of the Preparatory Department of Pennsylvania (now Gettysburg) College.

EICHELBERGER

- The name of Eichelberger is usually associated with the "Pennsylvania Dutch Country" but some of the family came over into Maryland.

- Eichelberger Cemetery Inscriptions:-
1. Motter Eichelberger, d 12/19/1850, 18/2/24 bd Taneytown Luth.
2. Martin Eichelberger, d 9/21/1855, a native of Jefferson County, Virginia, bd Taneytown Lutheran.
3. Samuel Eichelberger, s/o George M. & E.E., d 9/10/1887, 1/0/3 bd Creagerstown Lutheran and Reformed.
4. Virginia Eichelberger, d 5/6/1865 32/11/24 bd Creagerstown Luth & Reformed.
5. Abram J. Eichelberger, 1866-1928, w Minnie G. 1869-1953 bd Mt. Olivet Cem., Frederick
6. Francis M. Eichelberger, 5/14/1859 - 4/2/1933, w Lillie M. 8/12/1865 - 2/14/1932 - bd Mt. Olivet Frederick

- Dr. James W. Eichelberger, Sr., s/o James Eichelberger, b 6/17/1804, Abbottstown, PA, d 8/12/1895, bd Elias Lutheran, Emmitsburg, MD. m 1829, Anna Margaret Motter, d/o Lewis Motter, b 2/17/1805, d 8/19/1888/9, bd Elias.
- Dr. James W. Eichelberger - "Died, Emmitsburg, Maryland, on Monday, Aug 12, 1895, Dr. James W. Eichelberger, Senior, in the 95th year of his age. He was the oldest resident of Emmitsburg and a practicing physician since 1829. About 12 years ago he gave up his large practice because of his advanced years. Dr. Eichelberger came to Emmitsburg about 1820. For some years he was engaged in the store of Isaac Baugher, deceased. Later he entered the University of Maryland to study medicine. He graduated in 1827. At the time of his death he was the oldest graduate of that University. In 1829 Dr. Eichelberger married Anna Margaret Motter, the daughter of Lewis Motter, and sister of Lewis R. Motter, Esq. His wife died in 1889. Two sons and two daughters survive - Dr. James W. Eichelberger, Jr., Dr. Charles D. Eichelberger, Mrs. M.E. Ehrehart and Miss Marion F. Eichelberger. Dr. Eichelberger first practiced his profession at Woodsboro, for several years but about 1830 moved to Emmitsburg. ... Funeral services for Dr. Eichelberger were held in Elias Lutheran Church and interment was made in thae adjoining burial ground." - Republican Compiler August 13, 1895.

- Children of Dr. James W. Eichelberger and Anna Margaret Motter Eichelberger:-
1. Gustavus Milton Eichelberger, b 12/27/1828, died young, bd Emmitsburg Elias Lutheran
2. Dr. Charles D. Eichelberger, 3/2/1835-10/18/1910, physician, unmarried, bd Emmitsburg Elias Lutheran.
3. Marion F. Eichelberger, 5/7/1837 - 11/11/1911, unmarried, bd Emmitsburg Elias Lutheran.
4. Columbia Martha Eichelberger, 8/28/1839 - 12/21/1852 bd Elias.
5. Samuel William Eichelberger, b 10/5/1841
6. Dr. James W. Eichelberger, Jr., 12/5/1841 - 2/23/1913, m Sarah Minnie Hoke 1868-1942, son Charles Dicks Eichelberger, a pharmasist.
7. Anna Margaret Eichelberger, 1/3/1844-4/15/1891, bd Elias, m Eugene L. Rowe 2/6/1845-12/3/1916 bd Elias.
8. Motter E. Eichelberger, d 12/17/1850
9. Mary Elizabeth Eichelberger, bd Elias, m 8/5/1869, at Emmitsburg to Rev. Prof. C.J. Ehrehart of Gettysburg, PA.

- Dr. James W. Eichelberger, Jr., s/o Dr. James W. and Anna Margaret Motter Eichelberger, b 12/5/1841 - 2/23/1913, bd Elias Lutheran, m Sarah 'Minnie' Hoke, (1/12/1868-1/3/1942), d/o Peter and Frances Ann Rowe Hoke, bd Elias. Children:-
1. Charles D. Eichelberger, 5/6/1893-2/6/1938, never married, bd Elias Lutheran.

- "Lydia Eichelberger, d/o G.M. & Jane Eichelberger, d 9/20/1824, 8/2/6, also her infant brother, d 11/28/1818, aged 20 days." - bd Tom's Creek Presbyterian.

- Philip Frederick Eichelberger, b 1693 Germany, d 1776, emigrated 1728 from Ittlinger, near Sinsheim, county of Heidelberg, in the Grand Duchy of Baden. m2 Mary Magdaline, children:-
1. Leonard Eichelberger, b 1750 PA, d 1811, he was a farmer and wheelwright and Justice of the Peace. m Elizabeth, d 1/26/1817, 63/10/12, bd Elias, children:-
    1. George M. Eichelberger, b 1784 Carroll Co., MD., d 1/16/1854, Frederick, MD., bd Mt. Olivet Cem., He was Register of Will for Frederick County for 20 years. In 1814 Col. Eichelberger was one of the "Defenders of Baltimore". m Jane Grayson, d 2/4/1870, 75 yrs., bd Mt. Olivet Cem. Children:-
        1. Lydia, d 9/20/1824, 8/2/13, bd Mt. Olivet Cem.
        2. Miles, d 1/17/1841, 21/2/14. bd Mt. Olivet.
        3. Harvey, d 2/23/1893, 66 yrs. bd Mt. Olivet.
        4. Mary Jane, 1828-1860, bd St. John's Cath., Frederick, m Dr. H. Jernongham Boone.
        5. Grayson M. Eichelberger, leader of the Bar in Frederick County, Maryland, was Secretary of State under Governor Hicks and State Senator from Frederick County. b 1821 in Emmitsburg, d 2/17/1870, bd Mt Olivet Cem.

m. 5/21/1844 by the Rev. Solomon Sentman to
Amanda Baugher of Emmitsburg d/o Isaac Baugher,
merchant of Emmitsburg, d 7/24/1885, age 63,
bd Mt. Olivet Cem.

ELDER
- William Elder moved to the Frederick County area about 1728 from St. Mary's County, Maryland, where his ancestors had been located for three generations. He settled first at Zentz's Mill, three miles south of the college. His first wife, Ann Wheeler died there in 1739, he hollowed for her coffin one of those grand old chestnut trees ... and years later transferred her remains to the Elder family burial ground laid out on his farm, half a mile from Mt. St. Mary's College. Here he built a more permanent home with a house - chapel attached, which stood until 1862 and was known as "Elder's Station".

The old burial ground of the Elder family, laid out and set aside by William(1) Elder remains to this day - a memorial to that Roman Catholic pioneer. Inscriptions from that cemetery:-
1. "In memory of / William Elder, Sr. / Born 1707 / Died / April 22 1775."
2. "In memory of / Ann (Wheeler) Elder / wife of / William Elder, Sr. / Died August 11, 1739 / Aged 30 years."
3. "In memory of / Jacoba Clementina Livers / Elder / wife of / William Elder / Senior / Died September 19, 1807 / Aged 90 years."

References: - "Story of the Mountain", Meline & McSweeney, 1911, "History of Emmitsburg, Maryland", James A. Helman, 1906, "History of Western Maryland", J. Thomas Scharf, 1882.

- William(1) Elder, b 1707, in Lancashire, England or St. Mary's County, Maryland. d 1775, nr Emmitsburg, MD., bd Elder family cemetery. m1 Ann Wheeler, 1709 - 1739, bd 1 nr Zentz's Mill and later moved to Elder family Cemetery. m 2 1743, Jacoba Clementina Livers, d/o Arnold Livers, b 1717, d 1807, bd Elder family cemetery.

Children of William and Ann Wheeler Elder:-
1. William Elder, b 1729, Emmitsburg farmer and blacksmith, m 1752 Miss Sabina Wickham, d 1786, d/o Nathaniel and Priscilla Tyler Wickham.
2. Guy Elder, 1731-1805, Emmitsburg farmer, m1 1756 Elenor Wickham, d/o Nathaniel Wickham, m2 by 1760 Eleanor Ogle Beall, d/o Joseph Ogle, widow of Ninian M. Beall.
3. Charles Elder, 1730 1804, Emmitsburg farmer, m Julia Ward of Charles Co., MD.
4. Richard Elder, 1734-1790, Emmitsburg farmer, m Phoebe Deloyvier, d/o John Delozier.
5. Mary Elder, 1735-1798, bd Mt. Pleasant, m Richard Lilly s/o Samuel Lilly, lived at Hunting Creek, Frederick Co., MD.

Children of William and Jacoba Clementina Livers Elder:-
1. Elizabeth Elder, 1743-1820, lived nr Emmitsburg,
   m 1760 Richard Brawner (1736-1783) s/o Edward Brawner.
2. Arnold Elder, 1745-1812, bd Elder cemetery, Emmitsburg farmer, his land became a part of Mount Saint Mary's College. m Clotilda Phoebe Green, 1752-1833, bd Elder cemetery, d/o Francis, she m2 Roger Brooke.
3. Ann Elder, 1746-1806, m 1771, Henry Spalding (d 1816), American Revolution Soldier, s/o Basil and Catherine Green Spalding, lived nr Taneytown, both are bd at Taneytown St. Joseph's Catholic Cemetery.
4. Thomas H. Elder, b 1/4/1748, m 1771, Elizabeth Spalding, d/o Basil & Catherine Green Spalding of Charles County, Maryland. They had 11 children and lived in Harbaugh Valley for 28 years and then moved to Kentucky.
5. Ignatius Elder, b 1749, d ca 1800, Soldier in the American Revolution, Ensign 37th Battalion of Company Militia in 1776, m Elizabeth Brawner, d/o Edward Brawner, they moved to Kentucky.
6. Francis Elder, 1750/5 - 1816, American Revolution Soldier, Ensign in Col. Johnson's Battalion, m Catherine Spalding, (1766-1809), d/o Basil and Catherine Green Spalding, and lived in Frederick County, Maryland.
7. Aloysius Elder, 1757-1827, bd Elder Cemetery, lived on the Elder homestead, the 'Old church on the Hill' was built on his land in 1806 and Mt. St. Mary's College in 1808. m1 Elizabeth Mills (1757-1802), d/o Justinian Mills, bd Elder Cemetery, m2 Mary Josephine Green Hayden (1775-1842), d/o Philip Green, and widow of Bernard Hayden, bd Elder Cemetery.

- Basil Spalding Elder, s/o Thomas H. and Elizabeth Spalding Elder, and grandson of William Elder and Jacoba Clementina Livers Spalding, b 10/22/1773, nr Emmitsburg, d 10/13/1869, Baltimore, MD., m 11/18/1801, Elizabeth Snowden, Children:-
1. Eleanor Elder, became a Sister of Charity.
2. Mrs. Jenkins, d in Havava, Cuba in 1846.
3. Mrs. Baldwin, lived in Baltimore, d 1872.
4. Francis W. Elder, Baltimore, MD.
5. Basil T. Elder, St. Louis, Missouri.
6. James C. Elder, Baton Rouge, LA.
7. Joseph R. Elder, Denver, Colo.
8. Thomas S. Elder, New Orleans, LA.
9. William Henry Elder, Bishop of Cincinnati.
10. Charles D. Elder, New Orleans, LA.
and three children died in infancy.

- James Elder, moved to Kentucky, was born in Emmitsburg District in 1760, the s/o Guy Elder and grandson of William and Ann Wheeler Elder. He married Ann Richards and moved to Kentucky, where he settled on Hardin's Creek. His brother William Elder joined him a short time later and settled in the same area. James d 8/15/1845 and his wife Ann d 1/8/1857.

- Thomas H. Elder, b 1/4/1748, s/o William and Jacoba Clementina Livers Elder, m 1771 Elizabeth Spalding and lived in Harbaugh Valley, Frederick County, Maryland for 28 years. In 1799 they moved to Kentucky. Children:-
1. Anne (or Nancy) Elder, 7/1/1772 - 1844, unmarried.
2. Basil Spalding Elder, 10/22/1773 - 10/13/1869, m 11/18/1801 Elizabeth Snowden (d 1/20/1860)
3. Catherine Elder, b 3/7/1775, became the second wife of Joseph Gardiner, of Nelson Co., KY. Three of her step daughters became Sisters of Charity, of the Nazareth Community, and of these Sister Frances Gardiner was for many years Superior of the Sisterhood.
4. William Pius Elder, 5/4/1778 - 8/22/1799, d in Balt.
5. Clementina Elder, 6/16/1780 - 8/21/1851, m Richard Clarke.
6. Ignatius Elder, b 7/21/1782, m Monica Greenwell.
7. Teresa Elder, 3/1/1785 - 12/10/1816, unmarried.
8. Thomas Richard Elder, 6/14/1789 - 7/11/1835, m Caroline Clements.
9. Christiana Elder, b 10/30/1791, m John B. Wright.
10. Mary Elizabeth Elder, b 5/15/1794, m John Tarbee.
11. Maria M. Elder, b 4/11/1791?, m John Howell.

ELLIOT

- ELIZABETH ELLIOT, widow during the Civil War, lived in Emmitsburg, near or at the present office of the Emmitsburg Chronicle. During the Civil War, Maryland was a divided state. Many of its citizens sympathized with the South - many were slave owners. Mrs. Elizabeth Elliot was an ardent believer and supporter of the Confederacy. She could not go to war but she placed an important and active role in the struggle. Her home in Emmitsburg became a refuge for spys or agents of the South. Here they were hidden and cared for until such time as they could escape within their own lines. According to a fairly reliable tradition the famous Confederate espionage agent, Mrs. Greensleeves and her daughter - after the former was released from the old Capitol prison, Wash. D.C., stayed with Mrs. Elliot for a short time. Shortly thereafter the spy and her daughter were drowned in the Atlantic Ocean off Cape Fear - in an effort to escape a Union patrol and board a Confederate gunboat.

After 1875 Elizabeth Elliot name disappears from the tax lists and it is not known whether or not she died or sold her property and moved to another locality. It is interesting to note that Robert W. Chambers, historian and novelist, mentions Mrs. Elliot and her activities in his book "Operator No. 13."

EYSTER   EISTER   OYSTER

- Eyster - Eister - Oyster Family - The Oyster (or Eyster) Family first settled near Codorus, in York County, Pennsylvania, and was members of St. Micheal's (now St. Matthew's) Lutheran Congregation at Conewago (now Hanover).

- Eyster family members of St. Micheal's Lutheran, Hanover:-
1. George, s/o George & Madalena Eyster, b 6/8/1782.
2. Anna Maria, d/o George & Madalena Eister, 4/10/1784.
3. Barbara, d/o Peter Oister, b 5/14/1793.
4. Anna Maria, d/o Jacob & Catherine Eyster, b 4/7/1816.
5. Samuel, s/o Jacob Oyster, b 12/22/1817.
6. Elisa, d/o Jacob & Catherine Eyster, b 12/12/1819.
7. Sarah Jane, d/o Jacob & Catherine Eyster, b 2/5/1836.
8. Ellen Louisa, d/o Samuel & Sidney Oyster, b 6/24/1857.

- Andrew Eyster - b 1800, d 4/19/1872, 72 years, bd Emmitsburg Elias Lutheran, clock maker and silversmith of Emmitsburg. m1 Mary Margaret Winter 1801-1833, one child, John Thomas Eyster 1833-1921: m2 Livinia McNair, 8/6/1809-8/9/1869, bd Elias, she was the d/o Samuel & Livinia McNair. Children:-
1. John Thomas Eyster, 1833-1921, moved to California, bd Elias Lutheran, Emmitsburg.
2. Ellen C. Eyster, d 9/23/1881, 44/0/0, bd Elias.
3. Samuel Hueston Eyster, b 2/21/1842, d 8/24/1908, a Civil War Union Veteran of the Pennsylvania Reserves. bd Mt. View Cem., Emmitsburg.
4. Emma K. Scott Eyster Kelly, b 1844
5. George T. Eyster, 1847-1914, Emmitsburg jewler, m 1895, Fannie M. Frailey.
6. Hall Webster Eyster, b 6/24/1851

- Elisa Eyster, d/o Jacob & Catherine Eyster, b 2/5/1836, bp 1/30/1820 at St. Micheal's Lutheran, Conewago.
- Ellen Louisa, d/o Samuel & Sidney Oyster, b 6/24/1857, bp 1/23/1858 at St. Micheal's Lutheran, Conewago.
- George T. Eyster - "George T. Eyster has hung out, at his store, a large gilt watch, that indicates the time at 8:20 or 5:40 o'clock - as you please to read it. It goes by swinging." - Emmitsburg Chronicle May 5, 1883.
- "George T. Eyster, Executor for the estate of his sister, the late Ellen C. Eyster, of this place, has published due notice for settlement of said Estate." - Emmitsburg Chronicle Oct 15, 1881.
- George Eister took up lands located on Codorus Creek in what is now York County, Pennsylvania, in 1748.

- George T. Eyster, Emmitsburg jewler, b 9/23/1847, s/o Andrew Eyster, d 2/18/1914, bd Emmitsburg Mt. View, Civil War Soldier, Company C Coles Calvary. m 4/24/1895 by the Rev. Henry Mann, to Fannie M. Frailey (b 8/23/1863-2/20/1930. Children:-
1. Mary Ellen Eyster, b 12/3/1897, m Frederick D. Kime, a graduate of the U.S. Naval Academy, and held the rank of Rear Admiral.
2. Virginia Scott Eyster, m Allen B. Kime, brother of Frederick D. Kime.
- H.W. Eyster - "Married, in Shrewsbury, York Co., PA., by the Rev. Ephraim Miller - Mr. H.W. Eyster, of this place, to Miss Mollie Gingell, also of Emmitsburg, MD." - Emmitsburg Chronicle May 20, 1882.
- Hall Webster Eyster, s/o Andrew Eyster, b 1851, d 1927, bd Emmitsburg, Mt. View Cem. m 1882, Mary Mollie Gingell, 1863-1931, bd Mt. View. Children:-
1. Mary Violet Eyster, d 8/11/1884, 0/4/9, bd Elias.
- Jacob Oyster, d 12/8/1825, 64 yrs., bd Elias, the father of Samuel Oyster who is bd at old Tom's Creek. Jacob's wife's name is thought to be Maria Catherine.
- Jacob Oyster, s/o Jacob & Maria, b 2/4/1792, d 9/101794, 2/7/6 - bd Tom's Creek Lutheran & Reformed Cem.
- Jacob Oyster, d 12/8/1825, 64 yrs., bd Elias Cem.
- "John Oyster on May 12, 1748, took up fifty acres of land adjoining the lands of Martin Miller, located on a branch of the Codorus Creek, on the Susquehanna River, in York Co., PA." Land office of Pennsylvania.
- "John H. Oyster of near Washington City and Phebe Ann Flohr of Gettysburg, married 9/9/1846." - The Star & Sentinel - Sept 13, 1846.
- "John Thomas Eyster, b 1/23/1833, s/o Andrew & Mary Winter Eyster, went to California as a young man and lived there for the rest of his life. He died May 7, 1921 and his body was cremeated and the ashes were sent to his cousin, Columbia Winter. She arranged for their burial on his mother's grave at Emmitsburg Elias Lutheran Cemetery."
- "Mary Eyster, d 4/18/1843, aged 56/7/27. bd Harbaugh's Church, Sabillasville, MD."
- "Mrs. Mary Oyster, Died, near Washington City, on 1/11/1845, Mrs. Mary Oyster, the wife of George Oyster, for many years a resident of Georgetown, and a native of Emmitsburg, MD." - Gettysburg Star & Sentinel - Jan 20, 1845.
- Peter Eyster - "A.C. Musselman, of Fairfield, PA., has sold the farm of Peter Eyster, in Liberty Twp., Adams Co., PA., containing 98 acres, 150 perches, to James Bowling, for $2100." - Emmitsburg Chronicle Aug 1, 1881.
- Samuel Oyster, s/o Jacob & Maria, b 2/4/1792, d 9/10/1794, 2/6/7, bd old Tom's Creek Lutheran & Reformed Cemetery. - black slate stone with German inscription.

- Samuel Oyster, s/o Jacob Oyster, b 12/22/1817, bp 4/12/1818 at St. Micheal's Lutheran Church of the Conewago Settlement."
- Samuel H. Eyster, b 2/21/1842, d 8/24/1908, a Union Soldier of the PA Reserves, bd Emmitsburg Mt. View. He was unmarried and spent most of his life in California and paid only occassional visits to his home in Emmitsburg where he died. "Died 8/24/1908, Samuel H. Eyster, aged 67 yrs., burial in the Mt. View Cem." - M.F. Shuff Burial Records.

EYLER

- - Mrs. Joseph Eyler, d 7/2/1900, 28 yrs. - M.F. Shuff Burial Records
- William P. Eyler, 7/8/1862-3/3/1911, w, Barbara E., 7/18/1864-7/4/1908, bd Mt. View.

FLEMING

- Fleming Cemetery inscriptions at Tom's Creek Presbyterian:-
1. Robert Fleming, d 8/26/1818, 7 yrs.
2. Robert Fleming, d 6/17/1834, 69/0/7.
3. Mary Fleming, w/o Robert Fleming, d 6/5/1846 80 yrs.
4. Robert Fleming, s/o Robert & Mary, d 5/27/1833(or 53), 26 yrs.
5. Rueben Fleming, 5/3/1820-8/7/1831(71?)
6. Ellen Bruce Fleming, 2/22/1829-3/30/1905.

FORNEY

- The Forneys were an early and prominent family in York and Lancaster Counties, Pennsylvania. Adam Forney came to Penn's Province from Germany, settled in the vicinity of Manheim.
  In the Forney family Bible, Johann Adam(1) Forney wrote: "In the year 1721 on October 16th, I, Johann Adam Forney and Louisa Fornisin, with four children, arrived at Philadelphia in Pennsylvania."
  By 1731 Johann Adam Forney and his family were living on a plantation in Diggs Choice, in the vicinity of Hanover, York Co., PA. At that time it was known as the Conewago Settlement.
  Johann Adam Forney died in 1752 as the result of a wound suffered in a foray with the Indians. Six children were born to the old pioneer and his wife - four in "the old country" and two in Pennsylvania.

- Cemetery Inscriptions:- Tom's Creek Lutheran Churchyard:-
1. John Forney d 4/17/1848, 76/1/2
2. Christina, w/o John Forney, d 1/4/1855, 83/0/4
3. John A. Forney, 1/23/1847-12/26/1874
- Emmitsburg Elias Lutheran:-
1. Magdalena Forney 4/19/1843 - 8/25/1872
- Emmitsburg Mt. View:-
1. Susanna Forney, d 12/22/1872, 69/1/7

FOSTER

- Stephen Foster, the composer, m Jane Denny(5) McDowell, b 12/10/1829, the d/o Dr. Andrew(4) McDowell and his wife Jane Denny McDowell.

FRAILEY

- Oscar D. Frailey, of Emmitsburg, 1853-1932, bd Emmitsburg Mt. View Cem. m Clara Hoke, 1854-1933, d/o Peter and Frances Ann Rowe Hoke. Children:-
1. Richard E. Frailey 1883-1884, bd Elias.
2. Alice Madeline Racheal Frailey, b 1885
3. Carson Frayley, b 1887
4. George Clarence Frailey, b 1890.

GALT

Galt family - Piney Creek Presbyterian Records:-
1. Sarah Galt, wife of Capt John Galt, d 2/20/1864, aged 85 yrs. bd Piney Creek Presbyterian Cemetery.
2. Subscription List May 1, 1806 - Matthew Gault.
3. 1821, the Rev. Robert Smith Grier married William Jones to Mary Galt.
4. Membership List 1824 - Mathew Galt, Mary Galt, Elizabeth Galt, Susan Galt, Rebecca Galt, Sterling Galt, Margaret Galt, Samuel Galt and Mary Galt.
5. - those subscribing to the 'pastor's salary' - Matthew Galt, John Galt and Mary Galt - 1817.

- Edith Bolling Galt Wilson - MRS. WOODROW WILSON - "Mrs. Woodrow Wilson, the second wife of Presdient Woodrow Wilson, was first married to Norman Galt, of Washington D.C., but a descendant, in the fifth generation of Mathew Galt who founded the family in Maryland.

Mrs. Galt and the President, during the period of their engagement, visited the home of Sterling Galt, brother of the first husband of Mrs. Galt. Sterling Galt was a resident of Emmitsburg during the greater part of his life and worked hard for the progress of the town and its residents.

Norman Galt, son of Mathew Galt, married Edith Bolling. After Norman Galt's death Jan 1908 at Washington D.C. Edith Bolling Galt married President Woodrow Wilson. She wrote a book "My Memoir" which gave some history of the Galt family of Washington D.C. and Emmitsburg, Maryland.

Sterling Galt, brother-in-law of Mrs. Woodrow Wilson, by her first marriage, was a resident of Emmitsburg for many years, and died at his home in Emmitsburg. Mr. Galt was married twice - first to Harriet Wingard and after her death to Lucy Higbee.

- James Galt, s/o Matthew & Elizabeth Simpson Galt. Children:-
    1. Elizabeth Galt, m David Fisher
    2. Mary E. Galt Davis
    3. George Sterling Galt.
    4. William Galt
    5. James Veitch Galt
    6. Thomas Galt
    7. Matthew William Galt, m Mary Jane Galt

- John Galt, s/o Matthew & Elizabeth Simpson Galt. Children:-
    1. dau., m Mr. Ewing
    2. dau., m Mr. Dinsmore
    3. dau., m Mr. Brawner
    4. Elizabeth Galt Dysert
    5. Mary Galt Dysert
    6. Abner Galt
    7. son - probably died young

- Matthew Galt - Matthew Galt, the founder of the family in Maryland, m Elizabeth Simpson, were the parents of at least three sons, one son:-
1. Mathew Galt, m Mary ? , Children:-
    1. John Galt
    2. Peter Galt
    3. William Galt
    4. James Galt
    5. Joseph Galt
    6. Moses Galt
    7. Mathew Galt
    8. Elizabeth Galt
    9. Susannah Galt, m Wm Shaw
    10. Sterling Galt, m Margaret Grayson
    11. Rebecca Galt, m Benjamin Shunk
    12. Samuel Galt, m Mary Crockett
    13. Mary Galt, m Wm Jones

- Moses Galt, m Hannah Little, Children:-
    1. Samuel M. Galt, m Isabella Baer, d 7/2/1892, 69/11/5 bd Piney Creek Presbyterian Cem.
    2. Mary Galt, m Thomas Longley, bd Piney Creek "Thomas Longley d 7/7/1890, 72/9/10, Mary D. Longley d 6/18/1909, 75/3/9
    3. Catherine Galt, d 8/17/1871, 48 yrs., bd Piney Creek Presbyterian, m Jacob Koons.
    4. Rebecca Galt.

- Peter Galt s/o Matthew Galt. Children:-
    1. Lucretia Galt
    2. Mary Galt
    3. Dr. John Murray Galt, m Nancy Elizabeth Galt
    4. Washington Galt, bd Piney Creek Presbyterian Cem.

- Robert Galt - "Robert(1) Galt, the ancestor of the Pennsylvania Galts, left Ireland in 1710 and came to Pennsylvania. With the first Robert Galt came his son-in-law, William Wilson, and a grandson, Robert Armour. They landed at New Castle, Delaware. Robert left his family at New Castle while he journeyed into the colony of Pennsylvania; to seek lands for a plantation. He selected the area of Pequea, Lancaster County. He returned to New Castle for his family and on his return could not find the area of his first selection and eventually located on a well-watered tract further north.

James(2) Galt, s/o Robert, m Miss Alison. They had five sons;- Robert, John, William, James and Thomas Galt. William and John built what was known as "Galt's Mill".

Thomas(3) Galt, s/o James, m Isabel Wilson and went west to Cumberland County Valley and founded a farm near Carlise. But trouble with the Indians and they returned to Lancaster County. They then resided near New Holland. They were members of Pequea Presbyterian Church. They had tow sons;- James(4) and Alexander Galt.

The descendants of Alexander(4) Galt are the branch of the family known as the "Hill Galts" because they lived among the foothills of the Welsh Mountains.

- Samuel Galt, s/o Mathew and Mary Galt, m Mary Crockett, bd Piney Creek Presbyterian Cemetery, Harney, MD.

- Samuel M. Galt Family Bible:-
"Samuel M. Galt's Book - November 29, 1856. Handed down to his son, Robert W. Galt after the death of his father in 1892.
Marriages
Samuel M. Galt and Isabella Barr was married January 8th 1850.
Robert W. Galt and Alice T. Dorsey was married January 13th 1887.
Births
Albert Franklin Galt was born Dec 14th 1850.
James Barr Galt was born Sept 30th 1852.
Hannah Mary Galt was born April 19th 1854.
John Ross Galt was born June 2nd 1856.
Robert Walter Galt was born April 10th 1858.
Maggie Bell Galt was born April 1st 1860.
Jane Elizabeth Galt was born June 2nd 1862.
Deaths
Samuel M. Galt died Feb 10th 1892.
Isabella Barr Galt died July 2nd 1892.
Albert F. Galt died Sept 15th 1890.
James Barr Galt died April 9th 1919.
Hannah Mary Galt Weaver died Feb 16th 1928.
Robert Walter Galt died March 30th 1937."

- Sterling Galt, s/o Mathew and Elizabeth Simpson Galt, b 11/28/1796, d 11/19/1885, bd Piney Creek Presbyterian Cem. m Margaret Grayson, d/o Nathaniel Grayson, 11/17/1798 - 8/28/1851, bd Piney Creek.
Children:-
1. Nancy Galt, m Sr. John Murray Galt.
2. John Galt, m Elizabeth Handy
3. Mary Jane Galt
4. Mathew William Galt, - children:- Charles, Annie Galt Fendall, Walter Allen, Norman Galt, m Edith Bolling, Sterling Galt.
5. George Grayson Galt, 1/11/1832-2/20/1835, bd Piney Creek
6. Rev. Sterling Galt, d unmarried
7. Henry Galt, m Annie Moore
8. Margaret G. Galt, m Milton Valentine

- Rev. Sterling Galt, s/o Sterling and Margaret Grayson Galt, b 2/28/1837 - educated at Princeton College and Theological Seminary. He was licensed to preach by the Presbytery of New Brunswick in 1861. He began his labors at Newark and Red Clay

Creek, Delaware, within the bounds of the Presbytery of New Castle by which Dusbytery he was ordained in 1862. After three years in this, his only charge, he 'fell a victim to typhoid fever on 10/4/1865. He died at the home of his friend, the Rev. Thomas Love. He was buried from the residence of his brother in Washington D.C."

- Washington Galt, s/o Peter Galt and grandson of Matthew Galt. He is buried inside the lower gate into Piney Creek graveyard. He married Louisa Krise, d/o Abraham Krise and was buried at Piney Creek.

"Married, August 2, 1852, by the Rev. Mr. Aughinbaugh, Mr. Washington Galt of Frederick County, Maryland to Miss Louisa A. Krise, d/o Mr. Abraham Krise of Freedom Twp., Adams County, PA."

Washington Galt, b 8/17/1825, s/o Peter Galt, d 7/14/1890, 64/10/27, bd Piney Creek Presbyterian Cem., Harney, MD. m 8/2/1852, Louisa A. Krise, d/o Abraham, Lousia A. Krise Galt and her daughter Mary Jane Galt were first interred at Piney Creek but later removed to the Krise Plot at Gettysburg Evergreen Cemetery.

GAMBLE

- Joseph Gamble, 1865-1948, born at Emmitsburg, s/o Samuel and Emma R. Gamble, employed in Philadelphia, on retirement he returned to Emmitsburg and lived at the "old hotel in Emmitsburg". He was the grandson of David and Margaret Annan Gamble, bd Toms Creek Presbyterian.

GARDNER

-William P. Gardner, b 12/9/1822, d 3/22/1900, Jane M. Fleming, wife of William P. Gardner, d 7/22/1880, 66/10/9, bd Tom's Creek Presbyterian.

GAUGH

- Cemetery inscriptions at old Tom's Creek Lutheran and Reformed churchyard:-
1. Carrie Gaugh, d/o W. & C. Gaugh, d 3/31/1887, 10 days.
2. George Gaugh, d 11/16/1854, 78/10/2
3. Elizabeth, w/o George Gaugh, d 10/18/1858, 78/6/9.
4. Percival Gaugh, d 1/11/1877, 56/6/17.
5. Harriet Gaugh, w/o Percival Gaugh, 4/13/1822-5/31/1896.
6. Willie B. Gaugh, s/o W. & C. Gaugh, d 9/19/1887, 10/8/19.
7. Wilson A. Gaugh, d 7/18/1879, 30/4/18.

- George Gaugh, d 11/17/1851, 78/10/28, bd Tom's Creek Lutheran and Reformed churchyard. m Elizabeth, d 10/18/1858, 78/6/9, bd Tom's Creek Lutheran and Reformed. George, Elizabeth and Percival Gaugh are listed as members of Elias Lutheran Church, Emmitsburg, in 1851.

- Jonathan Gaugh and Catherine Eve Bowers, m 5/7/1835, at Mrs. Bowers house. Jonathan Gaugh d 8/22/1889, 78/8/0. Catherine E. Gaugh, w/o Jonathan, 3/22/1813-4/30/1865, both bd Utica Lutheran. Children:-
1. Addie E. Gaugh, 9/5/1860 - 4/10/1943

- Percival & Harriet Gaugh, a dau., Elizabeth Catherine, b 8/1/1849, bp 8/19/1850, Trinity Lutheran Records, Taneytown.

- Wilson A. Gaugh, d 7/18/1879, 30/4/18, m Mary V., both bd Tom's Creek Lutheran and Reformed churchyard. Children:-
1. William Barton Gaugh, b 12/31/1876, d 9/19/1887, bd Tom's Creek Lutheran & Reformed churchyard.
2. Effie Catherine Gaugh, b 12/5/1875

GEHRHART

- "Mrs. Benjamin Gehrhart, d 5/31/1894, 61 yrs." - M.F. Shuff Burial Records.

- Peter Gehrhart/Gearhart, 3/14/1844-2/5/1922, m Sarah ? , 8/2/1847-1/21/1906, both bd Emmitsburg Mt. View Cemetery.

GELWICKS

- Joseph Theophilus Gelwicks, 3/17/1843-3/22/1907, m Martha Isabella ? , 5/24/1844-7/11/1906, both bd Emmitsburg Mt. View Cemetery, "Mrs. J. Theophilus Gelwicks, d 7/11/1906, 63 yrs. J. Theophilus Gelwicks, d 3/22/1907, 65 yrs." - M.F. Shuff Burial Records.

GIBBS

- Harriet Gibbs, wife of William A. Gibbs, 8/18/1805 - 9/2/1882, 77/0/14. bd Tom's Creek Presbyterian.

GILILAND

- John Gililand - "Sacred / to the memory of / John Gililand / Died November 11, 1792 / Aged 4 years, 10 months, / and 3 days." Tom's Creek Presbyterian Cemetery.

GILLILAND

- Agnes Shields Gilliland - "Agnes Shields, the daughter of William(1) and Jane Bentley Williams Shields, was born December 1766. She was first married to Jacob Gilliland and after his death to Micheal Woods.
It is a known fact that Agnes Shields Gilliland, in company with 7 of her brothers and sisters emigrated to Tennessee. This probably took place after the death of her first husband for the Gillilands were an old and honored family in southeastern Pennsylvania and northern Frederick County, Maryland. It is also quite possible and highly probable that Jacob Gilliland died while

living in the vicinity of Emmitsburg, and was interred in a grave that is now unmarked - either in the Shield's family burial ground or in Tom's Creek Presbyterian churchyard."

- Betsy Gilliland/Gilland/Gilleland - "m June 1818, Mr. C. (Christian) Correll to Betsy Gilleland, by the Rev. Robert Smith Grier." (Note: Betsy Gilleland was the daughter of John Gilleland and Mary Hays Smith.)

- Jane Gilliland - "Jane Gilliland, m 4/1/1783, to James Shields, s/o William and Jane Bentley Williams Shields. Jane Gilliland was born Oct 15, 1764 and died Dec. 21, 1849. James and Jane Gilliland Shields emigrated to Tennessee after the American Revolutionary War."

- John Gilliland - "John Gilliland and his wife Jane, were the pioneer ancestors of the family in this country. They followed the tide of emigration in that day and settled near what is now the town of Biglerville, in Adams County, Pennsylvania.
According to the Family Bible they had the following children:-
1. James Gilliland was born August the 1st 1745. Went to Virginia.
2. Samuel Gilliland was born November the 6th 1747 - married Eleanor Vance - departed this life June 21st, 1811, aged 45 years."

- John Gilliland - "According to the record in an old Session Book of the Piney Creek Presbyterian Congregation, John Gilliland subscribed to the minister's salary in 1817."

- John J. F. Gilliland - "John J. F. Gilliland / Born January 28, 1832 / Died November 21, 1906 / Aged 74 years, 9 months, / and 23 days." "Annie M. Gilliland / the wife of John J. F. Gilliland / Died December 2, 1873 / Aged 37 years, 3 months, / and 18 days." "Sacred to the memory of / the Infant child / of John J. F. & Annie M. Gilliland". - Piney Creek Presbyterian Cemetery, Harney, MD.

Margaret Gilliland - 1824 Communicants List of Tom's Creek Presbyterian Church - lists - Margaret Gilliland.

GILLILAND - GILLELAN

- The Gillelans of Frederick County, Maryland, were a part of the pioneer family, who came from the Province of William Penn from the north of Ireland, and first settled in what is now Adams County, Pennsylvania.
In the Gettysburg "Star and Sentinel" for May 26, 1889 the following was published:- "Gilliland - When the Gillilands, one of our oldest families, first settled in this section, they took up their abode on the farm, now owned by William Brown, in Butler Twp. It was there on the outskirts of civilization, and a fort built there often gave the settlers protection from the Indians."

- Etta M. Gillelan - "Etta Mae Gillelan / Born 1867 / Died 1922." - Mt. View Cem.

- George Lawrence Gillelan - "Baptised - George Lawrence Gillelan, son of William and Magdelena Gillelan, born April 13, 1842, baptised June 4, 1842." - Trinity Lutheran Taneytown. "In memory of / George Gillelan / Born April 16, 1842 / Died Dec 4, 1911." - Emmitsburg Elias Lutheran Cem. George L. Gillelan was born on the old Hockensmith property, m Ida S. Ohler, d/o Samuel G. Ohler. "Ida S. Gillelan / wife of George Gillelan / Born May 23, 1852 / Died April 7, 1927." - Elias Lutheran Cem.

- George Thomas Gillelan - "Died May 24, 1841, George Thomas Gillelan, son of William & Magdelena Gillelan, aged 1 yr, 5 m, & 17 ds." - Taneytown Trinity Lutheran.

- George S. Gillelan - "In memory of / George S. Gillelan / Born August 23, 1880 / Died August 12, 1904." - Elias Lutheran Cem.

- Hannah S. Gillelan - "In memory of / Hannah S. Gillelan / Born 1836 / Died 1923." - Elias Lutheran Cem.

- Harry Morris Gillelan - "Harry Morris Gillelan / Born 1871 / Died 1943." - Mt. View Cem.

- John Thomas Gillelan - "In memory of / John Thomas Gillelan / Died January 7, 1834 / Aged 6 months and / 9 days." - Old Baptist (Taneytown Baptist) Churchyard, Taneytown, MD.

- Mary Gillelan - 1824 Membership List of Piney Creek Presbyterian Church - Mary Gillelan.
- Mary Gillelan - "In memory of / Mary Gillelan / Died March 26, 1829 / Aged 57 years, 8 months, / and 13 days." (1771-1829) - Harney Piney Creek Presbyterian Cemetery.

- Rhoda Gillelan - Miss Rhoda Gillelan, whose grave is to be found in Elias Lutheran churchyard, Emmitsburg, served as a nurse with the Armed Forces during WWI and was with the Nurse Corps in France. When she died she was accorded full military honors for service to her country. "Rhoda Hannah Gillelan / daughter of George and Ida S. Gillelan / Died January 26, 1957 / aged 71 years, 2 months / and 13 days." - Elias Lutheran Cemetery.

- Ruth B. Gillelan - "In memory of / Ruth B. Gillelan / Born August 20, 1882 / Died - ." - Elias Lutheran Cem.

- William Gillelan - "William Gillelan was the first of his family to live on the old Hockensmith Tavern property. William married Magdelena Hockensmith and lived on the Hockensmith property where they raised their family. They are buried at Emmitsburg Elias Lutheran Cemetery. "In memory of / William Gillelan / Died September 1, 1880 / Aged 71 years, 6 months, and 15 days."

"In memory of / Magdelena Gillelan / wife of William Gillelan / Died April 1, 1874 / Aged 71 years, 4 months, and / 28 days."

William R. Gillelan - "In memory of / William R. Gillelan / Born 1864 / Died 1926." "In memory of Margaret J. Gillelan / wife of William R. Gillelan / Born 1877 / Died 19--." - Elias Lutheran Cem.

GILLELAN

- Gillelan burials at Emmitsburg Elias Lutheran Cemetery:-
1. William Gillelan, d 9/1/1880, aged 71/6/15
2. Magdelena Gillelan, w/o William, d 4/1/1874, 71/4/26
3. George Gillelan, 4/16/1842-12/4/1911
4. Ida S. Gillelan, w/o George Gillelan 5/25/1852 - 4/7/1927.
5. Carrie Gillelan, d/o Geo. & Ida Gillelan 3/1/1875 - 5/13/1941
6. Rhoda Hannah Gillelan, d/o Geo. & Ida, d 1/26/1957, 71/2/13
7. Ruth B. Gillelan, b 8/20/1882 d   -
8. William R. Gillelan 1864 - 1926
9. Margaret J. Gillelan, w/o Wm R., 1877-19--
10. George S. Gillelan 8/23/1880-8/12/1904
11. Hannah S. Gillelan 1836 - 1923

- Gillelan burials at Emmitsburg Mountain View Cemetery:-
1. Charles Edgar Gillelan 1867-1937
2. Sarah Salome Gillelan, w/o Charles E., 1860-1934
3. Etta Mae Gillelan 1867-1922
4. H. Morris Gillelan 1871 - 1943

- Gillelan Family Bible Records, courtesy of Mrs. Ella Gillelan Shuff:-
Marriages
David S. Gillelan to Miss Virginia Flegel Dec 26, 1865.
Births
David S. Gillelan born May 26, 1834.
Mrs. Virginia Gillelan born April 18, 1843.
Charles Edgar Gillelan born May 12, 1867.
Willy Robert Gillelan born Jan 9, 1869.
Harry Morris Gillelan born April 30, 1871.
Anna Virginia Gillelan born Feb 7, 1876.

- Adam Sentman Gillelan - "Baptised Adam Sentman Gillelan, son of William and Magdalena (Hockensmith) Gillelan - born November 15, 1846, bp Dec 14, 1846." "Died - Jan 10, 1848, Adam Sentman Gillelan - son of William & Magdelena Gillelan - aged 1 year, 1 month, & 26 ds." - Taneytown Trinity Lutheran Records.

- Charles E. Gillelan - "Charles Edgar Gillelan / Born 1867 / Died 1937." "Sarah Salome Gillelan / wife of Charles E. Gillelan / Born 1860 / Died 1934." - Mt. View Cemetery.

- Carrie Gillelan - "Carrie Gillelan / daughter of George and Ada S. Gillelan / Born March 1, 1875 / Died May 13, 1941." - Elias Lutheran Cemetery.

- David S. Gillelan - "David S. Gillelan was married to Virginia Flegel on December 5, 1865. David was the son of William and Magdelena Hockensmith Gillelan. David S. Gillelan, along with other members of the family are buried at Elias Lutheran Churchyard, Emmitsburg. "In memory of / David S. Gillelan / Born May 26, 1834 / Died November 7, 1904." "Virginia Gillelan / wife of David S. Gillelan / Born 1843 / Died 1949." "Anna V. Gillelan / daughter of David S. and Virginia Gillelan / Born 1876 / Died -."

- William R. Gillelan - "In memory of / William R. Gillelan / Died January 26, 1834 / Aged 28 years, 9 months, / and 16 days."
- Old Baptist (Taneytown Baptist) Churchyard.

GRABILL - GRAYBILL

- Frederick Grabill - "Sacred to the memory of / Frederick Grabill / Died Nov 12, 1807 / Aged 9 months & 14 days." - Elias Lutheran Cem.

- John Graybill - "In memory of / John Graybill / Died February 17, 1836 / aged 61 years." - Elias Lutheran Cem.
- John Stewart Grabill - "Baptised John Stewart Grabill, son of John and Elizabeth Grabill, born December 27, 1832, baptised Jan 15, 1833, sponsors, the parents." - Taneytown Trinity Lutheran Church Records.

- Peter Grabill - Peter Grabill, Soldier of the American Revolution, of Tom's Creek Hundred, Frederick County, Maryland, bd Elias Lutheran Cemetery, Emmitsburg - at least 3 sons:- Peter, Frederick and John Grabill.

- Peter Grabill, s/o Peter Grabill, m 10/16/1841, Sarah Rudisill, d/o Tobias Rudisill of Taneytown. Children:-
1. Margaret Ann Grabill, b 11/25/1842
2. Sarah Jones Grabill, 1/3/1845-3/15/1853
3. Harry George Grabill, 8/12/1851 - 10/12/1863, bd Emmitsburg View Cem.

In the files of the Emmitsburg Chronicle under the date of Jan 19, 1889 is the obituary of Sarah Rudisill Grabill, wife of Peter Grabill:- "Died recently, Mrs. Peter Grabill, the d/o the late Tobias Rudisill of Taneytown, MD. Mrs. Grabill lived for many years at the old Grabill homestead at Locust Grove near Emmitsburg. Died at the home of her daughter at Mayberry, Carroll Co., MD. Burial at Baust Church."

- Samuel Grabill, m 12/20/1860 to Jeanet Ingle, both of Carroll County, Maryland.

GRAHAM

- Eliza Graham, d 10/27/1831, 22 yrs. - bd Piney Creek Presbyterian Cemetery, Harney, MD.

GRIER

- Grier family members interred at Tom's Creek Presbyterian churchyard near Emmitsburg:-
1. Ann Laverty, sister of Elizabeth Grier, d 3/6/1858, aged 74 yrs.
2. Sarah Jane Grier, w/o Rev. Robert S. Grier, d 3/14/1848, 37 ys.
3. Rev. Robert S. Grier, d 12/28/1865, aged 76 yrs.
4. Elizabeth Grier, w/o Rev. Robert S. Grier, d 9/25/1830, 37 yrs.
5. Jane G. Eppley, w/o Adam Eppley & d/o Rev. Robert S. Grier, d 6/23/1843, 23/10/19.
6. Effie S. Horner, d/o O.A. & A.M. Horner, b 10/11/1869, d 3/14/1870. (NOTE: granddaughter of Rev. Robert S, Grier.)

7. A. Margaret Horner, wife of Major O.A. Horner, & dau. of Rev. R.S. Greir, d 8/14/1872, aged 27/3/23.
8. Infant son of O.A. & A.M. Horner, 6/25/1867-4/27/1867?
9. Infant son of O.A. & A.M. Horner, 8/13/1868-9/10/1868
10. Major Oliver A. Horner, 6/10/1841-8/6/1897
11. Ann Elizabeth Annan Horner 8/31/1847-3/24/1935. (NOTE: second wife of Major Oliver Horner.)

- Rev. James Grier, b Bucks Co., PA., d 11/19/1791, converted early in life by Whitfield; 1772 graduated from Princeton College; 1776 ordained pastor of Deep Run Church, PA., he remained there until his death in 1791.

- Rev. John Nathan Caldwell Grier, s/o Rev. Nathan and Susannah Smith Grier; 1809 graduate from Dickinson College, Carlise, PA., study theology under his father; 1814 pastor of Forks of the Brandywine, for over 50 years; d 9/12/1880.

- Rev. Nathan Grier, b 1760, Bucks Co., PA., graduated from the University of Pennsylvania, studied theology under his brother the Rev. James Grier; 1786 licensed by the Presbytery of Philadelphia; 1787 ordained pastor of Forks of the Brandywine Church, remained there until his death 3/31/1814.

- Rev. Robert Smith Grier, b 5/11/1790, at Brandywine Manor, Chester Co., PA., the s/o Rev. Nathan and Susannah Smith Grier. d 12/28/1865, 76 yrs., bd Tom's Creek Presbyterian churchyard, near Emmitsburg, MD. He graduated from Dickinson College, Carlise, PA., 1813 obtained leave to labor in the bounds of the Presbytery of Carlise; 1814 pastor od Tom's Creek and Piney Creek Presbyterian Churches, near Emmitsburg, where he remained until his death 12/29/1865 at Emmitsburg. He was a licentiate of the Presbytery of New Castle, and also known for his artistry in wood carving. He married three times. m1 Elizabeth Laverty, d 9/25/1830, bd Tom's Creek Presbyterian Cemetery, Children:- 2 sons & 3 daus.:-
1. Jane Grier, d 6/23/1843, 23/10/19, bd Tom's Creek Presbyterian Cemetery, m 11/10/1827, Adam Eppley.
2. Susan Grier, m Rev. Father John H. Marsden, rector of Christ Episcopal Church, Huntington Twp., Adams Co., PA., bd Gettysburg Evergreen Cemetery.
3. Mary Grier, never married and lived in Emmitsburg.
m2 7/26/1841, Sarah Jane Annan, d 3/14/1848, 37 yrs., bd Tom's Creek Presbyterian Cemetery, Children, 1 son, 1 dau.:-
1. A. Margaret Grier (Maggie A.), d 8/14/1872, 27/3/23, bd Tom's Creek Presbyterian Cemetery. m 6/28/1866 at Carlise to Major Oliver A. Horner, of Emmitsburg, MD.
2. a son, died young.
m3 7/20/1858, Margaret B. Stewart, 6/26/1818 - 3/8/1902, bd Tom's Creek Presbyterian Cemetery, no children.

- Rev. Robert Smith Grier, Marriage Records:-
1. May 1816 --?-- Colestock to Polly Heagy.
2. August 1816 - James Wharton to Sarah Mains.
3. November 1816 - William Curren to Jane McGuigan.

4. November 1816 - Andrew Stewart to Nancy Bigham.
5. November 1816 - Jacob Wieart to Sally Shriver.
6. October 1817 - James Cunningham to Elizabeth Stewart.
7. December 1817 - Mr Alex. Horner to Miss McKee.
8. January 1818 - Mr. Guinn to Jane Majors.
9. January 1818 - John Harper to Eliza Horner.
10. January 1818 - William Ross to Peggy Bigham.
11. February 1818 - Charles Bigham to Margaret Agnew.
12. March 1818 - Mr. R. Gilson to Mary Smith.
13. April 1818 - Francis Reid to Margaret McIllhenny.
14. March 1818 - David Morrison to Harriet Landers.
15. May 1818 - Jonathan Harbaugh to Mary Street.
16. June 1818 - Mr. C. Correll to Betsy Gilleland.
17. June 1818 - Dr. Daniel Moore to Louisa Snatzell.
18. October 1818 - Mr. Thomas Hays to Betsy Armstrong.
19. January 1819 - Mr. Bergaw to Sally Wilson.
20. February 1819 - Mr. Isaac Fisher to Miss Row.
21. March 1819 - William McCreary to Nancy Caldwell.
22. April 1819 - Mr. Kelly to Betsy Wilson.
23. July 1819 - Timothy Evans to Betsy McKean.
24. November 1819 - Mr. Daniel Wetzel to Miss Lane.
25. January 1820 - N. Nut to Evalina Crabster.
26. February 1820 - Mr. Lomer to Miss Stevenson.
27. March 1820 - John Smith to Miss McGinn.
28. March 1820 - Mr. Begore to Miss Hunter.
29. August 1820 - Mr. Jones to Miss McClellan.
30. 1820 - Joseph Randolph to Miss Moore.
31. 1820 - Samuel Majors to Miss Sweeney.
32. 1820 - Solomon Linn to Miss Moor.
33. 1820 - Joseph Boner to Betsy Robinson.
34. 1820 - Mr. T. Cooper to Miss Barr.
35. 1820 - Rob. McKinney to Miss Breckenridge.
36. 1820 - N. Grayson to Eliza Ann Shields.
37. 1821 - Andrew Horner to Eliza Marshall.
38. 1821 - Dr. Rob. Moore to Miss Snatzell.
39. 1821 - William Rea to Miss Bigham.
40. 1821 - Robert McGurgan to Barbara McColester.
41. 1821 - Mr. Locklin to Sally Randolph.
42. 1821 - Eli Horner to Miss McKee.
43. 1821 - Solomon Bosserman to Sally Ecker.
44. 1821 - Jesse Davidson to Miss Faris.
45. 1821 - William Jones to Mary Galt.
46. 1821 - Robert Holt to Ursula Little.
47. 1821 - Samuel Baird to Elizabeth Floor.
48. 1821 - Gideon Seabrooke to Sally Harper.
49. 1821 - Thomas Brooke to Miss Eyler.

At this point the Rev. Grier, for some reason or other, gave up keeping a record of the marriages performed by him. He must have officiated at many others for he continued in the active ministry for some forty-five years after this (1821) but the record remains blank, unless he had other records now lost.

- Rev. Robert Smith Grier - Additional marriages by the Rev. Robert Smith Grier, as taken from the "Adams Sentinel":-
1. February 21, 1839 - Samuel McMillan, of Hamiltonban Twp., to Ann Fisher, of Freedom Twp.
2. September 17, 1839, Hugh F. McGaughy, of Martinsburg, Virginia, but formerly of Adams County, to Jane Walker, d/o Andrew Walker, of Freedom Twp.
3. January 8, 1850 - Samuel Galt, of Carroll Co., to Isabella Barr, d/o James Barr, of Mount Joy Twp.
4. October 8, 1851 - William Bigham, of Freedom Twp., to Margaret Horner, d/o Andrew Horner, deceased, of Cumberland Twp.
5. December 24, 1857 - Eli Horner, Esq., of Cumberland Twp., to Sophia Agnew, of Emmitsburg.
6. January 8, 1858 - Jacob Overholtzer to Margaret Clark, d/o John Clark, both of Liberty Twp.
7. December 14, 1858, Cambell Tipper, of Path Valley, Franklin County, Pennsylvania, to Amanda Horner, d/o John Horner, Esq., of Mount Joy Twp.
8. May 16, 1861, James McAllister, of Carroll County, Maryland, to Jane A. Barr, of Gettysburg.
9. January 7, 1864, James A.M. Smith, of Adams County, to Sophia Galt, of Carroll County, Maryland.

This marriage record is far from complete. In the years before marriage license was required such records were recorded in the majority of instances, only by the officiating minister. Some gave a certificate to the 'newly wed' others did not. Many church records have been 'lost, strayed, ot stolen' therefore newspaper files are more often than not, the only source remaining.

GROBP

- Rev. John G. Grobp, pastor of Elias Lutheran Church, Emmitsburg, d 5/29/1829, 75 yrs, bd Taneytown Lutheran Church Cemetery. m Elizabeth, d 4/15/1835, 69 yrs., bd Taneytown Lutheran Church Cemetery. "In memory of / Rev. John G. Grobp / Who departed this life / May 27th, 1829 / Aged 76 years." "In memory of / Elizabeth Grobp / wife of John G. Grobp / Died April 15, 1835 / Aged 69 years." Monuments erected by Abraham Sheets.

GUTHRIE

- Adam Guthrie, owned a large livery stable in Emmitsburg, known as "Guthrie and Beam". (Present location of the Emmitsburg Fire Company - 1970.) 10/12/1809 - 8/19/1858, bd Tom's Creek Presbyterian Cemetery. m Margaret Wagner, 5/29/1809-3/3/1894, bd Tom's Creek Presbyterian Cemetery. Children:-
1. Jane Guthrie, 1836 - 1911, m George F. Beam
2. Mary Louisa Guthrie, went west with friends 'in the days of the covered wagon'. She settled at Helena, Montana, and pioneered in library work. After her retirement she returned to Emmitsburg and lived with her sisters until her death in 1915. She is interred at Tom's Creek Presbyterian Cemetery. 1834-1915.

3. William Guthrie, 'lived in the wst'.
4. Susan C. Guthrie was a maiden lady and resided in Emmitsburg her entire life. b 1831

- Guthrie family members interred at Tom's Creek Presbyterian Cemetery:-
1. Adam Guthrie   10/12/1809-8/19/1858
2. Margaret Wagner Guthrie, wife of Adam Guthrie, 5/29/1809 - 3/3/1894
3. Margaret A. Guthrie 6/3/1850-8/14/1850
4. John W. Guthrie 1/25/1833-8/4/1853
5. George P. Guthrie, 3/2/1846-11/16/1853
6. Jane Guthrie Beam 2/15/1836-8/28/1911
7. Mary L. Guthrie 6/3/1834-5/20/1915
8. Sarah C. Guthrie   11/6/1831-2/6/1936

HARLEY

- William Harley, 9/30/1807-2/26/1891, 83/4/26, bd Tom's Creek Presbyterian Cemetery.

HAYS

- Hays family members interred at Tom's Creek Presbyterian Cemetery:-
1. "In memory of / Elizabeth Curren Hays / wife of / Joseph Hays / Born July 1, 1823 / Died April 20, 1909." Note: Elizabeth Curren Hays was the d/o William and Jane Curren.
2. "In memory of / Joseph Hays / Born August 13, 1828 / Died December 5, 1888."
3. "In memory of / Rev. Andrew T. Hays / son of / Joseph and Elizabeth Hays / Born December 22, 1856 / Died November 23, 18-6."
4. "In memory of / Willie Van Lear Hays / son of / Joseph and Annie Hays / Born May 14, 1859 / Died September 11, 1866."
5. "In memory of Elizabeth Hays / daughter of / Joseph and Elizabeth Hays / Born September 1, 1861 / Died August 30, 1863."
6. "In memory of / Elizabeth Hays / wife of Thomas Hays / died July 5, 1850 / Aged 52 years and 9 months."
7. "In memory of / Thomas Hays / Died July 10, 1843 / Aged 52 years, 1 month and 20 days."
8. "Sacred / to the memory of / John Hays / son of / T. and E. Hays / Died June 4, 1847 / Aged 6 years and 2 months."
9. "In memory of / John Thomas Hays / son of / Thomas and Elizabeth Hays / Died September 23, 18-- / Aged ?." Note: This stone is badly weathered and cannot be deciphered.

HEAGY

- Henry Heagy was married to Racheal Shriver, on Dec 5, 1821. Racheal Shriver was the youngest daughter of Lewis and Mary Sheets Shriver, b at her father's home, on Marsh Creek, on 1/12/1803. She died 2/4/1879 and is interred with family members, in Elias Lutheran churchyard, Emmitsburg.

Henry Heagy was the son of Jacob Heagy of Liberty Twp., Adams County, PA. In July of 1825 the estate of Jacob Heagy, deceased, was processed in the Orphans Court of Adams County and Henry Heagy is listed as one of his sons.
Obituary - "Died, Feb 4, 1879, in Freedom Twp., Adams Co., Mrs. Rachel Heagy, the d/o Mr. Lewis Shriver and the wife of Henry Heagy, aged 76 years and 23 days." "Died, Nov 7, 1881, at his residence in Liberty Twp., Mr. Henry Heagy, aged 84 years and 24 days."
"Inmemory of / Henry Heagy / Born October 11, 1797 / Died November 7, 1881." "In memory of / Rachel Shriver Heagy / wife of Henry Heagy / Born January 12, 1803 / Died February 4, 1879." "In memory of / Infant / Died October 29, 1822 / Amanda M.K. Heagy / Died February 26, 1838 / Aged 15 years, 6 months / and 28 days. Margaret R. Heagy / Died March 20, 1838 / Lewis P. Heagy / Died March 3, 1838 / Aged 7 years, 5 months / and 26 days. / Shriver Heagy / Died March 3, 1838 / Aged 2 years and 7 months. / Isaac T. Heagy / Died May 12, 1865 / Aged 27 years, 10 months / and 30 days. / Children of Henry and Rachel Heagy."
Amanda Maria Kitzmiller Heagy was the twin of the infant who died at birth. She was the firstborn of Rachel Shriver Heagy and was born 10/29/1822. Isaac T. Heagy, who is listed on the marker is interred at the end of the plot and the marker at his grave gives additional data. "Honor the brave / Isaac T. Heagy / Died May 12, 1865 / Aged 27 years, 10 months, and / 30 days. / Member of Company E, 99th Regiment / Pennsylvania Volunteers / Died in the Service of his Country / near Fredericksburg, Virginia."

HESS

- John E.E. Hess, m 12/2/1886 to Sallie Belle Ohler, d/o Isaac & Isiamiah Hockensmith Ohler.

HOCKENSMITH

- THE HOCKENSMITH TAVERN - It was at the Hockensmith Tavern that the name of the town, hither to known as "Poplar Fields" to Emmitsburg. Historian Helman writes of this historic event:- "The company had quite a merry time, having drunk to the health of the newly baptised town; they returned home full of sanguine expectations as to the rapid growth of the infant settlement. The population at that time consisted of seven families.'"
The actual site of the Hockensmith Tavern stood on the road from Emmitsburg to Taneytown, going east at the first bridge - brick house on one side of the road - barn on the other. The present house was built about 1804 by the Gillelans. At that time the tavern was torn down. It stood back of the house - down in the yard - near the old well.
Traditions states that George Hockensmith built the tavern and served as a "mine host' until his death. It was shortly thereafter that the property was sold to William Gillelan. Mr. Gillelan tore down the old tavern and erected the present brick house.

- Adam T. Hockensmith - "Adam Tobias Hockensmith, s/o Daniel and Elizabeth, b 2/16/1830, bp 3/21/1830. - Tom's Creek Lutheran Church Records.

- Conrad Hockensmith, the pioneer ancestor of the family in Maryland, is thought to have been among the "Monocacy settlers". The exact burial place of Conrad and his wife is not known - but it could be at the forgotten Monocacy Settlement churchyard. He was the father of:-
1. George Hockensmith, first of the family to live in the Emmitsburg district.
2. Jacob Hockensmith, Ensign in the Gamecock Company, American Revolutionary Soldier, m Elizabeth, d/o George and Christiana Smith.
3. Micheal Hockensmith
4. Henry Hockensmith, who attended the meeting protesting the Stamp Act in 1770 at Tom's Creek Hundred Schoolhouse.
5. Conrad Hockensmith

- Daniel Hockensmith, s/o John and Barbara Sluss Hockensmith, m Elizabeth Bowers. They were the parents of 3 children:-
1. Adam Tobias Hockensmith, m Margaret Ann Hitehashaw, 6 children
2. Isamiah Hockensmith, m Isaac Ohler, both bd Elias Lutheran.
3. Ivanna Hockensmith Hitchahew

- Daniel Hockensmith, d 9/18/1830, 30/3/25, bd Tom's Creek Lutheran

- Elizabeth Hockensmith, d 9/26/1906, 33 yrs. - M.F. Shuff Burial Records.

- HOCKENSMITH TAVERN - "It will be remembered that it was at the old Hockensmith Tavern that Emmitsburg recieved the name by which it is known 'even to this day'. Formerly known as Silver Fancy.

- Jacob Hockensmith, Ensign in the Gamecock Company of the American Revolution, and s/o Conrad, and brother to Lt. George Hockensmith, remained in the Emmitsburg district and raised a large family. m Elizabeth, d/o George and Christiana Smith of the "Cattail Branch" of Tom's Creek Hundred. Children:- 1. Henry; 2. Jacob; 3. Peter; 4. Elizabeth; 5. Mary, d unmarried, bd family plot at Tom's Creek Lutheran; 6. David; 7. Catherine, d unmarried, bd family plot Tom's Creek Lutheran; 8. Magdalena; 9. Polly Hockensmith McCleaf; 10. John Hockensmith, m Barbara Sluss; 11. William; 12. Sarah C. Hockensmith, d unmarried. Sarah C., Mary, and Catherine, together with their bachelor brother David, lived on the 'Hockensmith Farm' until all had died and were buried at Tom's Creek Lutheran cemetery.

- John Hockensmith, s/o Jacob and grandson of Conrad Hockensmith. m Barbara Sluss, d/o John Sluss. Children:-
1. Catherine Hockensmith, d unmarried, bd Tom's Creek Lutheran
2. Mary (Polly) Hockensmith, d unmarried, bd Tom's Creek Lutheran
3. Sarah Hockensmith, d unmarried, bd Tom's Creek Lutheran
4. Elizabeth Hockensmith Slaybaugh
5. John Hockensmith, d 5/11/1891, 86/11/17, m Elizabeth, d 2/9/1861, 68/3/3, both bd Tom's Creek Lutheran.
6. William Hockensmith, d 5/25/1864, 51/8/16, m Alice Amanda d 8/12/1858, 42/2/19, bd Tom's Creek Lutheran.
7. Daniel Hockensmith, d 9/18/1830, 30/3/25

KRISE

- Abraham Krise, s/o Henry Krise, b in New Jersey, 9/25/1771. He came with his family to the 'Monocacy Settlement' and lived there until after his marriage on 12/1/1799, to Ann Christina Kitzmiller. About 1800 Abraham moved to a farm containing some 750 acres in Liberty Twp., Adams County, Pennsylvania. Abraham d 4/20/1846, 74/7/14, and Ann Christina, b9/14/1777, d 4/3/1864, both bd Emmitsburg Mt. View Cemetery. Children:-
1. William Krise, m Hannah Ruff, lived in Maryland.
2. George H. Krise, m Eliza Otta
3. John Krise, d young, 8/1/1804-4/30/1825, bd Mt. View
4. David Krise, d young, 1806-1832, bd Mt. View.
5. Christian Krise, d unmarried
6. Lydia Krise, d unmarried
7. Abraham Krise, twin brother of Christian, m Annie Zimmerman, m2 Jane Tott. He was a native of Maryland, farmer of Adams County, PA., d Gettysburg 1880, bd Evergreen Cemetery.
8. Jacob Krise, d unmarried
9. Samuel Krise, 3/23/1814 - 4/29/1847, m Elizabeth Clabaugh, of Carroll Co., MD. (3/11/1824-3/24/1873), bd Emmitsburg Elias Lutheran Cemetery.

- Abraham Krise, s/o Abraham & Ann Christina Kitzmiller Krise, m1 Annie Zimmerman, m2 Jane Tott, Children:-
1. Louisa Krise Galt, m Washington Galt
2. Elizabeth Krise Carr
3. Calvin P. Krise
4. Samuel Krise.

- Henry Krise, the pioneer ancestor of the family, came to America before 1750. He first settled in New Jersey, later he came to the 'Monocacy Settlement', in Maryland, where both he and his wife died.

- Jacob Krise, d 5/11/1893, 77 yrs. - M.F. Shuff Burial Records.

- Lydia Krise, d 2/7/1895, 88 yrs. - M.F. SHuff Burial Records. Note:- a sister of Jacob Krise, both interred in the family plot at Mt. View.

- The Krise family lived in Freedom Twp., Adams County, PA., and were first buried in the Tract (Carrollsburg - Beard - Zimmerman) graveyard. Later three of these graves were moved to the Mountain View Cemetery.

LANDERS

- Landers burials at Tom's Creek Presbyterian Cemetery:-
1. Carrie Landers, w/o Charles Landers, d 4/24/1888, 23/7/27.
2. Mary Grier Landers, d/o Wm Crawford & Sarah Landers, 1/31/1863 - 6/1/1947.
3. Florence Bruce Landers, 8/30/1853-1/8/1912.

LANTZ

- Mrs. Vernon Lantz, d 10/5/1908, 26 yrs. - M.F. Shuff Burial Records. Fannie A. Lantz, w/o Vernon Lantz 1/5/1882 - 10/5/1908, bd Mt. View Cemetery.

LIVERS

- Arnold Livers, this Englishman by birth, had been an active and noted partisan of the unfortunate King James II. Upon the collapse of that monarch's cause he had been obliged to flee from his native land. He became the owner of a large estate in Maryland, called "Arnold's Delight", on Owings Creek, near Thurmont. His daughter Jacoba Clementina Livers, m 1744 to William Elder.

LIND LYNN LINN

- The Lynns of Maryland intermarried with the Harpers, of the branch of the family who founded the historic town of Harper's Ferry now in West Virginia.

- Johann Melchoir Lynn was a miller and owned 3 mills - one in what is now Adams County, PA. John and his wife Catherine Harper Lynn are buried at Emmitsburg Elias Lutheran Cemetery.

- Rev. Matthew Linn, b 1732, Cairn Castle, County Antrim, Ireland. He was educated at the University of Glassglow and was ordained by the Reformed (Covenantor) Presbytery of Scotland. For 13 years he was pastor of the Reformed Presbyterian Church of Aghadowey, County Londonderry, Ireland. In 1773, at the earnest desire of William Brown, of Paxtang, who went to Ireland for the purpose, he, in company with the Rev. Alexander Dobbin, came to America, arriving at New Castle, Delaware, in Dec 1773. In 1774 he became the first and only pastor of the Conventor Church at Paxtang (now in Daulphin County, PA.) also officiating at Stone Ridge, now in Cumberland Co., PA. Also took charge of the congregations of Greencastle, Chambersburg, Mercersburg and Great Cove. Here he died 4/21/1810? and was buried at Brown's Mill six miles south of Chambersburg near which he lived. He married Jennie Fulton, of Paxtang, who was b 1746 and d 4/1/1819. She was buried at Brown's Mill. Their son, John Linn, succeeded his father in the ministry. He died 1824 at Hagerstown, MD.

LONG

- Mrs. Philip Long, d 5/2/1906, 78 yrs. - M.F. Shuff Burial Records.

LONGWELL

- Col. Hamilton Longwell, d 2/25/1877, 85 yrs., Contractor on the Gettysburg Railroad. m 3/5/1838, Rebecca Wilson, of Adams County, PA., d 8/8/1866, 45 yrs., both bd Gettysburg Evergreen Cemetery. Children:-
1. Martha Agnew Longwell
2. Howard Longwell
3. Wilson Longwell
4. James Longwell

- Col. John K. Longwell wrote several interesting sketches pertaining to the good people of Gettysburg - of his day and generation. These were published in the old "Star And Sentinel". Col. John K. Longwell, b 10/18/1810, Adams Co., d 4/8/1896, He was born in Adams County, PA. and went to Taneytown, Maryland, in early 'manhood' and founded the newspaper in that town. m 5/6/1840, by the Rev. R.S. Grier, to Sarah 'Sallie' H. McKaleb, d/o Major John K. McKaleb, b 1/16/1814, d 12/1/1898, both are bd Piney Creek Presbyterian Cemetery, nr Harney.
Children:
1. Sallie Longwell, 2/10/1845 - 6/22/1905, bd Piney Creek Presb.
2. Jennie Longwell, d 9/11/1854, 12 yrs., bd Piney Creek
3. Joseph Augustus Longwell, d 9/6/1854, 6 yrs. bd Piney Creek
4. John E. McKaleb Longwell, d 6/18/1850, 10 yrs., bd Piney Creek Presbyterian Cemetery, Harney, MD.

- Joseph M. Longwell, formerly of Gettysburg, PA., d 8/21/1841, at Sommerville, Tennessee, in the 29th year of his age. - Gettysburg newspaper Sept 13, 1841.

- Matthew Longwell, d 9/12/1820, age 58 yrs., Merchant of Gettysburg. - Adams Sentinel 9/13/1820. Mrs Jane Longwell, widow of Matthew Longwell, d 8/21/1829, at Taneytown, MD., formerly of Gettysburg. - Adams Sentinel 8/26/1829.
Matthew Longwell, of Gettysburg, d 9/7/1820, 58 yrs., m 1/9/1810, at Taneytown, MD., to Jane Kleenhoop, of Taneytown. d 8/22/1829, 45 yrs., bd Piney Creek Presbyterian, Harney. Son;-
1. Col. John K. Longwell, 1810-1896, m 1840 Sarah H. McKaleb.

- Margaret Longwell, d 8/7/1879, 62 yrs. bd Piney Creek Presbyterian.

- Martha Agnew Longwell, known as 'Mattie', d 12/19/1914, at San Monica, California, aged 72 yrs. She was the d/o Major & Mrs. Hamilton Longwell, who lived on Baltimore St., Gettysburg. Her body was brought to Gettysburg for burial, She had 3 brothers, Howard, Wilson & James Longwell. - Compiler 1/2/1915.

- Sarah J. Longwell, d 1/5/1882, 66 yrs., bd Piney Creek Presbyterian Cemetery, Harney, MD.

MANNING

- Charles Augustus Manning, d 1909, m Emily Tiers, d/o Edward Tiers, and the sister-in-law of George Miles, the 'Mountain Poet'. Children; one son:- Harry F. Manning, m Nina Quinn.

MANSON

- Anna Maria Manson - "Sacred / to the memory of / Ann Maria Manson / daughter of / Johannan and Mary Ann / Manson / Died April 16, 1830 / Aged 7 months & 4 days." (Piney Creek Cemetery - Hays - Curren Family Plot.)

MARONEY'S COMPANY

- "Roll of Captain Philip Maroney's Company, Flying Camp, Maryland August 5, 1776 - List of the members of Captain Philip Maroney's Company, in the Flying Camp, August 5, 1776, enlisted in the Middletown District and elsewhere, Frederick County, Maryland.
Philip Marony, Captain, John Smith, Ensign - Enlisted men as follows:- Garah Harding, William Jacobs, John McCrery, Daniel Shehan, John Churchwell, George Holliday, George Hill (bd in the Piney Creek Presbyterian churchyard), William Gilmour, Patrick Murphy, Francis Quinn, Samuel Wheeler, John Shank, James McKinsie, Thomas Gill, William Calvert, John McClary, William Skaggs, John Marshall, Bennett Neall, John Test, Thomas Kirk, Jr., Ninion Nichols, William Cash, Jas. Burton, Thomas Burton, Thomas Hilleary, James Beall, John Brease, Patrick Scott, William McKay, Zadock Griffith, Henry Meroney, Henry Clements, Thomas Fenly, James McCormack, Patrick Cannon, Charles Philpoy (Taylor), James Lowther, Henry Berkshire (Deserted), John Maynard, James Beckett, James Tannenhill, John Miller, James Bryant, Micheal Arran, James Barrock, Christian Smith (of the Smith family of the 'Cattail Branch', near Emmitsburg, MD.), James Donack, James Kelam, George McDonald, James Hatchcraft, Jacob Holtz, Henry Smith (of the Cattail Branch), Richard Wells, Elisha Rhodes, Paul Boyer, Samuel Busey, John Kenneday, William Chandler, William Burton, Warren Philpot, Christopher Wheelan, James Buller, John Jones, James Carty, John Hutchison, Like Barnett, Samuel Silver, Edward Sehom, Robert McDonald, James McCoy, Richard Tounge, Herbert Shoemaker, John (?)yer, Richard Fletcher, Joseph McAllen, Thomas Harrison, John Alsop, Charles Dullis, Joshua Pearce (Pierce), Jacob Rhodes, George Kelly, William Louden, Frederick Beard (interred in Emmitsburg Elias Lutheran churchyard), Henry Fisher, James Hudson, Micheal Hall, John Price (Deserted), William Byer, Francis Freeman, John Cash, William Hollings, Jacob Burton, and William Barnett. - Enlisted men, 95, Officers, 2; Total, 97." Captain Philip Maroney kept a copy of his company roll, the famous Flying Camp, of the American Revolution, and it stayed in his family. One of his descendants moved to Louisiana, and this record was carried out of Maryland. In 1911 a descendant of Philip Maroney permitted a copy of the original roll to be made. This was attested to as authentic before a Notary Public and Judge John C. Motter. At that time a copy was also placed with the D.A.R.

MARSHALL

- James Marshall of Carroll's Tract, married Sarah Witherow d/o John Witherow & Margaret Barbour Witherow. Daus:-
1. Margaret Marshall Horner, d 12/23/1876 78/7/20, bd Tom's Creek Presbyterian, nr Emmitsburg, m Andrew Horner, d 6/29/1838, 63 yrs, bd Tom's Creek Presbyterian.
2. Elizabeth Marshall

MARTIN

- Rev. James Martin, pastor Piney Creek Presbyterian near Harney, Maryland. d 6/20/1795 Penns Valley, PA. m1 Annie McCullough, children:-
1. James, educated for the ministry, but was a teacher
2. Samuel
3. John
4. Martin
m2 Ellen Davidson of York Co., PA., no children.

1777 - member of the Associates Presbytery of PA., was received by the Synod and assigned to the Presbytery of Donegal
1780 - accepted a call to Piney Creek Presbytery, Harney, he remained at Piney Creek 8½ years.
1788 - applied to the Presbytery of Carlise 'for a release from his charge'.
1788 - pastor of East and West Penn's Valley, Warrior Mark and Half Moon in PA. Here he labored until his death on 6/20/1795.

He was a native of County Down, Ireland, but came to this country before the War of the American Revolution. At first, as the old Chronicle states, he 'labored for a season in South Carolina.' Piney Creek was his first "settlement" in this country, though he preached for many years in Ireland. He was one of the original members of the Presbytery of Huntingdon, which was set up on April 14, 1795. He died in his 67th year and was buried at Penn's Valley.

- Lewis Martin - "Died 2/24/1892, 20 yrs." - M.F. Shuff Burial Records. Note:- a son of James P. and Anna Margaret Martin, this young man is buried with his parents in the family plot at Mountain View Cemetery.

- Mathias Martin, came to Tom's Creek Hundred from Germantown, PA., m a d/o Peter Troxell, 1 known dau. Maria Magdalena Martin, m Lewis Motter.

MATTHIAS

- John Jacob Mattias had migrated from the Palatinate to Phila., PA., in 1733, and had immediately gone to the Monocacy Settlement. "Anna Margaretha Matthias d/o John Jacob Matthias bp 6/23/1734 by the Rev. Stoever at Monocacy Settlement."

MAXELL - MAXWELL

- Albert Heck Maxell, s/o Samuel & Jane Ferguson Maxell, m Columbia Hockensmith and were members of Elias Lutheran Church, Emmitsburg. Albert Heck Maxell and family along with his brother-in-law Robert Eli Hockensmith moved from the Emmitsburg area to Martinsburg, West Virginia. Children:-
1. William Fleming Maxell, b 6/27/1877
2. Samuel Robert Maxell, 3/5/1879 - 3/30/1879, bd Elias Luth.
3. Ella May Maxell, b 3/13/1880, m 12/8/1904, Cyrus Weller of Martinsburg, W.Va.
4. Charles Albert Maxell, b 7/24/1882.

- Henry Ferguson Maxell, b 1/5/1850, at Maxell's Mill, nr Emmitsburg, s/o Samuel & Jane Fergsuon Maxell., by trade a miller, m 5/27/1875, Jeminia Stansbury, d/o Nicholas & Amelia Stansbury. Children:-
1. Thaddeus Augustus Maxell, b 6/14/1876, d 1954, bd Mt View Cemetery, Emmitsburg, m Grace Baker (1881-1941), lived in Emmitsburg.
2. Maude Amelia Maxell Neely, m 6/5/1907, George McBeth Neely, of Fairfield, PA., both bd Fairfield Union Cemetery.
3. Roy Forest Maxell, b 9/30/1883, m 1/25/1911, Edna Fitez, of Emmitsburg.

- Samuel Maxwell - Maxell, b 12/17/1809, nr Waynesboro, PA., m ca 1842, Jane Ferguson (b 11/27/1811) in Franklin Co., PA. They moved into the Emmitsburg district ca 1846 - purchased the "Crabb's Mill" and became permanent residents of the district and members of the Lutheran Church. Maxell's Mill was a center of community activity - it contained a store, post office, blacksmith shop and a mill store. Samuel and Janes' children:-
1. Albert Heck Maxell, m Columbia Hockensmith, resided in the Emmitsburg area and later moved to Martinsburg, West Virginia.
2. Henry Ferguson Maxell, b 1/5/1850 at Maxell's Mill, m 5/27/1875 Jemina Stansbury.
3. Thaddeus (Theodore) Augustus Maxwell, unmarried, b 12/5/1843, nr Waynesboro, d 6/5/1864, bd Emmitsburg Elias Lutheran, Member of Cole's Calvary, killed by Sharpshooter at Piedmont, Virginia.
4. Mary Catherine Maxwell, b 3/22/1846, Franklin Co., nr Waynesboro, PA.
5. Henry Maxell, d early youth (1st child)
6. William Maxell, d in early youth
7. Samuel J. Maxell, Member of Cole's Calvary during the Civil War, d in Martinsburg, W.VA., m Miss Fleming.
8. Jane Maria Maxell Duckwall, m 7/15/1869 to John W. Duckwall, moved to Ohio.
9. Ann Eliza Maxell Rowe, m Charles Rowe, of Emmitsburg.
10. Francis Allison Maxwell, b 7/30/1843, d 4/29/1906, m Miss While, lived and died in York, PA., Francis bd Emmitsburg Elias Lutheran Cem.
11. Margaret C. Maxell Zimmerman, 1846-1884, m 11/12/1872, Ezra Rowe Zimmerman, 1847-1905, bd Mt. View Cem., Emmitsburg.
12. Mary Agnes Maxell, 1851-1915, m1 7/14/1872, John H. Sumwalt, who died 8/26/1872, m2 1/5/1875, N. Cronin Stansbury

MAXWELL
- William Maxwell, the pioneer ancestor of the family in Cumberland Valley, Pennsylvania. He served as a Major in the Provincial service during the French and Indian Wars. The fort known as Fort Maxwell was erected on his land. His wife's name was Susannah - her maiden name is unknown. William died in 1777 and both he and his wife are interred in the churchyard of Upper West Conocheaque. Children:-
1. James Maxwell, d 1807, unmarried. He was a lawyer and served as Captain, Magistrate and Assistant Judge.
2. Patrick Maxwell, m Hannah Whitehall, children:- William; James; Patrick; John; Racheal Maxwell m John Davis; Susannah Maxwell m John McClelland; Elizabeth Maxwell, unmarried.
3. Mary Maxwell McDowell, 1727-4/9/1805, m William McDowell, s/o William McDowell. Children:- William; John; Susan; James; Mary; Nathan; Alexander; Andrew; Margaret; Nancy; Patrick; Thomas McDowell.
4. Agnes Maxwell, m Thomas Brown
5. Ruth Maxwell, m William Reynolds and had 4 sons & 3 daus.
6. Catherine Maxwell, m Nathan McDowell, s/o William McDowell.

McCREA

- Ann McCrea, d 7/13/1866, 65 yrs. bd Piney Creek.

- Anna Mary McCrea, d 3/18/1823, 35/6/1, bd Piney Creek.

- Mary McCrea, d/o Elizabeth McCrea, d 10/1/1826, 14/9/1, bd Piney Creek.

- Sophia Thomson McCrea, d/o Thomson & Sophia McCrea, d 5/27/1849, bd Piney Creek.

McCREARY

- William McCreary, d 10/29/1839, 19/10/0, bd Tom's Creek Presbyterian, nr Emmitsburg.

McCULLOUGH

- Archie McCullough - see Eleanor Cochran Junkin.

McDOWELL

- The McDowell and Maxwell - Maxell families were intermarried. Members of the Maxwell - Maxell family moved from Franklin County, Pennsylvania to Frederick County, Maryland.

McDOWELL

- Dr. Andrew McDowell was a graduate from the medical department of the University of Pennsylvania in 1787, and for a brief period was professor of Latin and Greek in the University. He then settled in Chambersburg, PA., where he remained in active and successful practice for forty years. He finally reliquished his practice and moved to Mercersburg, where he died at the home of his son, Dr. John McDowell, on Jan 13, 1846.

Dr. Andrew McDowell s/o William and Mary Maxwell (Maxell) McDowell, b 1761, d 1/13/1846, at the home of his son Dr. John McDowell, of Mercersburg, PA. m 5/9/1793, Agnes McPherson. 8 children, 2 listed:
1. Dr. Andrew Nathan McDowell, physician, practiced in Pittsburg, PA. m 1824 Jane Denny Porter of Chambersburg, PA. He died 5/7/1849, leaving his wife and six daus. His youngest dau., Jane Denny McDowell m Stephen Foster, the composer.
2. Dr. John McDowell, Mercersburg, PA.

- Dr. John McDowell, s/o William and Mary Maxwell (Maxell) McDowell, b 1751, d 12/22/1820, 69 yrs., bd Waddell Presbyterian Graveyard, now Spring Grove, near Mercersburg, PA.
Dr. John McDowell, Doctor of Law, once principle of St. John's College, Annapolis, MD., and President of the University of PA. He was president of St. John's College, when George Washington sent his young step-grandson, George Washington Parks Custis to the school.

- William McDowell, s/o William McDowell, Sr., m Mary, d/o of Major William and Susanna Maxwell (Maxell). Children:-
1. Dr. John McDowell, 1751-12/22/1820, Presdident of St. John's College, Annapolis, MD.
2. Dr. Andrew McDowell, 1761 - 1/13/1846, at Mercersburg, PA. m 1793, to Agnes McPherson and had 8 children.

- William McDowell, Sr., d 1759, bd Donegal Churchyard, Lancaster County, PA. Children:-
1. William McDowell, Jr., m Mary, d/o Major William & Susanna Maxwell (Maxell)

McKALEB - McKELLIP

- Major John McKaleb of Taneytown, MD, d 1/2/1843, 77/6/0, bd Piney Creek Presbyterian, nr Harney, MD. m Mary Ann Clingan, d/o Rev. Mr. Clingan (Baptist), d 7/4/1816, 32/5/0, bd Piney Creek Presbyterian. Children:-
1. Margaret Ann McKaleb Ege, d 1/22/1851, 38/2/26, bd Piney Creek Presbyterian, nr Harney. m Col. Andrew G. Ege, who built "Antrim".
2. Sarah McKaleb Longwell, 1814-1898, m 5/6/1840 to Col. John K. Longwell, both bd Piney Creek Presbyterian Harney.
3. Joseph Augustus McKaleb, d 2/16/1845, 25/7/2, bd Piney Creek.
4. Joseph McKaleb, d 7/23/1802, 0/6/11, bd Piney Creek Presb.
5. Mary Jane McKaleb Annan, d 7/23/1825, 21/11/0, bd Piney Creek Presbyterian, Harney, she was the first wife of Dr. Samuel Annan.

McKALEB - McKELLIP

- Cemetery Inscriptions Piney Creek Presbyterian, Harney, MD.:-
1. Joseph McKaleb, d 2/5/1808, 75 yrs.
2. Martha, d/o Joseph & Mary McKaleb, d 1/1791, 19 yrs.
3. Mary McKaleb, wife of Joseph McKaleb, d 2/11/1811, 75 yrs.
4. Jane, d/o Joseph & Mary McKaleb, d 6/1796, 33 yrs.
5. John McKellip, d 3/10/1834, 80 yrs.
6. Ann, wife of John McKellip, d 12/14/1827, 64 yrs.
7. John McKellip, s/o John & Mary McKellip, d 7/1803, 15 months.
8. Sarah Jane, d/o James & Mary A. McKellip, 9/6/1843-3/8/1844.
9. James McKellip, d 5/4/1859, 55 yrs.

McKEE

- McKees, of Scotch descent. There are members of this clan buried in Upper Marsh Creek Presbyterian graveyard (Black's) and on one stone is embossed the McKees coat-of-arms.

- Cemetery inscriptions Tom's Creek Presbyterian, nr Emmitsburg, MD.
1. Thomas McKee, d 9/20/1843, 88 yrs.
2. Susanna, wife of Thomas McKee, d 5/9/1846, 72 yrs.

McNAIR

- The McNair Family - "Authorities on the clans of old Scotland record the fact that the McNairs were awarded a coat-of-arms in the year 1314 by King Robert the Bruce at the Battle of Bannockburn.

- Robert McNair - Robert(1) McNair was by blood a Scot - a descendant of the family fled from Scotland to Northern Ireland - and therefore known to history as "Scotch - Irish". Robert(1) McNair (or McNear -as recorded in early documents) had a wife named Agnes (or Ann). The baptism records of the First Presbyterian Church of Philadelphia record the baptism of three of Robert's Children:- "Baptised - Feb 1727, Alexander McNear, s/o Robert & Anne McNear. Baptised - Sept 28, 1730, Mary McNear, d/o Robert & Anne McNear. Baptised - Jan 8, 1732 - Robert McNear, s/o Robert & Anne McNear. (Children born in Philadelphia.)"

- Alexander McNair, b 1/8/1727 in Philadelphia, PA.,s/o Robert(1) & Anne McNair, bd at Tom's Creek Presbyterian Churchyard near Emmitsburg, MD. In 1761 Alexander was a resident within the bounds of "the manor of the Masque", York (now Adams) County, Pennsylvania. On 28 June 1762 he appears in the records at which time he volunteered for service in the Ninety-Fifth Regiment of Foot of the British Army. In 1761 he took part in an expedition against the Cherokee Indians, as an Ensign, it was instrumental in the capture of the Island of Martinque in 1762. From the years 1779 to 1783 he paid taxes on 360 acres of land, four horses and six cattle. During these years he was listed as living in Hamiltonban Twp., York Co., PA. When he wrote his will in 1790 he owned 375 acres of land in Pennsylvania and 10 acres in Maryland - adjoining his PA. holdings. During the American Revolution he served as a private soldier. In 1762 or 1763 Alexander married Margaret (?). Both are interred at Tom's Creek Presbyterian churchyard

McNAIR

and the inscriptions from the gravestones are as follows:- "In memory of / Alexander McNair / Died October 1, 1816 / Aged 90 years./ He was modest, meek, and good indeed. Courteous to all, helpful to those in need; a Careful father, and a loving friend; Peaceable was his end." "In memory of / Margaret McNair / wife of / Alexander McNair/ Died October 8, 1817 / Aged 85 years. / A pleasing form, a generous heart, A good companion, honest without art. Just in her dealings, faithful to her friends; Beloved thro' life, lamented in the end." Alexander & Margaret McNairs' children:-
1. Samuel(3) McNair, 1764-1828, m Lavina, both interred Tom's Creek Presbyterian Churchyard nr Emmitsburg.
2. Isabel(3) McNair Stevenson, m James Stevenson of Kentucky, two children:- Alexander McNair Stevenson, Margaret Stevenson.
3. Agnes(3) McNair Bigham, m Thomas Bigham of York (now Adams) County, PA.
4. Margaret(3) McNair - no further data.

- Samuel(3) McNair was born 1764, York County, PA., s/o Alexander(2) and Margaret McNair and grandson of Robert(1) and Anne McNair. From 12/1/1776 to 1/1/1777 Samuel appears in the records as a bombardier in the Arnold Battery of the Pennsylvania Navy. From 1779 to 1789 he paid taxes on cattle in Hamiltonban Twp., York Co., PA. In his father's will he fell heir to the family farm - some 385 acres. Like his father he was a farmer and added additional acreage to his farm. He married Lavina (?) and had 14 children. Samuel and Lavina were interred at Tom's Creek Presbyterian churchyard and the inscription from their tombstones as follows:- "Sacred / to the memory of / Samuel McNair / the son of / Alexander and Margaret / McNair / Died June 2, 1828 / Aged 64 years, 9 months / and 17 days." - "Sacred / to the memory of / Lavina McNair / wife of Samuel McNair / Born August 29, 1776 / Died Nov 30, 1842 / Aged 66 years, 3 months, / and 4 days." Their children as listed in the family bible:-
1. Elizabeth(4) McNair, d 7/1817, 3 yrs.
2. William(4) McNair, d 8/3/1820, 4 yrs.
3. Susan(4) McNair, d 1826, 2 yrs.
4. Margaret(4) McNair, m Benjamin Ellis, lived nr Lewisburg, PA.
5. Alexander(4) McNair, Doctor of Medicine, graduated from Jefferson Medical College in 1834, practiced in Philadelphia.
6. Eugenia(4) McNair, m Samuel Arthur
7. Agnes(4) McNair, m William McCallister, lived nr Emmitsburg.
8. Samuel Scott(4) McNair
9. Levinia(4) McNair, b 8/8/1809, d 8/9/1869, m 4/19/1836 Andrew Eyster of Emmitsburg.
10. Maria(4) McNair, m Mr. Parson, lived nr Emmitsburg.
11. Martha(4) McNair, m Mr. Toot, lived nr Emmitsburg.
12. Susannah(4) McNair

McNAIR

- Samuel Scott(4) McNair 1807-1875, b 1/21/1807 presumably on the McNair farm in Adams County, Pennsylvania, the s/o Samuel and Lavina McNair. d 2/7/1875, 68/0/16, bd Tom's Creek Presbyterian nr Emmitsburg, Maryland. m Statira C. Bigler, the neice of Gov. Bigler of California. Statira was b 8/1/1815, d 1/5/1885, 69/5/4. They were the parents of 11 children:-
1. Alexander(5) McNair, 10/12/1826-4/26/1904, Civil War Veteran, m 9/19/1865 Amelia Selina Jacobs (12/9/1840-7/10/1921).
2. Hiram(5) McNair, b 1838, served in the Civil War as an officer, graduated from Pennsylvania (now Gettysburg) College, m 6/11/1868 Nettie S. Hauer.
3. Samuel Newton(5) McNair, 1840-1909, Civil War Veteran and Post master of Emmitsburg, MD. m 2/16/1871 Mary Antionette Moutz (1839-1907) both bd Mountain View Cemetery, Emmitsburg.
4. William Burns(5) McNair, 1845-1920, m 1876 Mary Jane Eckenrode. He was a Civil War Veteran.
5. Ann Jane(5) McNair, d 5/5/1845, 2/8/0, bd Tom's Creek Presbyterian.
6. Watson W.(5) McNair, b 5/15/1847, Civil War Veteran, married and lived in the state of Iowa. No further data.
7. Jane(5) McNair, b 5/15/1847, twin of Watson, b 2/19/1859, bd Tom's Creek Presbyterian.
8. Ellen(5) McNair, b 9/7/1851, d unmarried in Baltimore, MD.
9. Robert(5) McNair, b 8/5/1853 - moved 'to the west'.
10. Harry(5) McNair, b 6/21/1859, m & lived nr Emmitsburg, MD., d 4/23/1908.
11. Margaret(5) McNair, twin of Harry, 6/21/1859 - 4/23/1868, bd Tom's Creek Presbyterian.

- Samuel Newton(5) McNair, b9/4/1840, s/o Samuel Scott(4) and Statira C. Bigler McNair, d 6/5/1909, bd Emmitsburg Mt. View Cem. He served in the Civil War in Cole's Cavary. He was severely wounded at Leesburg, VA., where a bullet passed through his leg. He was Postmaster at Emmitsburg. m 2/16/1871 Mary Antionette Moutz, b 4/10/1838, d 4/4/1907, 70 yrs., bd Mt. View. "Mrs. Samuel N. McNair, d 4/4/1907, 70 yrs." - MF Shuff Burial Records. Her family was associated with the 'old Mertz Tavern' on old Rt#15 between Emmitsburg and Greenmount. Children:-
1. Antionette(6) McNair, 3/21/1875-8/17/1878, bd Mt. View.

MILLS

- Abner Mills, d 1898, bd Mt. Joy Luth., Adams Co., PA., ml 12/17/1840, Catherine Maxell, of Mt. Joy Twp., m2 1/13/1863, Mrs Rebecca Sandoe. children:-
1. Samuel Mills, 1849-1849, bd Union Burial Ground, Waynesboro, PA.
2. Helen Catherine Mills, b 9/14/1849
3. Emma M. Mills, d 10/22/1864, 6/1/2, bd Mt. Joy Luth.
4. Sarah Jane Mills, b 10/6/1851

MILLS

- Cemetery Inscriptions, Mills family plot at Mountjoy Lutheran Church Cemetery, Mt. Joy Twp., Adams Co., PA.
1. Catherine Maxwell (Maxell) Mills, wife of Abner Mills, d 3/30/1861, 45/10/1. (NOTE:- a sister of Samuel Maxwell and d/o William & Catherine Maxwell, and first wife of Abner MIlls.)
2. Catherine Maxwell 3/7/1783 - 11/6/1851, 66/8/1. (NOTE:- the mother of Catherine Maxwell Mills, Samuel, and Martha Maxwell Allison, and the wife of William Maxwell.)
3. Emma M. Mills, d/o Abner & Catherine Mills, d 10/22/1864, 6/1/2.
4. Rebecca Mills, wife of Abner Mills, d 2/4/1904, 80/4/20.
5. Abner Mills, d 11/17/1898, 82/3/6.

MOORE

- The Moores probably came to Tom's Creek Hundred from the Marsh Creek Settlement in what is now Adams County, Pennsylvania.

- Cemetery Inscriptions, Moore family plot at Tom's Creek Presbyterian churchyard, nr Emmitsburg, MD.
1. Margaret Moore, d/o James & Jane S. Moore, d 6/13/1842, 31/1/8.
2. Jane Scott Moore, wife of James Moore, b 9/6/1786, d 5/9/1849, 62/8/3.
3. James Moore, 10/9/1785 - 10/19/1821.

- Mrs. Rebecca Moore - "Died, May 31, 1915, at her home near Mt. St. Mary's College, Mrs. Rebecca Delaney Moore, aged 71 yrs., 1 month, and 23 days. She was the daughter of the late Dr. Henry Deilman. Mrs. Moore is survived by two sons Harry A. Quinn and Edgar H. Moore. Three daughters - Mrs. H.F. Manning (Nina Quinn), Misses Georgia and Emma Moore, one brother Lawrence Deilman. Burial in the 'old Cemetery on the Hill'. - Emmitsburg Chronicle, June 14, 1915.

MORRISON

- Cemetery Inscriptions, Tom's Creek Presbyterian nr Emmitsburg:-
1. William B. Morrison, 2/21/1819 - 7/19/1890.
2. Penninah J. Morrison, wife of William B. Morrison, 9/21/1817 - 2/19/1913.
3. William Morrison, 6/20/1851 - 11/13/1934.
4. Helen E. Morrison, wife of William Morrison, 9/24/1846 - 3/9/1921.
5. John R. Morrison, s/o William & Helen, b & d 1887.
6. David A. Morrison, s/o Wm. & Helen, b & d 1882.
7. David Morrison, d 7/1866.
8. Harriet Morrison, wife of David Morrison, d 1/23/1871, 71 yrs.
9. Harriet Morrison, d/o D. & H. Morrison, d 6/18/1899, 76/8/19.

- Reuben Morrison, 4/5/1834 - 9/26/1906, m Elizabeth 'Betsy' Ohler, 11/19/1820 - 12/21/1891, d/o Thomas & Catherine Ohler, both bd Emmitsburg Elias Lutheran.

MORROW

- Cemetery Inscriptions, Lower Marsh Creek Churchyard, Adams Co., PA.
1. John Knox Morrow, d 5/1/1819, aged 3 yrs. (NOTE: a grandson of John and Mary Lockhart Morrow.)
2. Margaret, w/o James Morrow, d 5/9/1837, 46 yrs.
3. James Morrow, d 3/3/1826, 1 yr., s/o James & Margaret.
4. John Morrow, d 6/14/1829, 2 yrs., s/o James & Margaret.

- James Morrow, s/o John and Mary Lockhart Morrow, m 1815 to Margaret Knox (d 5/9/1837, bd Lower Marsh Creek, Adams Co., PA.) James was the last of his family to leave what is now Adams Co., PA., for the Ohio country. Children:-
1. John Knox Morrow, d 1819, 3 yrs.
2. James Morrow, d 1826, 1 yr.
3. John Morrow, d 1829, 2 yrs.

- Jeremiah Morrow, Covenanter, emigrated from Londonderry, Ireland, and settled in what is now Adams County, Pennsylvania. Jeremiah was an ordained Elder in the Rock Creek Society on 4/18/1753. He died 9/14/1758, aged 47 years. Sarah Morrow, his wife, died 12/19/1798, at the age of 76 years. They were interred in a graveyard located on the banks of Marsh Creek a few miles west of Gettysburg, possibly the McClellan family cemetery where rest so many of the early Covenanters. Their son:-
1. John Morrow, farmer, Marsh Creek, now Adams Co., PA., was a member and ruling Elder in the Associate Reformed Church, m Mary Lockhart.

MORT

- John Mort, 1854 - 1900, d 12/9/1900, 42 yrs. - M.F. Shuff Burial Record. Ida F., his wife, 1862-1940, both bd Emmitsburg Mt. View.

MOTTER

- Isaac Motter, b 10/26/1805, s/o Lewis & Mary Martin Motter, m 11/29/1826 Mary Ann Snively.

- Isaac M. Motter, Reformed Minister, s/o Lewis Martin Motter & Alice Rudisil, m 10/1878, Ada Serena Kunkel of Shippensburg, PA. Isaac M. Motter was born and reared in Emmitsburg, MD. Attended Mercersburg College, where he graduated in 1873. He graduated in Theology in 1876 and was ordained Oct 1876. The Rev. Motter was appointed president of the Board of School Commissions of Frederick County. He was also President of the Frederick and Woodsboro Turnpike Company. He had nine children.

- Jeanette Motter, "Died June 5, 1889, near this place, Jeanette Motter, the daughter of Joshua S. and Leathy A. Stokes Motter, aged 8 years, 5 months and 22 days. Little Jeanette died of lockjaw, which resulted from having a splinter into her foot. ... Burial was made at Mt. View Cemetery. - Emmitsburg Chronicle 6/8/1889.

MOTTER

- Joshua Motter, b 2/2/1801, s/o Lewis & Mary Martin Motter,
d 2/25/1875, bd Emmitsburg Elias Lutheran, m 3/7/1825, Harriet
Henkle, b 2/22/1808, d 3/16/1891, bd Emmitsburg Elias Lutheran.
Children:-
1. Isaac H. Motter, d 6/7/1841, 0/7/15, bd Emmitsburg Elias Luth.
2. Harriet H. Motter, 1844-1936.

- Lewis Motter 1775 - 1837 Several articles were written about Lewis Motter, each written here:- "Lewis Motter, the pioneer member of this family in Maryland was born in York County, Pennsylvania in 1775 and died in Emmitsburg, Maryland in 1837. He is interred with other members of his family in Elias Lutheran churchyard. Lewis was the son of Valentine Motter, who was also born in York County in 1752. The father (Valentine) died when his son, Lewis, was 'yet an infant' and the boy was raised by an uncle. Lewis removed to Frederick County, Maryland in 1798. He served in the War of 1812-1814 probably in the defense of Baltimore. He purchased the tanyard of Christian Flaught and carried on the business successfully until his death in 1837.
- Lewis Motter, b 1779, d 3/1/1837, bd Emmitsburg Elias Lutheran. Lewis Motter was the first of his family to settle in Emmitsburg. He was a tanner by trade and opened the first Tannery in Emmitsburg. The records from the family bible of Lewis Motter reads as follows:- "Lewis Motter moved to Emmitsburg on September 5, 1798. On January 15, 1799 Lewis Motter was married to Mary Magdalena Martin by the Rev. L. Hirsch." Children:-
1. "Joshua Motter, son of Lewis and Mary M. Motter, was born Feb. 2, 1801 and baptised on March 1, 1801 by the Rev. Lebright Hirsch. Confirmed May 5, 1822 by the Rev. D. Bossler. Married March 7, 1825 to Harriet Henkle by the Rev. John Winter of the lutheran church."
2. "Barbary Motter daughter of Lewis and Mary M. Motter, born April 25, 1803, baptised May 22, 1803 by the Rev Ruthrauff, Confirmed May 5, 1822 by the Rev. Bossler, married on Dec 19, 1822 to Charles Smith by the Rev. D. Bossler."
3. "Isaac Motter, son of Lewis and Mary M. Motter, was born Oct 26, 1805, baptised Nov 17, 1805 by the Rev. John Rahauser, Confirmed April 22, 1827 by the Rev. John Hoffman, married to Mary Ann Snively on November 29, 1826."
4. "Anna Margaret Motter, daughter of Lewis and Mary M. Motter, born (?) 17, 1808, baptised March 20, 1808 by Rev. Grubb, Confirmed April 29, 1827, married Dr. James W. Eichelberger on April 3, 1828 by Rev. D. Bossler."
5. "Elizabeth Motter, born November 19, 1810, baptised Feb 15, 1811 by the German Reformed minister, confirmed on April 22, 1827 by the Rev. John Hoffman, married to Andrew Annan, M.D., on April 27, 1830 by the Rev. J. Bossler."
6. "Magdalena Motter, born June 25, 1813, baptised June 30, 1813, died July 1, 1813, aged 5 days and 16 hours - 'and it pleased the Lord to take her to Himself'."
7. "Louis Martin Motter, born Feb 6, 1815, baptised March 14, 1815."
8. "William Motter born March 24, 1817, baptised May 4, 1817."
9. "Samuel Motter born Jan 11, 1822, Baptised, May 4, 1822."

MOTTER

-Lewis Motter, s/o Valentine Motter, d 1837. He was a tanner by trade and settled in Emmitsburg in 1798, purchased the tanyard of Christian Flaught. He also opened a store in part of his house and served as a Magistrate. He served in the War of 1812-1814.
m 1799 Mary Magdalena Martin. Children:-
1. Joshua Motter, 1801 - 1875, m 1825, Harriet Henkle, 1818 - 1891, both bd Emmitsburg Elias Lutheran.
2. Barbary Motter Smith, 1803 - 1884, m 1822, Charles Smith, both bd Emmitsburg Mt. View.
3. Isaac Motter, b 1805, m 1826, Mary Ann Snively,
4. Anna Margaret Motter Eichelberger, 1808 - 1888, m 1828 Dr. James W. Eichelberger, both bd Emmitsburg Elias Lutheran.
5. Elizabeth Motter Annan, 1810 - 1884, m 1830 Dr. Andrew Annan, bd Tom's Creek Presbyterian, nr Emmitsburg.
6. Magdalena Motter, 6/25/1813 - 7/1/1813.
7. Lewis Martin Motter, b 1815, m Alice, d/o Tobias Rudisill, both bd Emmitsburg Elias Lutheran.
8. William Motter, b 1817.
9. Samuel Motter, 1822 - 1889, m Mary Chadwick, both bd Emmitsburg Mt. View Cem.

- Lewis Martin Motter, s/o Lewis and Mary Magdalena Martin Motter, b 2/6/1815. He remained in Emmitsburg and followed his father's trade of Tanner and devoted much time to agricultural pursuits. As a Whig he was a member of the State Legislature in 1853-54. m 1840 Alice Rudisil d/o Tobias (also recorded as Ludwig) Rudisel of Taneytown. Children:-
1. Joshua S. Motter, 1848-1899, bd Mt. View Cem., m Leathy A. 1855-1939, dau. Charlotte Motter 1895-1948, bd Mt. View.
2. Isaac M. Motter, Reformed Minister, attended Mercersburg College, Mercersburg, PA., where he graduated in 1873. He graduated in Theology in 1876 and was ordained in Oct 1876.
3. Lewis Edwin Motter, removed to the West.
4. Carrie May Motter, m A.A. Kack.
5. Grace Motter, m Rev. George B. Reaser.
6. Ellen Motter, d unmarried.
7. Alice Motter, m Dr. Robert Annan, bd Elias Lutheran.
8. William Rudisil Motter, d 1/29/ 1848, 2/3/12.

- Samuel Motter, b 1/11/1821, s/o Lewis & Mary Martin Motter, d 3/21/1889, bd Emmitsburg Mt. View. m Catherine Mary Chadwick. "Samuel Motter - died 3/21/1889, aged 69 yrs." - M.F. Shuff Bur. Records. NOTE:- Samuel Motter, the founder and first editor of the Emmitsburg Chronicle - one of the town's more outstanding citizens. Mr. Motter was a descendant of that old pioneer, Lewis Motter, who for many years operated a tannery in the town. He was a graduate of Princeton University. He married Catherine Mary Chadwick, who after the death of her husband, 'ran the Chronicle', serving as both editor and business manager. Samuel began the Chronicle in 1879, he and his wife are interred at Emmitsburg Mt. View Cemetery.

MOTTER

- William Motter b 3/24/1817, s/o Lewis & Mary Martin MOtter, d 11/21/1892, bd Emmitsburg Elias Lutheran. m Hannah C., d 1/16/1883, 61/1/25, bd Elias Lutheran. Children:-
1. Mary Josephine Motter, d 3/14/1853, 7/3/18, bd Elias Lutheran.

MUNRO

- Munro, a Scotch family, interred at Tom's Creek Presbyterian churchyard, nr Emmitsburg:-
1. Isabella Munro, Sr.   5/7/1749 - 8/12/1846.
2. Robert G. Munro   11/3/1768 - 11/3/1823.
3. Isabella Munro, Jr.   11/1780 - 8/31/1823.

MURDOCK

- William Murdock - Among the early Scotch settlers at Tom's Creek is William Murdock and his two wives. He lived in the "Tract", Carroll's Tract what is now Adams County, Pennsylvania. His plantation must have been very close to the Maryland - Pennsylvania Line for the family attended the church at Tom's Creek. William Murdock was an Elder and a member of the Session. In addition he was a man of substance, the owner of many acres of land - well cultivated - a power among his neighbors. The graves of William Murdock and his two wives are located at Tom's Creek Presbyterian churchyard and are marked by a marble "altar" tomb. The inscription follows:- "Mary Murdock of William / Died March 22, 1810 / Aged 65 years. / Also William Murdock / Died March 1, 1820 / Aged 76 years / Also Ann Murdock of William / Died November 28, 1848 / Aged 92 years."

OGLE

- There is no more Honored name in Maryland than that of Ogle. Both men and women of this family have been outstanding. They helped shape the History of Maryland. On the Eastern SHore - at Annapolis - Ogle graves are to be found and the history of the clan is most interesting.

- Benjamin Ogle, d 6/20/1822, 62 yrs., bd Tom's Creek Presbyterian, nr Emmitsburg.

OHLER

- The Ohler family - Phillipp Ohler, the pioneer ancestor, emigrated to Pennsylvania and came to Maryland with the Monocacy settlers. His name appears on the roll of the Monocacy church. He came to this country on the ship "Minerva" and landed Oct 10, 1768 and gave his name as Phillipp Jacob Ohler. In 1794, Elizabeth Ohler, d/o Phillipp and Dorothea Ohler, b 1793 and was baptised by the pastor of Taneytown Lutheran church. Children:-
1. George Ohler, m Rosanna Ott.
2. John Ohler
3. Elizabeth Ohler

OHLER

- Andrew Jackson Ohler, s/o James & Christena Ohler, b 9/5/1833.
- Cemetery Inscriptions Tom's Creek Lutheran & Reformed Graveyard:-
1. Catherine, w/o Thomas Ohler, 9/19/1791-1/25/1873.
2. David S. Ohler, d 11/25/1851, 21/4/9.
3. David S. Ohler, s/o J.T. & A.C. Ohler, d 8/7/1873, 0/0/17.
4. Fannie V. Ohler, d/o J.T. & A.C. Ohler, d 8/20/1864, 0/8/7.
5. Frederick Ohler, d 1/11/1869, 82 yrs.
6. Margaret Ohler, w/o Frederick, d 8/13/1873, 73 yrs.
7. George Ohler, d 11/1/1826, 38 yrs.
8. George Adam Ohler, d 9/7/1912, 87/7/18.
9. Sarah Jane Ohler, w/o George Adam Ohler, d 4/13/1917, 80/4/10.
10. Minnie Ohler, d/o George Adam & Sarah Jane Ohler, d 7/6/1864, 0/5/15.
11. Harriet Ohler, 5/9/1836-4/9/1895.
12. Helen May Ohler, d/o Emory & Katie T. Ohler, 8/11/1904-9/24/1904.

- David Ohler, bd Emmitsburg Elias Luth 2/22/1824-12/9/1909.

- David Samuel Ohler, d 11/29/1831, 21/4/9/.

- Elizabeth Ohler, b 8/14/1793, bp 4/15/1794, d/o Phillip Jacob & Dorothea Ohler - Taneytown Lutheran Church Records.

- Esther Elizabeth Ohler, d/o George & Margaret Ohler, b 5/10/1844.

- George Ohler, s/o Phillipp Jacob Ohler, m Rosannah Ott. He died comparatively young and was buried in the Tom's Creek Lutheran churchyard. The inscription follows:- "In memory of / George Ohler / Died Nov. 1, 1826, / Aged 38 years." Rosannah Ott Ohler was interred in the family plot of her son, Samuel George Ohler, in Elias Lutheran churchyard. "In memory of / Rosannah Ohler / Died Feb 3, 1876, / Aged 80 years, 4 months, / and 3 days." Children:-
1. Samuel George Ohler, of Emmitsburg, m 1, Susannah Singer, on 10/29/1840, d at childbirth, bd Elias Luth., m2, 1/3/1851, Susan Adaline Rowe, d/o Joseph & Susannah Baker Rowe. 5 children:-
    1. Ida Ohler, m George Gillelan, both bd Elias.
    2. Flora Belle Ohler, unmarried, bd Elias.
    3. Rose Ohler, m Martin V. Valentine, both bd Harney, MD.
    4. Jacob Rowe Ohler, m Anna Stansbury, bd Elias.
    5. Edwin Ohler, m Mary Lambil, bd Elias.
2. Elizabeth Ohler, m David Little, 4 children, 2 sons, 2 daus.
3. Frederick Ohler.

- George Ohler, s/o Philip Jacob & Dorothea Ohler, m Margaret, son:-
1. Thomas Ohler, m Catherine, son:-
    1. John Thomas Ohler, b 12/8/1831, bp 5/9/1832, at Taneytown, d 1/25/1917, m Ann Shorb, 8/28/1833 - 12/7/1919, both bd Keysville Cem.

- Hettie Ohler, m John Fuss, both bd Tom's Creek Methodist:- "In memory of / John Fuss / Died 14 Feb 1890 / Aged 65 years and 5 days." "In memory of Hettie Fuss / wife of John Fuss / Died Sept 21, 1887 / Aged 59 years, 5 months / and 20 days." "In memory of / John T. Fuss / son of John and Hettie Fuss / Died Jan 8, 1874 / Aged 21 yrs. 2 mos. and / 3 days."

OHLER

- George Adam Ohler, was the father of Cameron and Beecher Ohler-both bd Mt. View Cem., Emmitsburg.

- George Adam Ohler, d 9/7/1912, 89/7/15, Sarah Jane Ohler, w/o George Adam Ohler, d 4/13/1917, 80/4/18, Minnie Ohler, d/o George Adam Ohler & Sarah Jane Ohler, d 7/26/1864, 0/5/15, all bd Tom's Creek Lutheran.

- George Adam Ohler's wife, Catherine, d 9/1/1823, 64 yrs., bd Elias Lutheran Emmitsburg.

- Isaiah James Ohler, 1843 - 1925, bd Tom's Creek Lutheran, s/o James & Christina Ohler, b 2/21/1843.

- Issaac Ohler, s/o John & Dorothea Ohler, m 12/8/1846 by the Rev. Benjamin Keller to Isamiah Hockensmith - both of Frederick County, Maryland. They were members of the Lutheran churches at Taneytown and Emmitsburg and are buried at Emmitsburg Elias Lutheran. The inscriptions from their tombstones reads as follows:- "In memory of / Isaac Ohler / Born April 12, 1812 / Died December 2, 1873." "In memory of / Isamiah Ohler / Born January 3, 1826 / Died November 24, 1902." Children:-
1. Elizabeth Catherine Ohler, twin, b 1/28/1849.
2. Ezra Levi Ohler, twin, b 1/28/1849.
3. Emma Jane Ohler, b 2/1 /1851
4. Mary Ellen Ohler, b 7/17/1855, m Denton A. Watchter.
5. Alice Virginia Ohler, b 10/27/1858, d 12/16/1876 (9/16/1878?), 19/11/19, bd Elias.
6. James Henry Ohler, b 9/21/1861.
7. William Daniel Ohler, b 2/13/1864.
8. Sallie Belle Ohler, b 5/16/1867, m 12/2/1886 to John E.E. Hess of Carroll County, Maryland.

- Jacob Ohler, s/o George Adam & Catherine Ohler, b 12/31/1800.

- Jacob Ohler, b 12/13/1833, d 5/24/1920, m Emaline (?), b 9/29/1839, d 7/19/1911, both bd Emmitsburg Mt. View Cem. Children:-
1. William Morris Ohler, d 8/27/1861, 8/5/5, bd Mt. View.

- John Ohler, s/o Phillip Jacob & Dorothea Ohler, m Dorothea, Child:-
1. Samuel Ohler, m Catherine Groff, raised a large family, both bd Emmitsburg Elias Lutheran.
2. Hannah Ohler
3. Micheal Ohler
4. Sarah Ohler
5. Isaac Ohler, m Isamiah Hockensmith, bd Emmitsburg Elias Lutheran.
6. David Ohler.
7. Joseph Ohler
8. Levi Ohler
9. John Ohler.

- John Thomas Ohler, 12/8/1831-1/25/1917, m Anna Catherine Shorb, 7/28/1833 - 12/7/1919, both bd Old Tom's Creek Lutheran. Children:-
1. Anna C. Ohler, d 8/9/1857, 0/1/19.
2. Helen Ohler, m Elmer Valentine.

OHLER

- Children of John Thomas & Anna Shorb Ohler, con'd:-
3. Harry Ohler, m 1/24/1897, Effie B. Stambaugh, both of Emmitsburg.
4. Emory Ohler, m 1/24/1893, Kattie Williar of Emmitsburg.
5. Maud Ohler, m Jacob Stambaugh.
6. Alice Jane Ohler, m Harry Mushower.
7. Edward Ohler
8. George Ohler
9. Elizabeth Ohler, m Denton D. Wachter.

- John Thomas Ohler Family Bible:- Births:-
John Thomas Ohler b 12/5/1831
Ann E. Ohler b 7/28/1833
David S. Ohler b 6/21/1853 d 8/7/1855
Anna C. Ohler b 8/28/1856 d 8/9/1857
George W. Ohler b 11/5/1857
Mary E. Ohler b 4/18/1859
Alice Jane Ohler b 1/20/1862, m Wm Harry Munshower
Fannie V. Ohler b 12/13/1863
Helen M. Ohler b 3/5/1865, m Elmer Valentine
Edward T. Ohler b 6/9/1869
John E. Ohler b 8/25/1871
Harry B. Ohler b 5/6/1874, m 1897 Effie B. Stambaugh
Maude R. Ohler b 5/23/1877, m Jacob Stambaugh

Deaths:-
John Thomas Ohler, d 1/26/1917, 85/1/18
Anna C., w/o John Thomas Ohler, d 12/7/1919.
David S. Ohler, d 8/7/1855, 0/1/17.
Anna C. Ohler, d 8/4/1857, 0/11/2.
Fannie V. Ohler, d 8/20/1869(?), 0/8/7, bd Tom's Creek Lutheran.
George W. Ohler, d 4/30/1929
Mary E. Ohler Wachter, d 2/5/1941, bd Mt. Tabor Lutheran, Rocky Ridge.
Edward Ohler, d 7/22/1958.
Helen Ohler Valentine, d 8/15/1953, bd Mt. Tabor Lutheran.

- Joseph Ohler, 2/7/1827 - 9/12/1913, bd Emmitsburg Elias Lutheran.

- Louise Ohler, m 11/8/1853, Ephraim Buffington.

- Mary Catherine Ohler, m 12/22/1857, Andrew Jackson Ohler.

- Samuel Ohler, d 8/5/1889, 82/8/4, bd Emmitsburg Elias Lutheran.
m 12/19/1842, Samuel Ohler of Frederick County, MD., and Catherine Graff of Adams County, PA. Catherine d 7/9/1899, bd Elias Lutheran.
Children:-
1. David Ohler, b 2/1/1844
2. Amanda Susannah Ohler, b 4/13/1845
3. Wm Henry Ohler, b 12/2/1846
4. Harriet Marenda Ohler, b 4/15/1848
5. Ellanaro Francis Ohler, b 4/24/1850
6. John George Ohler, d 7/5/1863, 12/9/0.

OHLER

- Thomas Ohler, d 12/10/1843.

- Thomas Ohler & Catherine Ohler, Children:-
1. Mary (Merry) R. Ohler, b 11/27/1819, m Henry Bishop.
2. Elizabeth 'Betsy' A. Ohler, b 11/19/1820, m Reuben Morrison, both bd Emmitsburg Elias Lutheran.
3. Catherine Ohler, b 5/11/1822, m Hiram Forney.
4. George A. Ohler, b 1/20/1825.
5. Esther Ohler, b 4/1/1828.
6. Louisa Ohler, b 5/12/1830, m Ephriam Buffington, children:-
George H. 1869-1872; Luther S. 1870-1872.
7. John Thomas Ohler, b 12/8/1831, m Ann Shorb, both bd Tom's Creek Lutheran, nr Emmitsburg.

Family Bible:-
Merry R. Ohler, b 11/27/1819.
Elizabeth A. Ohler Morrison, b 11/19/1820.
Catherine Ohler, b 5/11/1822,. m Hiram Forney.
George A. Ohler, b 1/20/1825.
Esther Ohler, b 4/1/1828.
Louise Ohler Buffington, b 5/12/1830.
John Thomas Ohler, b 12/8/1831, m Ann Shorb.

OVERHOLTZER

- Members of the Overholtzer family are interred in the 'Tract Graveyard', sometimes called 'Carrollsburg', 'Cochran', 'Annan', or the 'Zimmerman' graveyard.

- Lewis Overholtzer, 1/21/1836 - 8/21/1908 - bd Emmitsburg Mt. View Cemetery. Lewis A. Overholtzer, d 8/20/1908, 73 years. - Shuff Burial Records. Mary Jane, w/o Lewis A. Overholtzer, d 6/2/1866, 33/11/24, bd Mt. View. Rebecca Ann, d/o Lewis A. & Mary J. Overholtzer, bd Mt. View.

PATTERSON

- Patterson family plot at Tom's Creek Presbyterian Graveyard, near Emmitsburg:-
1. George Patterson, d 4/9/1850, 75 yrs.
2. Matthew Patterson, d 3/27/1851, 80 yrs.
3. Elizabeth Snitzel, d 7/4/1857, 47 yrs.
4. William Patterson, s/o Geo. M. & L. Patterson, d1/21/1861, aged 1 month.
5. Lydia Patterson, d 3/19/1880, 81/9/2.

- John Patterson, 8/18/1818-1/1/1904, bd Tom's Creek Presbyterian.

- Robert H. Patterson, 5/23/1831 - 10/30/1916, bd Tom's Creek Presbyterian.

PAXTON

- Clara E. Paxton - "In memory of / Clara E. Paxton / daughter of S.C. and / E.J. Paxton / Died June 21, 1859 / Aged 1 month & 10 days."- Tom's Creek Presbyterian, near Emmitsburg.

- Emily J. Paxton - "In Memory of / Emily Paxton / wife of Samuel C. Paxton / Died January 20, 1879 / Aged 45 years, 2 months / and 12 days." - Tom's Creek Presbyterian.

John William Paxton - "In memory of / John William Paxton / Died May 24, 1860." - Tom's Creek Presbyterian.

- Samuel C. Paxton - "In memory of / Samuel C. Paxton / Died April 29, 1885 / Aged 57 years, 7 months / and 17 days." - Tom's Creek Presbyterian.

- Rev. William Paxton - Rev. Dr. William Paxton, one of the early ministers of Tom's Creek Presbyterian church. He lived at Millerstown (now Fairfield), PA., from that point ministered, for a time, to three churches, namely Lower Marsh Creek, Piney Creek and Tom's Creek. He was a native of Chestnut Level, Lancaster County, Pennsylvania. He was interred at Lower Marsh Creek.

- William Paxton - "In Memory of / William Paxton / Died September 21, 1853 / Aged 62 years." - Tom's Creek Presbyterian.

PINEY CREEK PRESBYTERIAN CHURCH, near Harney, Maryland.

1817 - According to the record in an old "Session Book" of the Piney Creek congregation, the following persons subscribed to the minister's salary in 1817:- "John Adair, Samuel Adair, Francis Alison, William Alexander, Isaac Armstrong, James Barr, William Breckenridge, James Black, Clotworthy Birnie, Daniel Baldwin, William Beard, the Widow Breckenridge, Margaret Brannon, Thomas Cornal, William Cornel, John Crabbs, Elijah Currens, William Currens, Jesse Corbel, Smith Cornel, Archibald Clingan, William Clingan, John Crabster, John Crabster, Jr., Isaac Darborrow, John Darby, James Drummond, John Ferguson, William Ferguson, Matthew Galt, John Galt, John Gilliland, Andrew Guin, George Guin, Mary Gordin, Moses Galt, Alexander Horner, Hannah Hill, Joseph Hunter, William Horner, Andrew Horner, John Horner, Philip Heagy, Joseph Hays, Susanna Hunter, George Heagy, the Widow Jamison, John Jamison, John Jones, James Linn, Samuel Linn, Robert Love, Robert Leech, Abraham Lonal, Thomas Lorimore, Samuel Linn, Jr., Susanna Little, Robert McCreary, John McAlister, James McAlister, John McKaleb, John McKalip, Thomas McCune, John McIlhenny, Moses McIlvane, Robert Major, John McKinny, Thomas McCune, John McIlhenny, Elizabeth McCrea, Thomas McCrea, Samuel Musgrove, James McIlhenny, William Paxton, Thomas Paxton, Robert Robinson, Francis Reid, James Ross, Samuel Smith, James Smith, William Stevenson, William Shoemaker, George Six, Nicholas Smith, Hugh Shaw, George Sink, Obadiah Smith, Jno. Thomson, Samuel Thomson, Robert Thomson, Hugh Thomson, William Wilson, Mary Walker, Charles Wilson, Jr., James Wharton, Fanny Weems, Andrew Walker, James Stevenson, and Abraham Shoemaker."

PINEY CREEK PRESBYTERIAN CHURCH

1814 - 1836 - John Adair was treasurer of Piney Creek Church from 1814 to 1822 and he was followed in the post by James Barr who served from 1823 to 1836. It is interesting to note that the position of "Doorkeeper" was filled, in turn, by Abraham Shoemaker, James Ross, and Elijah Currens.

1824 - According to an old record (Session) the following were members of the Piney Creek Presbyterian church on January of the year 1824:- The four Elders at that time were Alexander Horner, John McAlister, Samuel Thompson, and James Barr. The following were listed as members of the congregation:- Alexander Horner, Elder, Sarah Horner, John Horner, Eli Horner, Robert Thompson, Mary Thompson, Elizabeth Thompson, Ann Thompson, Eleanor Thompson, Andrew Walker, Robert McCreary, Ann McCreary, Maria McCreary, Sarah Horner, James Horner, James Black, Philip Heagy, Esther Guinn, Margaret Linah, William Walker, William Stevenson, Peggy Stevenson, John McAlister, Elder, John W. McCalister, Betsy McCalister, Mary McCalister, Elizabeth Henery, Frances Weems, Jane Cornell, Margaret Paxton, William Paxton, Carolina Barris, Jane McCrea, Elijah Baldwin, Mathew Galt, Mary Galt, Elizabeth Galt, Susan Galt, Rebecca Galt, Abraham Linah, Sterling Galt, Margaret Galt, Samuel Galt, Mary Galt, Mary Jones, Elizabeth McCrea, Thompson McCrea, Samuel Thompson, Elder, Archibald Clingan, William Clingan, Elizabeth Clingan, Hugh Thompson, Margaret Snyder, Elijah Baldwin, Elizabeth Baldwin, Mary Baldwin, Kizech Baldwin, Rachel Miller, Sarah Drummond, James Smith, Sarah Smith, -(?)- Alison, Martha Alison, Mary Ann Alison, Isabella Barr, James Barr, Elder, Margaret Barr, Sally Barr, Mary Cornell, Esther Cornell, Sarah Galt, Martha Breckenridge, Margaret Birnie, Hester Birnie, Clotworthy Birnie, Hester Birnie, Jun., Rose Birnie, John McKelob, Mary Jane Annan, John McKellip, Ann McKellip, Mary Gillelan, Sarah Clanbach, Catherine Musgrove, John Ferguson, Sen., John Ferguson, Rebecca Ferguson, John Adair, Esther Adair, Sarah Adair, Samuel Adair, Hannah Adair, Frances Alison, Margaret Reid, Margaret Reid, Jun., Mary Reid, Weems Black, Elizabeth Larrimore, Lucinda McCalister, Thomas McCune, Thomas McCune, Jr., Mary McCune, John Thompson, Andrew Cuin, Margaret Hunter, Susanna Hunter, John Hunter, Andrew Horner, Margaret Horner, William Horner, William Horner, Elizabeth Horner, Nancy Bently, John Darby, Catherine Darby, Elizabeth Smith, Mary Wilson, Mary Wilson, Jane Wilson, John Wilson, Betsy Larrimore, George Guin, Elizabeth Baldwin, John McClanahan, Ann McClanahan, James McCalister, James McCalister, Jr., Mary McCalister, Alexander McCalister, James McIlhenny, Jun., Maria McIlhenny, Sally McIlhenny, Robert McKinney, Susanne McKinney, Esther McKinney, James Smith, Jane Longwell, Sally Jamison, Miss Jamison, Kelly (colored), and Jack (colored).

1825 - May of the year 1825 saw an increase in membership; Catherine Harris, Susan Jamison, Sarah and William Thompson, Rebecca Wilson, Betsy Donwiddie Amelia Rhinedollar, Sophia Deukart, Robert Fleming and Miss Eliza Graham. In 1830, the Session received Jacob Shoemaker, who became a most useful member, and was ordained to the Eldership in 1838. Both Jacob and his wife Margaret are interred in Piney Creek churchyard.

PINEY CREEK PRESBYTERIAN CHURCH

- The Rev. John Slemmons, A.M., was born in Chester County, Pennsylvania. His parents were emigrants from the north of Ireland and strict members of the Presbyterian church. He was a graduate of Princeton College and was licensed by the Presbytery of Donegal in 1762 or 63. He was called to the Lower Marsh Creek Presbyterian church on the third Saturday of November, 1764. He also received calls from Tom's Creek (Emmitsburg) and Piney Creek about the same time. On May 23, 1765, Rev. Slemmons declared his acceptance of the call to Lower Marsh Creek, and was ordained and installed by the Presbytery of Carlise, on October 30, 1765.
Like all the early ministers the Rev. Slemmons worked "long and hard". He frequently supplied Tom's Creek and Piney Creek, both before and after his 'settlement' at Lower Marsh Creek. His relation to the latter church was dissolved in 1774. He was pastor of Slate Ridge and Chanceford at the time of the organization of the Presbytery of Baltimore in 1786. Rev. Slemmons gave up his active career in the ministry because of ill health. He bought a farm in the vicinity of Piney Creek church, above the Mason and Dixon Line, and there spent his later years. This probably accounts for his grave and that of his wife in the Piney Creek churchyard.
Mrs. Slemmons was the daughter of the Rev. Joseph Dean, a co-laborer of the Tennents. Mr. Dean and his immediate family are interred in the Neshaminy church burial ground. Two brothers and a sister of Mrs. Slemmons, as well as the children of one of the brothers, are interred in the Lower Marsh Creek Presbyterian churchyard.

- The Rev. Robert Smith Grier - The long pastorate of the Rev. Grier was "quiet and uneventful". Rev. Simonton, however, has this to say pertaining to that worthy "shepard of the Lord":- " It is here deemed worthy of record that Mr. Grier possessed a peculiar talent for carving in wood, ... They included carvings in miniature of spread eagles, of horses and other animals ... They served as interesting mementoes of a genius, which, with proper direction and culture, might possibly have produced some great works of art, but which he devoted to the nobler art of winning souls to Christ, and of polishing gems for the Redeemer."
Many fine examples of Rev. Grier's art remains to this day in the Emmitsburg, Harney and Gettysburg neighborhoods. They are now treasured and valued as historical heirlooms. The retirement of the Rev. Grier from the pastorate of the 'united congregations' must have left both churches in somewhat of a quandry. Few among his people could remember any other minister ... For a few months they were supplied by the Rev. Daniel B. Jackson. In 1866 they were visited by the Rev. Isaac M. Patterson and this resulted in a 'call' being made to this minister. He was installed at Piney Creek on November 13, 1866.

- Rev. Isaac M. Patterson, installed November 13, 1866, and was minister for the next seven years. During his pastorate a parsonage property was bought, enlarged and improved. Both churches were remodeled and refurnished. A substantial stone wall was erected enclosing the Piney Creek churchyard. At the time it was built the cost was $1000.00.

The second church built at Piney Creek is still standing and is in use. ... In addition the burial ground is very well kept ... It alone is well-worth a 'walking tour' and careful study. Visit old Piney Creek Church and graveyard and appreciate what history has to offer in your own neighborhood.

REEVES

- Jacob Reeves, Soldier, d 1/23/1906, 70 yrs. - M.F. Shuff Burial Records. Jacob H. Reeves / Company C., 165th PA. Militia. bd Mt. View, Emmitsburg.

REIFSNIDER

- John Reifsnider, d 9/10/1908, 76 yrs., Soldier. - M.F. Shuff Burial Records. John I. Reifsnider / Company C., 1st P.H.B. Calvary - Margaret Ellen Reifsnider, w/o John I. Reifsnider, d 4/13/1865, 26/2/14 - Emmitsburg Mt. View Cem. Insc.

REINEWALD

- Rev. Dr. Charles Reinewald, D.D., b 10/20/1860, in Duncanville, PA., s/o Joseph Lewis and Catherine Sommer Reinewald, and pastor of the Emmitsburg Elias Lutheran Church.

- Joseph Lewis Reinewald (the name Reinewald means 'Pure Forrest"), b 10/24/1824, Darmstadt, Germany, e 1852, taking ship at Havre, France, for New York. He traveled to Pittsburg, PA., went to Hollidaysburg, PA., and soon after settled at Duncansville, PA. He was a tanner by trade. m 1855, in Hollidaysburg, PA., to Catherine Sommer, b 1833, Stutt, Germany, e from Havre, France and made her home with her uncle Frederick Weidler.   Children:-
1. Mary M. Reinewald
2. Charles Reinewald, D.D.
3. Matilda Reinewald Elliot, m Wm J. Elliot
4. Henry J. Reinewald, of Phila., PA.
5. Emma Reinewald Kirkham, m Joseph Kirkham

RHEA

- Rev. Joseph Rhea, the first 'settled' pastor of Piney Creek Presbyterian Church near Harney, Maryland.
1770 - became member of the Presbytery
1771 - Pastor of Piney Creek Presbyterian church
1775 - visited Virginia
1776 - resigned as pastor of Piney Creek Presbyterian church
9/20/1777 - Rev. Rhea died and was buried in the Piney Creek churchyard. The inscription from the marker at his grave:- "Sacred to the memory of the Rev. Joseph Rhea who died 1777 Aged about 62 years. Erected at the request of a grandson of the deceased, in 1839 by the Elders of Piney Creek Church where he preached seven years." Mr. Rhea was a native of Ireland. Piney Creek was his only pastorate in this country. The statement that he preached seven years in this church is incorrect for he was there less than five years. However he supplied the congregation sometime before he was 'regularly settled' and this period may be included in the time he served the congregation.

ROBERTSON

- G.W. Robertson, Co. "C", 6th MD INF, b 5/10/1824, 57/5/15, bd Tom's Creek Presbyterian, nr Emmitsburg. (The soldier's death date is not given.)

ROBINSON

- Micheal Robinson, (colored), d 1/17/1913, (no age given), bd Emmitsburg Mt. View. - M.F. Shuff Burial Records.

ROW - ROWE

- The Row Family - According to a family tradition - three brothers left Germany and emigrated to Pennsylvania about the middle of the eighteenth century. They landed at Philadelphia and from that point they went their separate ways. One, Andrew Row, came to Lancaster County, Pennsylvania, and there took up a plantation. He was married about 1742 to a distant cousin, one Sally Row. It is believed that Andrew was one of the "Monocacy Settlers". From that point three of Andrew's sons, Micheal, Arthur and George moved on into Tom's Creek Hundred (Emmitsburg area).

- Arthur Row, s/o Andrew & Sally Row, 1753-1823, m Sarah Ann Row, 1760-1828, both bd Tom's Creek Lutheran and Reformed graveyard near Emmitsburg. Arthur was a soldier of the American Revolution. Children:-
1. Samuel Row
2. George Row
3. Frederick Row
4. Abraham Row
5. Micheal Row
6. John Row
7. Joseph Row, m Susan Baker
8. Elizabeth Row, m Thomas Redford
9. Jacob Row, Soldier War 1812-14
10. Julian Row, m Frederick Flohr
11. Barbara Row, m John Young

- Cemetery Inscriptions Emmitsburg Elias Lutheran:-
1. Charles F. Rowe, 7/29/1830, 7/29/1830 - 2/21/1911
2. Ann Eliza Maxell, w/o Charles F. Rowe, 3/6/1836 - 8/21/1926
3. Susan F. Rowe, only d/o Charles F. & Ann Eliza Rowe, 10/21/1860 - 2/13/1882.

- James A. Rowe, s/o Joseph Rowe and Grandson of Arthur Row, m Sarah (Sallie) Hoke, Children:-
1. Edward Norman Hoke Rowe, b 1856, m Mary C. Clabaugh, 1855-1938
2. Fannie Belle Rowe, b 1858, m Walter W. White, of Adams Co., PA.
3. Howard M. Rowe, 1861-1936, m Mary Alma Overholtzer, 1862-1925 both bd Emmitsburg Mt. View Cemetery.

ROW - ROWE

- Micheal Row, 1750-1831, s/o Andrew & Sally Row, m Christina Smith d/o George and Christiana Smith. Children:-
1. Catherine Row Henry
2. Micheal Row
3. Mary Row Hartzell
4. Elizabeth Row Zollinger
5. Lucy Ann Row, m John Sluss
6. William Row
7. Margaret Row
8. Samuel Row
9. Sarah Row Fisher
10. John Row
11. Christiana Row Weant
12. Joseph Row
13. George Row

- Nathaniel Rowe, the Gunsmith of Emmitsburg, was the son of George and Anne Mary Rowe. He learned his trade of gunsmith under John Armstrong, the first gunsmith in Emmitsburg. Both were masters of their craft. m Elizabeth Rowe, d/o Jacob and Susan Baker Rowe, and his first cousin.

SEABROOK

- "Doctor Seabrook - Dr. Alice M. Seabrook, of Adams County, PA., daughter of the late William C. Seabrook, of Liberty Twp., was among the graduates last Thursday May 9, 1895, of the Woman's Medical College, of Phila., PA. Before being permitted to practice her profession, however, she must pass an examination before the PA. State Medical Board in June next. Miss Seabrook is a young lady of superior gifts and education."
- Emmitsburg Chronicle, May 17, 1895.

- Dr. Alice M. Seabrook, M.D., d/o William Chamberlain Seabrook and Catherine Zimmerman Seabrook. In old Elias churchyard is interred the ashes of Dr. Alice Seabrook, pioneer woman physician and surgeon. In the same plot are also buried her father, and her mother and three of her brothers, all of whom died of diptheria in 1859. Her grave is marked - very simply- "Dr. Alice M. Seabrook, M.D., Born 1856 Died 1936." Dr. Seabrook made a definate contribution for the betterment of all mankind for to her is attributed the design for the incubator used in the care of premature babies. During her years as head of the Woman's Hospital, in Phila., Dr. Seabrook must have seen many children, born prematurely, die - because medical sciences did not know how to deal with the problem. She determined to do something and with the help of the electrician at the hospital the incubator was designed and built. Her invention was given to the world - freely - a gift of untold value. Alice Mary Seabrook was born on her father's farm in Liberty Twp., Adams COunty, PA. the fifth child and only daughter of William C. and Catherine Zimmerman Seabrook. She and a younger brother, Elisha A. Seabrook, were the only children to survive in this somewhat tragic family. Four others had died - before attaining their sixth birthday. In that day the only profession open to women was that of schoolmistress. Alice Seabrook passed the examination given by the County Superintendant of Schools and became a teacher. She taught at Walkers School and at Liberty Hall School, both in Liberty Twp. Later the young teacher went as an instructor to the Indian School, Carlise, PA. It was Captain Pratt, superintendant of the Indian School, who persuaded the young teacher that she should study medicine. Four years later Alice Seabrook was graduated from the Women's Medical College at Phila. A short time later she was appointed to head the staff of Women's Hospital - at that time a part of the Medical School.

SEABROOK

- Dr. Seabrook - The institution, under Dr. Seabrook's guidance, grew - not only in size but in its range of services. Later Dr. Seabrook was appointed to the Pennsylvania State Board of Medical Examiners - the first woman in the history of the state to hold the position. A heart condition forced Dr. Seabrook to retire from active practice a few years before her death. After this she made her home in Califonia. Here, in her home near Hollywood, she died in 1936. Her body, at her request, was cremeated, and the ashes returned to Emmitsburg, MD. and interred at the Seabrook family plot at Elias Lutheran Churchyard. Her ancestral background:-
(1) Hans & Ann Zimmerman
(2) Peter (1752-1823) & Maria Shirk Zimmerman, early settlers of Carrolls Tract, Adams County, Pennsylvania.
(3) Joseph (1783-1823) & Mary Wiekert (1789-1855) Zimmerman
(4) William Chamberlain Seabrook & Katherine Zimmerman Seabrook
(5) Dr. Alice Seabrook

- Alice M. Seabrook, M.D., was born 4/20/1856, the fifth child and only daughter of William Chamberlain and Fanny Catherine Zimmerman Seabrooks, of Carrolls Tract. At the age of 18 she was teaching at country schools, one being the "Tract School". In 1884 she began teaching at the Carlise Indian School and it was Capt. Pratt, of that institute, who persuaded her to study medicine. She borrowed money and in due time received the degree of 'Doctor of Medicine'. Immediately after her graduation from the Women's Medical College, Phila., she went to the Methodist Hospital as Chief of Nurses. After a few years in this post she became Medical Superindendant of Women's Hospital, in Phila., and here she remained until her retirement. While here she designed the incubator for premature babies. She was also appointed to the Pennsylvania State Board of Medical Examiners, a post she held until her retirement, due to a heart condition, in 1920. Among her many friends made during her long life was an Englishwoman, Miss Dolly Hopper, who came to Woman's Hospital for treatment. They traveled together to just about every part of the world. After Dr. Seabrooks retired the two went to California - bought a home near Hollywood and there lived the remainder of their lives. Dr. Alice Seabrooks died in her 80th year - on March 10, 1936. Her body was cremeated and sent to Emmitsburg, MD., and interred at the family plot at Elias Lutheran churchyard. "Dr. Alice M. Seabrooks, M.D., 1856-1936. Pax Vobiscum." She was a descendant of the famed Madame Marie Warenbuer Feree of the Pequea Settlement, Lancaster County, Pennsylvania."

SCARBOROUGH

- Rev. William Scarborough, m Margaret Birnie, d/o Rogers & Amelia Harry Birnie. Children:-
1. Joseph J. Scarborough, 1860-1935, m Margaret Goss, 1868-1942.
2. Rogers Birnie Scarborough, 1862-1869
3. William Scarborough, b 1868, m Harriiet Angel, b 1881

SCOTT

- Francis Scott, d 1766, m Margaret Craig, who d 1741. Children:-
1. Francis Scott, 1698-1770
2. Rev. Hugh Scott, 1704-1736
3. Jean Scott, d 1771
4. Dr. Upton Scott, 1722-1814
5. Margaret Scott, b 1717, m Clotworthy(1) Birnie
6. dau., m Mr. McCord
7. Elizabeth Scott, d 1773, m Paul Reid
8. John Scott

Francis Scott Key, lawyer, poet, Churchman, and author of the national anthem of the United States, was a descendant of this Scott family. Many of his Scott and Key ancestors are interred in or near Annapolis.

- Dr. Upton Scott, 1722-1814, s/o Francis Scott and Margaret Craig Scott, died at Annapolis, MD. He was the first president and one of the founders of the Maryland Medical Society.

SEITZ

- Mrs. Stewart Seitz, d 1/27/1907, aged 28 yrs. - M.F. Shuff Burial Record

SENTMAN

- Rev. Solomon Sentman, d 12/10/1871, at Gettysburg, PA., bd Evergreen Cemetery, Gettysburg. He was the pastor of Elias Lutheran Emmitsburg, Taneytown, Fountaindale and possibly Sabillasville. m2 Sallie A. Lehman. Children:-
1. Sallie A. C. Sentman, 4/19/1839-5/3/1866, Taneytown, MD. m 11/3/1859 in St. Peter's Lutheran church, Barron Hill, Montgomery Co., PA, to Andrew McKinney.
2. Clara S. Sentman, 5/2/1842-11/22/1873, Phila., PA., m 2/21/1872, Phila., PA., to James J. Metcalfe
3. Amanda Isabella Sentman, 9/29/1841-5/26/1904, Balt., MD., m 11/21/1875, Germantown, PA., to William N. Thomson, and moved to Baltimore, MD.
4. Pearson Peterson Sentman, 3/15/1861 - 8/8/1900, at Gap, Lancaster County, PA. m 10/20/1892, at Gap, PA., to Martha Jane Parke.

SHAW

- Hugh Shaw, d 8/3/1844, 67 yrs., bd Piney Creek Presbyterian, m Elizabeth, d 12/13/1844, 77 yrs., bd Piney Creek Presbyterian

- Moses Shaw, 1/6/1760 - 2/8/1849, 83/12, m Grizelda Jamison, d 5/9/1832, 63/7/0, both bd Piney Creek Presbyterian.

- Thomas Shaw, d 1865, 37 yrs., m Susan E., d 8/5/1904, 75 yrs., both bd Piney Creek Presbyterian.

SHAW

- William Shaw, d 2/20/1871, 78/11/19, m Susannah Galt, d/o Mathew and Elizabeth Simpson Galt, 3/31/1792 - 7/22/1871, 79/3/22, both bd Piney Creek Presbyterian, near Harney. Children:-
1. Samuel Shaw, d 3/15/1835, 10 yrs., bd Piney Creek Presbyterian
2. Thomas Shaw, 2/21/1828 - 8/17/1865, 37/5/26, bd Piney Creek
3. Joseph Shaw, 12/7/1826 - 4/24/1865, 38/4/17, bd Piney Creek.

SHEETS - SHEADS

- Abraham Sheets, 11/17/1797 - 9/9/1887, 89/9/22, bd Taneytown Lutheran Cemetery. "Mr. Abraham Sheets, of Emmitsburg, Maryland is about to erect a monument in Taneytown Lutheran churchyard to the memory of the Rev. John Grobp, one of the early Lutheran ministers in that region." - Gettysburg "Star and Sentinel" Aug. 19, 1880.

Burials at Taneytown Lutheran Cemetery:-
1. Isaac Sheets, 5/24/1795 - 12/19/1888, 93/6/23.
2. Abraham Sheets, 11/17/1797 - 9/9/1887, 89/9/22
3. Father / Jacob Sheets d 1/27/1826, 65/5/26, also Mother / Hannah Sheets, wife of Jacob Sheets, d 5/5/1852, 85/4/11
4. Catherine SHeets, wife of Jacob Sheets, d 3/13/1803, 73/4/11
5. Jacob Sheetz, d 10/27/1806, 81 yrs.
6. Elizabeth Koons, wife of William Koons, d 6/5/1867, 74/3/18. Also Jacob Sheets d 11/11/1866, 76/4/2.

- Daniel Sheets, s/o George, m Barbara(Barbary) Ann, both bd Emmitsburg Elias Lutheran:- "Daniel Sheets 15 Apr 1815 - 26 June 1900, Barbara w/o Daniel Sheets, 4 Dec 1818 - 14 Oct 1897. "Died, Tuesday a week, at his home in Emmitsburg, Mr. Daniel Sheets, in the 86th year of his age. Mr. Sheets arrived in Emmitsburg in 1874. Prior to that time he lived in Freedom Twp., Adams County, PA. His father and grandfather were residents of Frederick County, MD. He is survived by the following children:- Mrs. John T. Hosplehorn, Mr. Sentman Sheets, Mrs. Abraham Krise, Mr. David Sheets and Mr. Harry Sheets. Daniel Sheets was a lifelong member of Elias Lutheran Church and served that congregation in many official capacities. He was Secretary of the cemetery board for many years. Funeral services were held in the Lutheran church with interment in the adjoining burial ground." - Emmitsburg Chronicle July 4, 1900.   Children:-
1. Lydia A. Sheets, b 2/4/1848, m 6/6/1870, John T. Hosplehorn, both bd Emmitsburg Elias Lutheran.
2. Florence Virginia Sheets, 1851-1853, bd Elias Lutheran.
3. Isadore M. Sheets, d 4/15/1855, 1/7/11, bd Elias Lutheran.
4. Barbara E. Sheets, d 11/24/1862, 16 yrs., bd Elias Lutheran.
5. David Myers Sheets, b 4/13/1842
6. Jacob Sentman Sheets, b 10/13/1843

SHEETS

- David and Margaret Sheets. Children:-
1. Riley Sheets, b 4/30/1838
2. Mary Jane Sheets, b 2/16/1840
3. Matilda Ann Sheets, b 5/10/1844
4. Alfred Sheets, 10/2/1845 - 9/20/1847
5. David Sentman Sheets, b 7/20/1848

- George Sheets - the miller, was one of the first of his family to live in the Emmitsburg district. George Sheets was one of the earliest men to settle in that section, 1746 or earlier.

- George Sheets, d 6/5/1852, 82/5/8 (death records), d 6/7/1852, 82/5/8 (Cemetery inscriptions). m Ann Elizabeth (Ella M.), d 10/5/1853, 80/3/20, both bd Emmitsburg Elias Lutheran. Children:-
1. Daniel Sheets

- Hannah Elizabeth Sheets, d/o Jacob & Mary Sheets, b 10/31/1843.
- Harriet Virginia Sheets, d/o John & Savilla Sheets, b 4/12/1845.
- Harriet Ida Isadora Sheets, d/o Frances Sheets, b 7/1/1861.
- Harry Pitzer Sheets, s/o David M. & Mattie R. Sheets, b 7/20/1870.
- Jacob Sheets - Sheads, Soldier of the American Revolution, bd Taneytown Lutheran with members of his family.

- Jacob Sheets, d 1/27/1826, 65/5/26, m Hannah, d 5/5/1852, 85/4/11, both bd Taneytown Lutheran Cemetery. Inscriptions:- "In memory of / Father / Jacob Sheets / Died January 27, 1826 / Aged 65 years, 5 months,/ and 26 days. / A Soldier of 1776. / Enlisted under Washington as he passed through Taneytown. / Also / Mother / Hannah Sheets / wife of Jacob Sheets / Died May 5, 1852 / Aged 85 years, 4 months, / and 11 days. / Erected by Abraham Sheets." "In memory of Elizabeth Koons / wife of William Koons / Died June 5, 1867 / Aged 74 years, 3 months, / and 18 days. / Also / In memory of / Jacob Sheets Died November 11, 1866 / Aged 76 years, 4 months, / and 2 days. / Erected by Abraham Sheet

- Lizzie Sheets & Nathan Angell, m 3/21/1872, by the Rev. E.S. Johnson.
- Lydia F. Sheets & Joseph A. Baker, m 9/28/1874, by Rev. E.S. Johnson.
- Miranda Sheets, bd 3/26/1846, 7/7/8.

- Peter Sheets - Sheads, came to this country from Germany before the American Revolution and settled near Germantown and later into York County, Pennsylvania. One of his sons came into Maryland with the Monocacy Settlers.

- Sarah C. Sheets & Geo. G. Maring, m 11/26/1861.

- Susan E. Sheets & George H. Grove, m 9/30/1856, by Rev. Henry Bishop.

SHIELDS

- William(1) Shields, b 7/14/1728, County Armaugh, Ireland, e 7/26/1739, arrived at Newcastle, Delaware, d 1797, bd Shields Family Cemetery nr Emmitsburg, MD. m 4/25/1754, Jane Bentley Williams, d/o John Williams, b 8/16/1736, Lancaster Co., PA., d 1806, bd Shields Family Cemetery nr Emmitsburg, MD. 11 Children.

SHIELDS

- William(1) Shields, by profession was a surveyor and practiced his craft in Frederick County, Maryland. Historian Helman describes William shields as "a surveyor true to his compass". Later in life, when he "reached his sixties", he gave up his work as a surveyor - probably due to the 'infirmities of age'. By this time he had become 'a landowner of considerable means'. In addition he had acquired slaves, had fathered eight sons and three daughters, and described himself as 'a farmer'. The late Mrs. Charles Hoffman (Emma Gertrude Hunter), of Emmitsburg, a descendant of William Shields, and a tireless researcher into the Shields genealogy, found reason to believe that her ancestor was a brother-in-law of Samuel Emmit, the founder of Emmitsburg.

- William(1) Shields, Pioneer, Surveyor, Soldier, Farmer. William(1) Shields was of "Scotch-Irish" descent. He was born in 1728 in the County of Armagh in Ireland. At the age of nine years he emigrated to Newcastle, Delaware in 1737 along with his father and brother, both died on that voyage. Little is known of his early life. It is believed that while he was a resident of Cecil Co., MD., he served as an apprentice with a surveyor since he followed that profession. He became a farmer later in life. In 1748 he moved to Tom's Creek Hundred, the area which became known as the Emmitsburg district of Frederick County. In 1754 he married Jane Bentley Williams, the daughter of John Williams. To this union eleven children were born - all in Frederick County.
William recieved his first land holdings in the Emmitsburg area in 1757, the land in Hampton Valley, land west of Carrick's Knob. In 1762 & 1767 he purchased land in the region west of the present town of Emmitsburg. Later, between 1781 - 1797, he bought additional tracts. In 1787 he purchased from Samuel Emmit, 106 acres of land west of and adjoining the west end of Emmitsburg. He continued the town and named it Shield's Addition He wrote his will November 30, 1789 and it was entered to probate shortly after his death. The welfare of his wife was uppermost in the writing of his will and he directed that "... Jane, My Beloved Wife, is to have one-third of my Personal Estate and also one-third part of my Real Estate, the Mansion House where I now live to be included in her third part ..."

- William Shields Family Bible: - "William Shields was born in the County of Armagh, in the Kingdom of Ireland, on Sunday the fourteenth day of July in the Year of our Lord 1728 - Embarked aboard a sloop Commanded by Captain Alexander Smith on the twenty-sixth day of July 1737 being the Ninth year of his age. Arrived at Newcastle State of Delaware on the First Day of August Next Ensuing. On the Voyage lost his Father and Brother Robert, who was taken away by the unrelenting hand of death. Dwelt in Newcastle County six years - then Removed into Cessil (Cecil) County State of Maryland. Remained there four years Next Ensuing - then removed to Frederick County, State of Maryland aforesaid in the year 1748 - and was married on the twenty - fifth day of April 1754 to Jane (Bentley) Williams the daughter of John Williams - who was then late from Chester County, Pennsylvania. Sade Jane was born in Lancaster County, Pennsylvania, in North America on the sixteenth day of August 1736."

SHIELDS

- Children of William(1) Shields and his wife Jane Bentley Williams Shields:-
1. John(2) Shields, 3/20/1755 - 1/22/1833, m Mary McCollum, 2/18/1769 - 4/20/1820. They were the parents of eight children and emigrated to Tennessee.
2. James(2) Shields, 6/12/1757, Frederick Co., MD. - 8/30/1840, Greene Co., Tenn. Served as a Surgeon (Sergeant) in his father's Militia Company during the War of the American Revolution. Later reported to have been commissioned a Captain in the Continental Army. m 4/1/1783, to Jane Gilliland (Gilleylen), who was born 10/15/1764 died 12/21/1849, d/o John Gilleylen and Hester Roome Gilleylen. They were the parents of 11 children. After the close of the American Revolution the family emigrated to Tennessee.
3. Henry(2) Shields, 11/3/1759 - 9/12/1826, emigrated to Tenn., m Esther Waddell.
4. William(2) Shields, b 10/8/1761, m1 1785, Elizabeth Coulter, d 1794, 4 children; m2 1798, Ann Patterson, 6 children, d 4/7/1808, when her son, Patterson(3) Shields, was born; m3 1810, Ann McKissie, d 1811, one dau., Margaret, d age 15; m4 1813, Betsy McDonald, 5 children. William and a number of his children settled in Ohio.
5. Samuel(2) Shields, b 3/13/1764, m Jane Montgomery and/or Margaret Ware. Emigrated to Greene Co., Tenn., sometime after the American Revolution.
6. David(2) Shields, b 6/12/1769, m Rachel Waddell, settled in Tennessee, where he reared his family of five.
7. Banner(2) Shields, b 10/28/1772, m Margaret Ware of Blount Co., Tenn.
8. Agnes(2) Shields Gilliland, b 12/30/1766, m1 Jacob Gilliland (Gilleylen), s/o John and Hester Roome Gilleylen), and after his death m2 to Micheal Woods. Agnes, in company with 7 of her brothers and sisters, emigrated to Tennessee. This probably after her first marriage for the Gililands were an old and honored family in southeastern Pennsylvania and Frederick County, Maryland. It is also quite possible that Jacob Gilliland died while a resident of the Emmitsburg vicinity and was interred in a grave, (at the Shields Family Cemetery or Tom's Creek Presbyterian Cemetery), that is now unmarked. It is interesting to note that there are several Gilliland graves in Piney Creek Presbyterian graveyard. Perhaps the Gililands buried in this churchyard.
9. Mary(2) Shields, b 1/2/1775, m John Blair. Moved to Tennessee after 1806.
10. Margaret(2) Shields, b 10/2/1783, m Evan Evans, of Welsh descent. They lived and died in Greene County, Tennessee and were the parents of 2 children.
11. Ebenezer(2) Shields, b 12/27/1778, the only one of his family to live his entire life in the Emmitsburg vicinity. He was a somewhat complex character. Traditiions of some of his 'doings' are still repeated in his home neighborhood. Some are good and others are just the opposite. As was to be expected Ebenezer's reputation has been handed down to posterity, in part by ledgends. There is even a ghost story associated with his name and person. It is said that on dark, moonless nights, the ghost of Ebenezer may often be seen riding horseback up and down old Route 15 south of Emmitsburg.

SHIELDS

Apparently he did not rest 'easy in his grave' but desired to be 'up and doing'. He was buried in the family burial ground and his gravestone can be seen at that site to this day.
Ebenezer(2) Shields was the father of at least four sons for he named this number in his will. They were as follows:- Jefferson(3) Shields, John Henry(3) Shields, Andrew Jackson(3) Shields and William Vanburren(3) Shields.
The second son, John Henry(3) Shields, m Eva Benchoff. John Henry is buried at Emmitsburg ELias Lutheran, his wife Eva is buried at Burns Hill Cemetery, Waynesboro, PA.

SHOEMAKER - HOCKENSMITH

- Shoemaker Family Bible, c/o Mrs. Ella Gillelan Shuff, Emmitsburg, MD.
Births:-
- Levi Hockensmith b 4/7/1824, bp 5/1/1834, by Rev. John Grubb.
- Isamiah Hockensmith, b 1/3/1826, bp 1/21/1826 by Rev. John Hoffman.
- Adam Tobias Hockensmith, b 1/21/1835, bp by Rev. Daniel Hincle.
- Hannah Joanna Hockensmith, b 1/21/1828, bp 3/23/1828 by Rev. John Hoffman.
- Adam Tobias Hockensmith, b 2/16/1830 by 3/1830 by Rev. John Hoffman.
- Daniel Lawrence Shoemaker, b 2/16/1835, bp by Rev. Daniel D. Hincle.
Marriages:-
- Hannah Joanna Hockensmith was married Sept 3, 1841.
Deaths:-
- William Bowers Shoemaker, d 11/1/1847, 10/3/29.
- Levi Hockensmith, d 2/28/1847, 23/10/21.
- Daniel Shoemaker, d 3/11/1852, 40 yrs.
- Elizabeth Shoemaker, d 10/4/1882, 82/1/21.
- Egbert Hafey Courtney, s/o D.L. Shoemaker & May G. Shoemaker, b 10/24/1857, d 11/15/1889, 32/0/22.
- Daniel Lawrence Shoemaker, d 1/30/1897, 61/11/14
- John M. Shoemaker, d 7/9/1914, 74/11/10.
Births:-
- William Bowers Shoemaker, b 7/3/1837, bp by Rev. Ezra Keller.
- John Maxell Shoemaker, b 9/11/1839, bp by Rev. Ezra Keller.
- Jerimiah David Shoemaker, b 7/17/1842, bp by Rev. Solomon Sentman.

SHORB

- Tom Shorb, a member of the Roman Catholic Church, was buried in the Tom's Creek Methodist churchyard - after night. He lived in a little house located on the Krise farm. He was brought to the burial ground in a spring wagon and buried without a service of any kind. The following Sunday the Methodist minister announced that a burial had been made in the churchyard and no rites were held. At that point he asked the entire congregation to follow him to the burial ground and assist him in the burial service. This was done and Tom Shorb received the blessing and last offices of the church.

SHUFF

- Charles O. Shuff, 12/12/1861 - 2/12/1917, bd Tom's Creek Presbyterian. He married Sarah Gibbs, who was 'buried in the west'.

SHUNK

- Benjamin Shunk, m Rebecca Galt, d/o Mathew Galt, Children:-
1. Mary Shunk, m John McKellip
2. Aberillia Shunk, 'married and had issue'.

SHRIVER

- Andrew Shriver, first settled in the Conewago Settlement, in the vicinity of Christ Reformed Church, near Littlestown, PA. He was a shoemaker by trade.

- George Lewis Shriver, s/o Lewis and Mary Sheets Shriver, was married twice, first to Sarah Krise, 2 children, and after her death married 2nd Mrs. Mary Fisher Rife, a widow, and had three children.

- Lewis Shriver, 1750 - 1816, bd Emmitsburg Elias Lutheran. m Mary (Maria) Sheets (Sheads), d 1849. Children:-
1. Jacob Shriver
2. Elizabeth Shriver
3. Barbara Shriver
4. Frederick Wm. Shriver
5. Mary Shriver
6. Susannah Shriver
7. Catherine Shriver
8. George Lewis Shriver
9. Anna Shriver
10. Christian Shriver
11. Sarah Shriver
12. Rachel Shriver, m 1821, Henry Heagy, bd Elias.

- Lewis Shriver was born 1750 and d 7/12/1815. He m Mary (Maria) Sheets (Sheads), who d 8/1849. After the death of her first husband she m 2nd Peter Weikert.
Lewis and Mary were the parents of 12 children. Lewis lived in Cumberland Twp., in what is now Adams County, PA., about three miles north of the Mason and Dixon Line, nr Marsh Creek on the Emmitsburg - Gettysburg Road. He was a Soldier of the War of the American Revolution and was bd in Emmitsburg Elias Lutheran churchyard. The inscription from the marker at his grave follows:-"In memory of / Lewis Shriver / Died July 11, 1815 / Aged 65 years."

- Lewis Peter Shriver, grandson of Lewis Shriver, m Rebecca C. Rowe, d/o Jacob Rowe, Soldier of the War of 1812-14. They were the parents of a large family but lost 5 of their children to diptheria.

SIMONTON

- Rev. William Simonton wrote the historical discourse "Historical Sketch of the Presbyterian Churches of Emmitsburg and Piney Creek".

SINGER

- Ann Elizabeth Singer & Uriah Yingling, m 4/11/1850, by the Rev. Solomon Sentman. - Taneytown Lutheran Records.

- Charlotte Singer, second wife of John Hoover, and d/o John and Sarah Singer.

- Eva Singer, Mrs., - d 1/15/1842, 56/6/0. - Taneytown Lutheran Records.

- Mary Singer - d/o Samuel Singer, sister of John Singer, aunt of Charlotte Singer Hoover and Susannah Singer Ohler, and wife of Mathias Zacharias. Buried Elias churchyard, Emmitsburg. The Inscription from the black slate stone is as follows:- "In memory of / Mary Zacharias / wife of Mathias Zacharias / and daughter of Samuel Singer / Died April 11, 1824 / Aged 33 years and 15 days."

- Samuel Singer, Soldier of the War of the American Revolution, late of the Monocacy Settlement, was the first of his family to settle in the Emmitsburg vicinity. He was the father of John Singer who was born in 1779. He was bd in Emmitsburg Elias Lutheran churchyard and the inscription from his tombstone reads:- "In memory of / Samuel Singer / Died July 29, 1818 / Aged 70 years." Also buried at Elias Lutheran is Samuel's son John and members of his family, as follows:-
1. "In memory of / John Singer / Died March 24, 1849 / Aged 70 years and / 3 months."
2. "In memory of / Sarah Singer / the wife of John Singer / Died January 13, 1893 / Aged 92 years, 3 months. / and 26 days."
3. "In memory of / Charlotte Hoover / the daughter of John and Sarah / Singer / Died August 13, 1905 / Aged 76 years, 4 months, / and 14 days." Charlotte was the second wife of John Hoover.
4. "Sacred / to the memory of / Susannah Singer Ohler / wife of Samuel G. Ohler / Died October 25, 1845 / Aged 24 years, 3 months, / and 27 Days." Susannah was the first wife of Samuel G. Ohler, they were married 10/19/1840, by the Rev. Benjamin Keller. She was buried in the family plot of her grandfather, Samuel Singer.

SKILES

- Skiles family burials at Tom's Creek:-
1. Hopkins Skiles - "In memory of / Hopkins Skiles / Born November 12, 1797 / Died May 20, 1872 / Aged 74 years, 6 months / and 8 days."
2. Lettice Skiles - "In memory of / Lettice Skiles / wife of / Hopkins Skiles / Died July 20, 1859 / Aged 53 years, 2 months / and 10 days."
3. Thomas A. Skiles - "Sacred / to the memory of / Thomas A. Skiles / son of / H. & L. Skiles / Died May 29, 1847 / aged 11 months."
4. William E. Skiles - "In memory of / William E. Skiles / Born March 23, 1834 / Died June 24, 1890."

SLEMMONS

- Rev. John Slemmons, b Chester County, Pennsylvania.
- 1762-3 — graduated from Princeton University and licensed by the Presbytery of Donegal.
- 1764 — pastor of Lower Marsh Creek Presbyterian (nr Gettysburg), Tom's Creek (Emmitsburg) and Piney Creek (Harney).
- 1765 — pastor of Lower Marsh Creek Presbyterian.
- 1774 — pastor of Slate Ridge and Chanceford. He bought a farm in the vicinity of Piney Creek where he retired. He and his wife were interred at Piney Creek.
- 1814 — died 6/1814, 80 yrs., bd Piney Creek Presbyterian
- 1823 — his wife, Sarah Dean, d/o Rev. Joseph Dean, d 6/2/1823, 75 yrs., bd Piney Creek Presbyterian.

SLUSS

- Capt. Micheal Sluss, a soldier of the War of 1812 - 1814, his wife, Lucy Ann Row, d/o Micheal & Christiana Smith Row. Son:-
1. John Sluss, m Susan Smith, interred at Tom's Creek Lutheran and Reformed cemetery, nr Emmitsburg.

SMITH

- Charles Smith, d 4/15/1847, 55/8/25, bd Emmitsburg Mt. View, m 12/19/1822, Barbary Motter, d/o Lewis & Mary Martin Motter, b 4/25/1803, d 1/10/1884, 80/8/15, bd Mt. View. Children:-
1. Emma Alice Smith, d 2/8/1855, 10/9/23, bd Mt. View.

- Ella J. R. Smith - "In memory of / Ella J. R. Smith / daughter of Stephen and Frances / Smith / Died August 14, 1837 / Aged 2 months and 3 days."

- George Smith, 1720 - 1793, 73 yrs., his wife Christiana, 1720 - 1790, 70 yrs., both bd Tom's Creek Lutheran and Reformed graveyard, nr Emmitsburg. George Smith was the first man to receive a patent for land in Tom's Creek Hundred, Frederick Couinty, Maryland. He called his plantation "The Cattail Branch". George and his wife, Christiana were the parents of 11 children, - 4 boys and 7 girls. According to the Historian Helman:- "The first patent in this vicinity was to George Smith, on March 21, 1746, for five hundred acres, near the lands of Ohler, Eckard, Hockensmith and others. He was born 1720 and died 1793. The survey is called 'Cattail Branch". George was the father of 11 children - 4 boys and 7 girls."
George and members of his family are interred at Tom's Creek Lutheran and Reformed graveyard, near Emmitsburg. In Tom's Creek graveyard, near the center of the plot, stands the George Smith Memorial. The inscription that is cut thereon:- "To the Memory / of our Ancestors / They were / amongst the / Earliest Settlers / in this Locality / March 16th, 1746. / A patent was / granted for a / Tract called / Cattail Branch / where they lived and died. / George Smith / Born 1720 / Died 1793. / Christina Smith / Wife of George Smith / Born 1720 / Died 1790."

SMITH

- Children of George and Christiana Smith   (11 children, 5 known):-
1. John Smith, Soldier of the American Revolution, a Sergeant in Capt. William Blairs Gamecock Company, d 5/12/1783, bd Tom's Creek Luth. and Reformed graveyard, nr Emmitsburg.
2. a dau., m John Crabbs, Corporal in the Gamecock Company during the American Revolution, and owned one of the first mills built on Tom's Creek.
3. Elizabeth SMith, m Ensign Jacob Hockensmith, of the Gamecock Company, both bd Tom's Creek Lutheran and Reformed graveyard.
4. Christiana Smith, m Micheal Row, Soldier of the American Revolution. both bd Tom's Creek Lutheran and Reformed graveyard.
5. Susan Smith, m John Sluss, both bd Tom's Creek Lutheran and Reformed graveyard.

- Maria Smith - "In memory of / Maria Smith / daughter of Stephen & Frances Smith / ... (?)" - bd Pineycreek Presbyterian, nr Harney.

- Mary Smith - "Sacred / to the memory of / Mary Smith / Born March 11, 1793 / Died January 17, 1859 / Aged 65 years, 10 months / and 6 days." - bd Piney Creek Presbyterian, nr Harney.

- Stephen Smith, 2/25/1813 - 9/3/1881, m Frances, 7/9/1827 - 2/10/1888, both bd Piney Creek Presbyterian, nr Harney. Their son :-
1. John W. Smith, d 5/26/1872, bd Piney Creek Presbyterian:- "John W. Smith died May 26, 1872, Aged 19 yrs. 4 mos & 1 day." He was the only son of Stephen and Frances Smith at the time of his death he was a student in Pennsylvania (now Gettysburg) College - a candidate for the ministry.

SONNINGER

- Bertha Sonninger, d 3/26/1908, 23 yrs. - M.F. Shuff Burial Records.

SPENCE

- John Spence, d 10/24/1894, 65 yrs., Civil War Soldier. - M.F. Shuff Burial Records.

SPRINGER

- Edwin Springer, 9/25/1821 - 8/16/1899, bd Mt. View, Emmitsburg. Edwin Springer, d 8/15/1899, 79 yrs. - M.F. Shuff Burial Records.

- Mary M., wife of Edwin Springer, 11/7/1823 - 5/26/1905, bd Mt. View, Emmitsburg.

STAMBAUGH

- Jacob Stambaugh, m Maude Ohler, children:- Anna, Frank, Ruth m Otis Showmaker, Freda m David Scott.

STOKES

- Henry Stokes, 1825 - 1911, one of the early magistrates of Emmitsburg was active in just about every public work of his time. In regard to Mt. View Cemetery he was Secretary of the first Board and

STOKES

many years had charge of the sale of burial plots. He also worked on one of Emmitsburg's early murder cases, the magistrate in the Munshour - Wetzel case.
Henry Stokes, 1/17/1825 - 5/20/1911, bd Mt. View. Henry Stokes, d 5/20/1911, 86 yrs. - M.F. Shuff Burial Records. m Mary J., 10/25/1824 - 11/29/1914, bd Mt. View. Children:-
1. Mary Lizzie Stokes, d 11/23/1859, 1/11/ 20, bd Mt. View.

SUMWALT

- Burials Mt. Hope Cem., Woodsboro, MD.
1. Isaac Sumwalt, Aged 77 yrs. (no dates)
2. Rachel Sumwalt, Aged 88 yrs. (no dates)
3. Runyon Sumwalt, Aged 10 yrs. (no dates)

- John Sumwalt, 11/29/1849 - 8/26/1872, bd Emmitsburg Elias Lutheran. m 7/4/1872, at Emmitsburg Elias Lutheran, Mary Agnes Maxell, d/o Samuel & Jane Ferguson Maxell, of Maxell's Mill. She was b 1851 and remarried after her husbands' death to A. Cronon Stansbury on 1/5/1875.

- Runyon Sumwalt, d 1855, bd Tom's Creek.

SWEENY

- Burials at Tom's Creek Presbyterian, nr Emmitsburg:-
1. Christina Sweeny, w/o James, d 3/26/1854, 42/4/22
2. Amos T. Sweeny, s/o James & C. Sweeny, 3/16/1854 - 7/4/1854.
3. Columbia Alice Sweeny, d/o James & C. Sweeny, d 4/26/1865, 14/7/1.

THORNDALE SCHOOL

- Thorndale School, located east of Taneytown, Maryland, was the home of the Birnie Family but it also was a private academy for young ladies - organized and run by the Birnie sisters. Because of its excellent reputation it drew pupils not only from the immediate neighborhood but also 'boarding students' from distant points.
Thorndale Seminary For Young Ladies Under the Care of the Misses Birnie At Their Residence, Near Taneytown, Carroll County, Maryland. Thirty - seven miles from Baltimore.
The course of Instruction Comprises the usual Branches of an English Education, with Needlepoint. The pupils have the advantage of daily association with the Falculty, and are under their constant care and supervision. Particular attention is given to religious instruction in the study of the Scriptures forming a part of the regular exercises of the School. Mathematics taught by Mr. Rogers Birnie.
The year is divided into two Sessions of twenty-one weeks, once commencing on the second Thursday in May, the other on the second Thursday in November. Terms - Boarding and Tuition, per session - $110.00. The above payable in advance. Music, and the use of Piano, per session - $25.00, Drawing and painting - $10.00, French - $10.00, Use of Library - $ .50. Pupils will be received at anytime, but not for a shorter period than one session. The number being limited, a notice of two months

THORNDALE SCHOOL

is required before the removal of a scholar. References:- Rev. Dr. R.J. Breckenridge, Danville, Kentucky, Dr. R.J. Johns, Alexandria, Virginia, Rev. Dr. W.B. Sutton, Harpers Ferry, Virginia, Rev. Dr. Backus, Baltimore, Maryland, Mr. Joseph Cushing, Baltimore, Maryland, Dr. John Ridout, Annapolis, Maryland." - from a brochure.

Thorndale School flourished well over a hundred years ago ... education was not the easy matter that it is today. Private schools and academies were the rule rather than the exceptions. Thorndale was a 'finishing school' with a thin layer of academic studies for young ladies of better families.

TOMSON

- William Tomson, d 7/4/1800, 89 yrs. - Piney Creek Presbyterian Cemetery, Harney, MD.

TOM'S CREEK PRESBYTERIAN CHURCH AND CHURCHYARD, near Emmitsburg:-

- In January of the year 1824 there was a list of the communicants of Tom's Creek Presbyterian church made. It reads as follows:-
"James, Crocket, John Witherow, William Long, and William Bigham, Ruling Elders. William Grayson, Agnes Grayson, David Morrison, Harriet Morrison, Patrick Reid, Fielding Donaldson, Kitty Donaldson, William Ferguson, Miss Ferguson, Charles Bigham, Margaret Bigham, William Long, (Edler), Mary Long, Hugh Patterson, Nathaniel Grayson, Eliza Ann Grayson, Mary Emmit, Sarah Emmitt, Margaret Long, Marton Hill, Jane Williams, Margaret Holmes, Abigail Emmitt, Elizabeth M. Hays, Margaret Gilliland, Margaret Agnew, Jane Eichelberger, Jane McKeehan, Jane Faries, Sarah Hover, Betsy Hunter, Nancy Armstrong, Miss Danner, Margaret Witherow, Mary Danner, James Paxton, Cassandra Paxton, James Crocket (Elder), Margaret Ferguson, Margaret Knox, Mary Knox, Margaret Annan, Hannah Robinson, Martha McKeehan, Susan Little, Mina Armstrong, Molley Patterson, Jane Patterson, John Stewart, Rosanna Stewart, James Moore, John Witherow (Elder), Jane Witherow, Sarah Witherow, Eleanor Ross, William Curren, Jane Curren, Lavinia Curren, Robert McGuigan, Barbary McGuigan, Peggy Nolton, William Bigham (Elder), Phebe Bigham, Phebe Bigham, Jun., Kitty Bigham, Hannah Law, Esther Clark, Sarah Crockett, Hannah Morrison, Melcher Sheaner, Elizabeth SHeaner, Elizabeth Jordan, Polly Day (colored), Nancy Boens (colored), Ellen Boens (colored), Jane Armstrong, Sally Breckenridge, Polly Breckenridge, WIlliam Breckenridge, Samuel Witherow, Polly Witherow, Betsy Shriver, Nancy Linn, Joseph Kerr, David Kerr, Sally McKinley, Barnabas McSherry, Sr., Peggy McKee, Nancy McKee, Nathaniel Randolph, Eliza Randolph, Joseph Randolph, Sally Randolph, Peggy Caldwell, Peggy Caldwell, Jun., John Myers, Nancy McCreary, Elizabeth Grier, Joseph Clark, Betty Hasslet, Sophia Dumfee, John Gezelman, and John McKee."
- The above should prove of great historical and genealogical value to all interested in old Tom's Creek Presbyterian church and graveyard.
The Rev. Robert Smith Grier, who, as his tombstone states, was the "Pastor for fifty-two years of the United Churches of Tom's Creek and Piney Creek" left a list of the marriages performed by him during the years of his ministry. Because it is so little known it is of great interest and value:-
1. Mr. -(?) Storey to Miss Stevinson.

TOM'S CREEK PRESBYTERIAN CHURCH - Marriage Records of Rev. R.S. Grier:-

2. "Barnabas McSherry to Dorcas Work, Adams County, January 1815."
3. "March 1815 - William Clingan to Elizabeth McGuffin - Maryland."
4. "May 1815 - James Thomas to Margaret Robinson - Maryland."
5. "1815 - John Myers to Martha Caldwell."
6. "1816 - Abraham Linard to Margaret Black."
7. "1816 - George Rupert to Mary McCleaf."
8. "March 1816 - David Stauffer to Mary Clabaugh."
9. "March 27, 1816 - Alexander Laughlin to Hannah Neil."
10. "March 29, 1816 - Nathaniel Stinchcomb to Elizabeth Blair."
11. "April 1816 - James Blair to Peggy Hunter."
12. "May 1816 - Jacob Myers to Polly Foot."
The list of marriages ... will be continued in this series next week."

TROXELL

- Frederick W. Troxell - "M 2/27/1849, by the Rev. S. Sentman, Frederick W. Troxell, of Gettysburg to Sarah Jane Rowe, of Frederick County, MD." "Baptised Frederick William Troxell - son of Frederick W. Troxell (deceased) and Sarah Jane Troxell, born 9/11/1851, baptised 12/4/1851. - Rev. S. Sentman." "In memory of / Frederick W. Troxell / Died August 5, 1851 / Aged 40 years, 4 months / and 7 days."
Frederick W. Troxell, m Sarah J. Rowe, d/o Joseph and Susanna Baker Rowe, of Emmitsburg. Frederick was a teacher at the Preparatory Dept. of Pennsylvania (now Gettysburg) College. The family made their home in Gettysburg where their first son Charles Troxell was born. Before the birth of their second son, Frederick William, the father died and was interred in the old Lutheran churchyard at Gettysburg. This plot was located east of the jail (now the county library). The body of Frederick W. Troxell was later moved from Gettysburg to Mt. View Cemetery, Emmitsburg.
Mary Ann Rowe, the sister of Sarah Jane Rowe Troxell, was married to Detrick Zeck, who came to Emmitsburg from York Co., PA. Mary Ann Rowe Zeck died young and was buried at Emmitsburg Elias Lutheran churchyard. Detrick Zeck married a second time to his first wife's sister, Sarah Jane Rowe Troxell. The second Mrs. Zeck predeceased her husband and was buried in the Zeck family plot at Elias. There was no issue to this second marriage.

- James W. Troxell, - ... 'was born in Frederick County, MD., on 4/1/1831 He was a graduate of Dickenson College, Carlise, PA., in 1856. Four years later he received the degree of Master of Arts from that Institution In 1866 Mr. Troxell was married to Miss Mary E. Zacharias, who survives him, together, with 6 daus. & one son. Burial was made in Mt. View Cem.'
Emmitsburg Chronicle - 2/5/1904.
James W. Troxell, 4/1/1831 - 2/2/1904, 72/10/0. m 1866, Mary E. Zacharias, 2/10/1841 - 12/1/1915, both bd Emmitsburg Mt. View Cem.

- Peter Troxell emigrated from the Palatinate, to the Huguenot Colony in White Hall Twp., in what is now Lehigh Co., PA. He was a member of the Egypt church. Children:-
1. John Troxell, served as a Lt. during the American Revolution.
2. Peter Troxell - served as a Soldier during the American Revolution. m Magdalena Shriver about the year 1776, both buried at Tom's Creek Lutheran and Reformed churchyard, near Emmitsburg, MD.

WACHTER

- Denton A. Wachter, 7/3/1857 - 1/26/1931, m 2/16/1866 to Mary E. Ohler, 7/17/1855 - 2/5/1941, d/o Isaac & Isamish Hockensmith Ohler.

WADDLE

- Joseph Waddle, d 5/10/1892, 62 yrs. - M.F. Shuff Burial Records. NOTE: Grave marked at Mt. View Cem., Emmitsburg - the stone giving the year of his birth as 1829. Sarah Waddle, the wife of Joseph, who is buried beside her husband, was born 1830 and died 1921.

WADDLES

- Sarah Waddles, d 1/29/1908 - 80 yrs. - M.F. Shuff Burial Records.

WANTZ

- Mrs. Robert Wantz, d 1/22/1907 - 37 yrs. - M.F. Shuff Burial Records.

WAYBRIGHT

- Waybright Marriages
1. Abraham Hesson & Ann Margaret Waybright, both of Adams Co., PA., m. 12/22/1851 by the Rev. Solomon Sentman.- Elias Lutheran.
2. John J.J. Hunter & Margaret E. Waybright both of Adams Co., PA., m. 3/27/1884 by the Rev. E.S. Johnston. - Elias Lutheran.
3. Newton McHoner & Sarah E. Waybright, both of Adams Co., PA., m. 11/9/1856 at Trinity Lutheran, Taneytown, MD.

- Waybright Family Bible
Births
Jacob Fickes Waybright was born April 19, 1840.
Lucinda Catherine Sharets was born July 10, 1843.
Franklin Abraham Waybright was born January 23, 1870.
Anna Margaret Waybright was born June 24, 1871.
Emma Amelia(?) Waybright was born May 8, 1873.
Margaret Mary Waybright was born November 26, 1877.
Harriet May Waybright was born March 5, 1880.
Marriages
Jacob Fickes Waybright was married to Lucinda Catherine Sharets on January 6, 1869 by the Rev. Peter Bergstresser - at her father's house.
Anna M. Waybright was married to William C. Durboraw on December 12, 1893 by the Rev. W.G. Winnick - at her father's house.
Emma A. Waybright was married to Ernest W. Ritter November 24, 1896 by the Rev. W.G. Minnick - at her father's house.
Oliver J. Waybright was married to Lousia Swartz on December 14, 1897.
Margaret Mary Waybright was married to Walter Shoemaker (?) 27, 1900 by Rev. Minnick.
Harriet M. Waybright was married to Ernest R. Shriver on December 9, 1902 - by the Rev. W.G. Minnick at her father's house.

WAYBRIGHT

- Waybright Family Bible:-
Deaths
Lucinda Catherine Sharets wife of Jacob Fickes Waybright died 15 minutes of 12 o'clock at noon February 23, 1911 from a paralitic stroke and died instantly. Aged 62 years, 7 months, and 13 days. Franklin Abram Waybright died June 6, 1943, Aged 73 years.

- Abraham Waybright, s/o Jacob and Margaret Fickes Waybright, d 1/10/1879, 79/2/19, m Margaret, d 12/14/1880, 72/7/22, both bd Gettysburg Evergreen Cemetery. Children:-
1. Margaret Waybright Hunter, d 1/1/1915, m John J.J. Hunter, 10/31/1859 - 9/30/1904, both bd Gettysburg Evergreen Cemetery.

- Abram Waybright, m Anna M. -?-, Children:-
1. Samuel Abraham Lincoln Waybright, b 12/3/1866
2. Robert Lewis Waybright, b 12/6/1874

- Jacob W. Waybright, s/o Micheal & Margaret Widler Waybright, 3/1/1768 - 7/13/1856, m Margaret Fickes, 2/3/1775 - 3/16/1834, both bd originally at Tom's Creek Lutheran and Reformed graveyard near Emmitsburg, but removed in 1894 to Evergreen Cemetery, Gettysburg, PA.

- Harriet Rebecca Waybright, b 2/6/1846, d/o Abraham & Margaret Waybright.

- Micheal Waybright, 1728-1820(?), m Anna Margaret Widler (Margaret Anna Widler) 1735 - 1801, both bd Tom's Creek Lutheran and Reformed graveyard, near Emmitsburg. Children:-
1. Jacob Waybright, m Margaret Fickes, both bd Gettysburg Evergreen Cemetery (both originally bd at Tom's Creek).

WEANT

- David Weant, of Frederick Co., MD., d 4/30/1888, 72 yrs., Civil War Veteran, Company E, 7th MD Infantry. m 12/23/1841, Lydia Ann Gaugh of Carroll Co., MD., d 3/27/1883, 74/10/26, both bd Tom's Creek Lutheran and Reformed graveyard, near Emmitsburg. "In memory of / David Weant / Died April 30, 1888 / Aged 72 years / A member of Company E (?) - 7th Maryland Infantry." "In memory of / Lydia Ann Weant / wife of David Weant / Died March 27, 1883 / Aged 74 years, 10 months, / and 26 days."

WAYGAND

- William Weygand, d 7/28/1908, 60 yrs. - M.F. Shuff burial Record.

WEIKERT

- Peter Weikert, m Maria Sheads (Mary Sheets), first wife of Lewis Shriver who died in 1816. Maria d 1849.

WHITE

- Walter W. White, m Fannie Belle Rowe, d/o James A. and Sarah Hoke Rowe. Children:-
1. John Dinwiddie White, b 1900
2. Sarah Ann Ruth WHite, b 1903

Williams

- The Williams family were among the early settlers in Tom's Creek Hundred and were members of the Presbyterian church. The Williams family intermarried with the Shields clan. There is a tradition that Henry Williams was a soldier of the American Revolution. The Williams family plot at Tom's Creek Presbyterian (near Emmitsburg) is enclosed by an old fashioned iron fence. Within are two altar stones which bear the following inscriptions:- "In Memory of My Parents / Henry Williams / and Jane Williams / The former was born in 1743 / and died in 1820 / The latter was born in 1779 / and died in 1854." "In memory of / Washington Williams / son of Henry and Jane Williams / Born 1817 / Died 1822."

WINTER

- Winter family Cemetery Inscriptions:-
Emmitsburg Elias Lutheran
1. George Winter, s/o Jacob & Margaret, 11/11/1805-11/17/1895.
2. Jacob Rowe Winter, s/o Henry & Mary Anne Rowe Winter, 10/19/1856 - 9/25/1857.
3. Jacob Winter, 1771-1846.
4. Margreta Gerver, w/o Jacob Winter, 1771-1848.
5. Mary Margaret Winter Eyster, w/o Andrew Eyster, 9/4/1801-2/10/1833, and her son John Thomas Eyster, 1/23/1833-5/7/1929.
6. Joanna Troxell Winter, w/o Henry Winter, 8/13/1812-7/12/1848.
7. Margaret E. Winter, d/o Henry & Joanna, d 7/22/1848, 0/5/9.
8. Mary Magdena Winter, d 4/6/1856, w/o George Winter.
9. George Winter, 1783- 2/1/1850.
10. Anna B. Winter, d 6/22/1866.
11. Henry Winter, d 8/4/1844, 76/3/13.

Harbaugh Family Graveyard, east of Sabillasville, MD.
1. John Harbaugh, of Jacob, 5/27/1764-6/18/1834.
2. Elizabeth Winter, w/o John Harbaugh of Jacob, d 8/10/1827, 64 yrs.

Mt. Olivet Cem., Frederick, MD.
1. Harry Johns Haller, 1858-1942, Veteran of the Indian Wars, 12th Infantry Regiment, U.S. Army.
2. Frances Winter Haller, w/o Harry Johns Haller, 4/12/1864 - 1955.
3. Harry Francis Haller, s/o Harry J. & Frances Winter Haller, 10/11/1894 - 8/28/1926.

Mt. View Cem., Emmitsburg
1. Harry H. Lantz, 9/5/1851-5/21/1914.
2. Mary C. Winter, w/o Harry H. Lantz, 8/4/1854 - 1/10/1931.
3. Charles R. Lantz, s/o Harry H. & Mary Winter Lantz, 1893-1950.
4. Harvey C. Winter, 5/16/1830 - 3/9/1914.
5. Tereasa Winter, w/o Harvey C. Winter, 6/16/1826 - 1/24/1898.

WINTER

St. Luke's (Winter's) Lutheran Church, nr New WIndsor, Carroll Co., MD.
1. Catherine Winter, d 8/20/1851, 77/10/0.
2. Christian Winter, d 3/9/1810, 25/3/0.
3. George Winter, Sr., d 8/6/1831, 45/11/7.
4. Elizabeth, w/o George Winter, Sr., d 1/16/1866, 73/1/20.
5. J. Winter, d 10/13/1731 (probably 1831), 61 yrs.
6. Jacob Winter, d 12/1/1845, 58/1/18.
7. John Winter, d 6/3/1827, 43/5/26.
8. Joseph Winter, 2/9/1797 - 12/3/1863.
9. Martin W nter, d 7/7/1876, 72/6/6.

- Columbia Winter, d/o Henry & Mary Ann Rowe Winter, 4/10/1853 - 6/23/1937, bd Emmitsburg Elias Lutheran. She was a millener in Emmitsburg.

- Francis Winter - "Emmitsburg Chronicle - 1/19/1894 - About the year 1760 Francis Winter, one of the earliest settlers in what is now New Windsor, Carroll County, Maryland, received an application from German colonists near Lancaster, Pennsylvania, for land for farming purposes and for the prospective erection thereon of a Lutheran church of the Ausburg Confession. ... In 1772 a log church was erected, but was not organized as a congregation until Jan. 6, 1783, under the pastorial care of Rev. Johann Daniel Schroeter. On May 31, 1784 the first officers of the church were elected and installed. They were, according to the old records, as follows:- Elders, Francis Winters and Henry Crowl; Deacon Jacob Haintz and George Spangler. Pastor Johann Daniel Schroeter. ... Officially the church is known as "Saint Luke's" but to the people in that part of Frederick County it is more commonly called 'Winter's Church". Francis Winter was the father of Jacob Winter. Jacob Winter m Margarite Gerver and they were the parents of Henry Winter and Mary Margaret Winter who m Andrew Eyster.
George Winter 1783-1850, m Mary M., d 1856, both bd Emmitsburg Elias Lutheran.'

- Henry Winter, s/o Jacob and Marguerite Gerver Winter, and a grandson of Francis Winter. He was a Lieutenant in the Mexican War from the company raised in Emmitsburg and vicinity. By trade he was a wagonmaker. His first wife, Joanna Troxell, 8/13/1812 - 7/2/1848, died young, his second wife, m 9/4/1849, Mary Anna Rowe, d 12/5/1907, 92/2/25, d/o Jacob Rowe, bd Emmitsburg Elias Luthean. Children:-
1. Margaret E. Winter, d 7/22/1848, d/o Henry & Joanna
2. Susanna Winter, b 6/6/1850, d/o Henry & Mary Ann
3. Mary Frances Winter, b 9/14/1851
4. Columbia Winter, b 4/15/1853
5. George Jacob Rowe Winter, 10/19/1856 - 9/23/1857, bd Elias Luth.

- Jacob Winter "In memory of / Jacob Winter / Born December 9, 1810 / Died August 29, 1811." - bd Emmitsburg Elias Lutheran.

- Jacob Winter, s/o Francis and Margarite Gerver Winter. Children:-
1. Henry Winter, wagonmaker of Emmitsburg.
2. George Winter, 1805-1895. a member of Emmitsburg Elias Lutheran church. "Buried, George Winter, died Nov 17, 1894, aged 88 yrs." - Elias Records. "In memory of / George Winter / son of Jacob and Margaret Winter / Born November 16, 1805 / Died November 17, 1895 / aged 89 years." - Elias Cem. Inscription.
3. Mary Margaret Winter, 9/4/1801 - 2/10/1833, bd Elias Luth.

WINTER

Mary Margaret Winter m 4/15/1828 to Andrew Eyster of Emmitsburg, their son John Thomas Eyster 1833-1929, bd Emmitsburg Elias Lutheran.

- Susan Winter, d/o Henry & Mary Ann Rowe Winter. She and her sister Columbia Winter (known as 'Lum'), conducted a millinary business in Emmitsburg for many years. Miss Susan Winter and her sister, Miss Frances (Frank) Winter, are buried side by side in Elias churchyard. The inscriptions follow:- "In memory of Susanna Winter / Born June 15, 1863 / Died April 4, 1907." "In memory of / Mary Frances Winter / Born September 14, 1851 / Died August 23, 1904." Miss "Frank" Winter, as she was known to her friends in Emmitsburg was a teacher and at one time conducted a private school in Emmitsburg. In addition she was an artist of some talent.

WITHEROW

- Cemetery Inscriptions, Lower Marsh Creek Presbyterian, Adams Co., PA.
1. John Witherow, d 3/9/1857, 12 yrs.
2. Margaret Witherow, d 12/13/1855, 19 yrs.
3. S. McClean Witherow, d 12/15/1857, 21 yrs.
4. Elizabeth Witherow, d 3/21/1751, 12 yrs.
5. Elizabeth Witherow, d 3/17/1774, 68 yrs.

- John Witherow, of Tom's Creek Hundred, Maryland, m Margaret Barbour, Children:-
1. Major Samuel Witherow, d 1/27/1832, 64 yrs., bd Lower Marsh Creek Presbyterian, Adams CO., PA., m Rachel
2. Jane Witherow Cooper Williams, 1779-1854, bd Tom's Creek Presbyterian, nr Emmitsburg. m 1 Robert Cooper, died young, m2 Henry Williams, 1743-1820, bd Tom's Creek Presbyterian, nr Emmitsburg.
3. Sarah Witherow Marshall Horner, m1 James Marshall of Carroll's Tract, 2 daus., m2 Alexander Horner.
4. Elizabeth Witherow Harper, m John Harper, they were the parents of 5 children:- John, James, Samuel, William and Margaret Harper.
5. Margaret Witherow, d unmarried, 9/1/1846, 58 yrs., bd Tom's Creek Presbyterian, nr Emmitsburg.
6. David Witherow, lived on or near the original Witherow plantation in Frederick County, Maryland. In 1818 he and his younger brother bought a mill on Marsh Creek in Adams Co., PA., known as "Witherow Mill", near Fairfield.

Marriages
1. Hugh Culbertson, of Culbertson Row, Franklin Co., PA., m 6/15/1815, and Sally Witherow of Carroll's Delight, Adams County, PA.
2. Wm., Crawford Rhea, Hamiltonban Twp., and Eliza Witherow, m 1/9/1833.
3. Maxwell Shields, Liberty Twp., & Rebecca Witherow, Hamiltonban Twp., m 1/9/1833.
4. James Patterson & Bettsey Witherow, m 10/26/1797, Hamiltonban Twp., by Rev. Alexander Dobbin.

WITHEROW

- Mary Witherow, only remaining dau. of Samuel Witherow, of this borough, d 9/19/1842, 22 yrs. - Gettysburg Newspaper record.

- Major Samuel WItherow, s/o John & Maragret Barbour Witherow, d 1/27/1832, 64 yrs., m Rachel, d 10/5/1826, 55 yrs., both bd Lower Marsh Creek Presbyterian, Adams Co., PA. "Died Oct 5, 1826, in the 55th year of her age, Mrs. Rachel Witherow, wife of Major Samuel Witherow, of Carroll's Delight, Adams Co., PA." Children:-
1. Moses Witherow, d 9/24/1823, age 27, bd Lower Marsh Creek Presbyterian. "Died, Sept 4, 1823, Mr. Moses Witherow, the son of Major Samuel Witherow of Hamiltonban Twp., Adams Co., PA., in the 26th year of his age." - Gettysburg newspaper record.
2. Samuel Witherow, Jr., m 8/11/1829, Jane Eliza Maginly, d/o James Maginly, dec'd, of Hamiltonban Twp., Adams CO., PA. Jane died 4/14/1857, 49 yrs., bd Lower Marsh Creek Presbyterian.
3. William Witherow, m 12/12/1820, Rachel Hutcheson, d/o Samuel Hutcheson of Gettysburg, PA.
4. Margaret Witherow, d 10/19/1847, 44 yrs., bd Lower Marsh Creek Presbyterian, m 3/14/1821, Samuel Knox.

- Samuel J. Witherow, "Died 2/21/1833, Samuel James Witherow, the son of John Witherow of Millerstown, Adams County, PA." - Gettysburg newspaper records. "Samuel James Witherow, d 2/21/1833, aged 3 yrs." - Cemetery inscription, Lower Marsh Creek Presbyterian.

WHITMORE

- David Whitmore, d 5/8/1889, 79/1/24, m Rebecca, d 2/25/1906, 89/9/2, both bd 1, Whitmore family burial ground on Tom's Creek, stones were later removed to Emmitsburg MT. View Cemetery.
"Mrs. David WHitmore, d 2/24/1906, 90 yrs." - M.F. Shuff Burial record. David Whitmore, d 5/4/1889, 75 yrs. - M.F. Shuff Burial record. Note: Both interred in the Simon Whitmore plot at Mt. View.

- Deaths - Burials
1. Susan Whitmore, d 10/27/1851, 78/10/28. Elias Records.
2. Milton Whitmore, d 4/3/1915, 66 yrs. bd Mt. View.
3. Sarah Cover Whitmore, w/o George Whitmore, d 6/6/1847, 67/3/5, bd Haugh's, nr Ladiesburg, MD.
4. George Whitmore, d 4/29/1848, 64/10/16, bd Haugh's, nr Ladiesburg
5. Mrs. Susan Whitmore, d 10/27/1851.
6. Simon Whitmore, d 3/17/1889, 84 yrs. - M.F. Shuff Burial Records.
Whitmore family burials - see Cemeteries, Whitmore family burial ground.

- John Jacob Whitmore, 1868-1940, m Clemmie F., 1878-1938, both bd United Brethern, Thurmont, MD.

- Marriages
1. Isaac Dotterer & Catherine E. Whitmore, both of Frederick Co., Md., m 2/12/1901.
2. Frederick W. Brockman Jr., of Baltimore, & Mary B. Whitmore of Emmitsburg, m 11/10/1913.
3. Samuel D. Witherow, & Rebecca Stambaugh, both of Carroll Co., m 8/5/1847.

WINEGARTEN

- Mrs. George Winegarten, d 11/15/1912, 31 yrs. - M.F. Shuff Burial Records.

ZACHARIAS

- Christian(3) Zacharias, s/o Mathias(2) and Anna Stockslager Zacharias, b 3/19/1802, d 10/2/1875, bd Zacharias family cemetery - later removed to Emmitsburg Mt. View Cemetery. m 5/12/1836, Sarah Picking, d/o John Picking, b 6/1/1812, d 9/10/1865, bd Mt. View. "Mrs. Zacharias passed all but the last few years of her life near the place of her birth and on the farm of her husband at the Stoney Branch ... she reared 4 sons and 3 daus ... She was buried in the family burial ground ..." - Emmitsburg Chronicle. Sarah Picking Zacharias, d/o John Picking and granddaughter of John & Esther Burns Picking of the vicinity of Zora, Adams County, Pennsylvania.   Children:-
1. Mathias Picking Zacharias, 9/15/1837 - 8/1/1883, m Emma Potts of Hillsboro, VA., he was bd at the family burial ground but later removed to Mt. View Cemetery. Mathias P. Zacharias, d 8/1/1882, 44/10/16.
2. Esther Ann Zacharias, 1/30/1839 - 9/18/1912, unmarried, lived at Chambersburg, PA., bd Emmitsburg Mt. View.
3. Mary Elizabeth Zacharias, 2/10/1841-12/1/1915, bd Emmitsburg Mt. View, m James W. Troxell, d 2/2/1904, 72/10/0. They lived nr the Zacharias homestead near Emmitsburg.
4. John Flavius Zacharius, 11/1/1842 - 1/28/1868, m Ann Rebecca Miller of Frederick, MD. (1835-1908), both bd Frederick Mt. Olivet Cem.
5. Sarah Adelaide Zacharias, 4/14/1847, d 2/21/1926, unmarried, lived Chambersburg, PA., bd Emmitsburg Mt. View Cem.
6. Christian Thomas Zacharias, 5/29/1849 - 12/23/1919, m Margaret Stokes of Emmitsburg, both bd Emmitsburg Mt. View.

- Christian Thomas(4) Zacharias, 1849-1919, s/o Christian(3) and Sarah Picking Zacharias, b 5/29/1849, d 12/23/1919, m Helen Margaret Stokes, b 12/14/1851, d 4/16/1900, both bd Emmitsburg Mt. View. Children:-
1. Henry M. Zacharias, 12/8/1881 - 7/21/1884, bd Mt. View.
2. Horace E. Zacharias, 1/12/1889 - 1/30/1889, bd Mt. View.
3. Maurice C. Zacharias, 12/9/1890 - 5/8/1891, bd Mt. View.

- Hettie Zacharias, d 9/5/1912, 74 yrs. - M.F. Shuff Burial Records.

- Mathias(1) Zacharias, b 1753, Germany, d 10/7/1773, Stoney Branch, Motter Station, Frederick Co., MD., emigrated ca 1753. m ca 1752, Elizabeth Margaret Kuhn, both bd Zacharias family cemetery - later moved to Emmitsburg Mt. View Cemetery.
Mathias Zacharias with his bride of a little over a year, Elizabeth Margaret Kuhn Zacharias, landed at Philadelphia, Pennsylvania, on September 28, 1753, on the ship "Halifax", Capt. Thomas Coatam, from Rotterdam, but late from Cowe (England). These people came from Elsoff in Wittgenstein (Palatinate, Germany), and they were accompanied by a brother of Mrs. Zacharias, one Johannes Kuhn.
A little over a year after their arrival in Philadelphia, they were in Frederick County, Maryland, and awarrant was issued to Mathias for 125 acres of land, located on "Stoney Branch", near what is now Motter's Station. The warrant was dated Dec 10, 1754. His land was warranted Dec 10, 1759 and on April 14, 1760 a resurvey conveyed 85 additional acres to his grant and a deed was issued for the same on Sept 29, 1762.

ZACHARIAS

Mathias named his plantation "Mon Dollar". On April 18, 1762 he appeared before the Provincial Court and received his certificate of naturalization.

With his own hands Mathias cut a home from the wilderness. He built a house and other necessary buildings, cleared land for fields, and all unknowing, helped to lay a foundation for this great nation. On one part of his plantation, just west of the house, he set aside land for a family burial ground. The first burial in the Zacharias family burial ground of which is recorded was Mathias Zacharias himself. He died Oct 7, 1773 and two days later was interred 'on his farm'. His remains along with other buried there, were removed to Mountain View Cemetery, near Emmitsburg in the early part of the Twentieth century. His grave was probably marked with a native stone, as were so many others, for no regular grave marker exists at the present time for the pioneer.

By his last will and testament, dated Oct 6, 1770 and entered to probate Nov 20, 1773, Mathias devised his entire estate to his wife and three children. Children:-
1. Mathias(2) Zacharias II, b 7/5/1757, m Anna Stockslager.
2. Anna Elizabeth Catherine(2) Zacharias, b 5/15/1759
3. Maria Elizabeth Catherine(2) Zacharias, b 3/11/1766

- Mathias(2) Zacharias II, b 7/5/1757, s/o Mathias(1) and Elizabeth Margaret Kuhn Zacharias. He is listed in Capt. Benjamin Ogle's Company of the Continental Army during the American Revolutionary War. This unit was raised in the Emmitsburg, Graceham and Thurmont district. Referring to family tradition he was present at the seige of Yorktown in 1783 and acted as one of the guards who escorted the Hessians captured there when they were taken to York, PA.

After the war he returned to the Zacharias home farm. These lands, some 254 acres, remained in the Zacharias family for about 160 years. Mathias married Anna Stockslager, b 10/25/1759, d/o Albertus Stockslager.
6 Children:-
1. John(3) Zacharias, 4/4/1788 - 10/28/1832, bd on the family ground, remains later removed to Mt. View Cem.
2. Mathias(3) Zacharias III, 9/8/1789 - 7/13/1849, bd at the family burial ground - later removed to Mt. View.
3. Christian(3) Zacharias, 3/4/1802 - 10/1/1875, m Sarah Picking

- William Jackson Zacharias, 3/18/1852 - 12/8/1933, bd Chambersburg, Pa. m 3/20/1883, Mary Jane Boyd, 2/23/1859 - 12/5/1906. William studied law and was admitted to the Bar and practiced at Chambersburg. He had one sister, Helen, and three brothers, John L., Ralph L., and Richard M. Zacharias.

ZIMMERMAN

- The Zimmermans came to America and to the Province of Pennsylvania with that intrepid pioneer, Madame Mary Ferree (Marie Warenbuer Ferree), who received her grant of land in what is now Paradise Township, Lancaster County, PA., from the founder, William Penn. She was a French Huguenot, who fled from France to Germany because of religious persecution. Two of her daughters married into the Zimmerman, or Carpenter, family. Madame Ferree visited William Penn in London, laid out her case before him and received her grant.

Peter Zimmerman (or Carpenter) a grandson of Madame Ferree, took up land in Carroll's Tract, in what is now Liberty Township, Adams County,

ZIMMERMAN

Pennsylvania. He bought his platation from the 'Chrochan - Annan' families.

Peter Zimmerman and his wife Mary Shriver are bd at 'Zimmerman's Graveyard'. They were the parents of 11 children.

There was apparently a migration of Earl Township, Lancaster Co., PA., families to the locality of 'Tract', now Liberty Township, Adams Co. between 1775 and 1800. Besides Peter Zimmerman and family, there were the Martins, Oberholtzers (Overholtzers) and Weavers. These families settled on the Cochran tract of land.

In Flat Run near the Maryland line on what is now know as the old Reed farm, the Zimmermans, a Swiss family who subsequently anglicized their name to Carpenter, settled in 1765.

- Anna Zimmerman, d/o Joseph and Mary Weikert Zimmerman, m Abraham Krise.

- Catherine Zimmerman, d/o Joseph and Mary Weikert Zimmerman, m William C. Seabrook, and were the parents of Dr. Alice Seabrook.

- Ezra Rowe Zimmerman, 1847-1905, m 11/12/1872, Margaret C. Maxell, 1846-1884, d/o Samuel & Jane Ferguson Maxell, both bd Emmitsburg Mt. View Cemetery. Children:-
1. Luther Maxell Zimmerman, b 6/10/1873, d infancy, bd Mt. View.
2. Thaddeus Elmer Zimmerman, b 10/19/1875.
3. Edna Mae Zimmerman, b 5/10/1879, d infancy, bd Emmitsburg Elias - later Mt. View.
4. Charles Francis Zimmerman, b 12/28/1881, d infancy, bd Elias - later Mt. View.

- Joseph Zimmerman, s/o Peter and Mary Shriver Zimmerman, m Mary Weikert and were the parents of 9 children.

- Joseph Zimmerman, 1816 - 1888, s/o Joseph & Mary Weikert Zimmerman, m Elizabeth Rowe, 1823 - 1907, bd Emmitsburg Mt. View. "Mrs. Joseph Zimmerman, d 2/11/1907, 82 yrs." - M.F. Shuff Burial Records.

- Mary Zimmerman - "In 1765, nine year old Mary Zimmerman, engaged in picking berries on the banks of Flat Run, in the vicinity of her home, was captured by a roving band of Indians. A neighbor was a witness to the abdication but could do nothing accept carry the tragic news to the girls family. Pursuit followed but the Indians and their captive disappeared into the wilderness.

Some ten years later the Indians were defeated in a skirmish with the whites and among the captives returned was Mary Zimmerman, now a young lady, with a half-breed son. She had married an Indian warrior and like so many captives was most reluctant to return to her own people. However she with her son was returned to the Zimmerman home in Liberty Carroll's Tract and gradually adjusted to life as lived by those who has long morned her as dead.

Several years after her return home Mary Zimmerman married a young farmer, one George Lowman, who also lived in the Tract. Seven Children were born to this marriage and in addition the half-breed son, now known as John Lowman, was a part of the household.

George Lowman died in 1800 and in his will left his step-son one-fourth of his estate. Mary Zimmerman Lowman lived to be over ninety years of

ZIMMERMAN

age and died on the farm - located not far from where she had been taken captive. Her half-breed son, John Lowman, died in 1826, never married, and in his will left his estate to his half-brothers and sisters. The Lowmans are interred in the southeast corner of the Zimmerman burial ground - along with pioneer members of the Zimmerman family. Thirteen fieldstones - without inscriptions - mark these graves.

- Peter Zimmerman, s/o Hans and Anna Zimmerman, b 1752, Earl Twp., Lancaster Co., PA., d 10/22/1823, 'Tract', Liberty Twp., Adams Co., PA. m 2/20/1776, Maria Shirk, 1756 - 2/27/1828, both bd on their farm plantation, Zimmerman family burial ground 'Carrollsburg Cemetery'.
Children:-
1. Peter Zimmerman, II, b 1777, m Catherine Lowman.
2. Nancy Ann Zimmerman, 11/6/1778 - 10/24/1864, m David Elker, 9/9/1771 - 12/17/1839.
3. John Zimmerman, b ca 1780, m1 Rebecca Lowman, sister of Catherine Lowman, m2 Ida Maria
4. Joseph Zimmerman, 6/6/1783 - 3/28/1823, m Mary Weikert, 1/30/1789 - 4/1855, lived in Liberty Twp., both bd 'Carrollsburg Cemetery.
5. Barbara Zimmerman, b ca 1785 - d ca 1829, m David Weaver.
6. Samuel Zimmerman, 2/1/1787 - 8/19/1838, bd Carrollsburg Cemetery, m Esther -(?)- , bought his father's farm and sold 150 acres to his sisters, Esther, Elizabeth and Judith, and also sold 80 acres to Abraham Krise.
7. Mary Zimmerman, 1788 - 2/3/1862, m Henry Welty, b 1787, d 8/18/1854, resided in Liberty Twp., both bd 'Carrollsburg Cemetery'. Children:-
    1. Henry Welty, m Lydia Eiker, & moved to Indiana.
    2. Susan Welty, m Henry Martin.
    3. Nancy Welty, m Eli Shockey, lived in Washington Co., MD.
    4. Mary Welty, m John Shank, lived in Adams Co., PA.
    5. Elizabeth Welty, never married.
    6. David Welty, 1817-1839, bd 'Carrollsburg Cemetery'.
    7. John Zimmerman Welty, 1829 - 1899, m Harriet, 1828-1898, both bd 'Carrollsburg Cemetery'.
8. Esther Zimmerman, 6/1792 - 10/1844, unmarried, bd Carrollsburg Cem.
9. Elizabeth Zimmerman, 6/28/1795 - 11/2/1880, unmarried, bd Carrollsburg Cemetery.
10. Judith Zimmerman, 10/24/1797 - 5/12/1832, unmarried, bd Carrollsburg Cemetery. Judith along with her two sisters, Esther and Elizabeth lived on their farm in Liberty Twp., originally a part of their father's farm and are bd at Carrollsburg Cemetery. This cemetery is located on what was originally their land and was sold to a group of neighbors by Elizabeth in 1822 for $1.00.
11. Susanna Zimmerman, m John Arthur.

INDEX

-A-
AARRON, Micheal, 60
ADAIR, Esther, 78
  Hannah, 78
  John, 77, 78
  Samuel, 77, 78
  Sarah, 78
ADELSPERGER,
  Alice Duphorne, 1
  Annie Mary, 1
  Barbara Lucy, 1
  Esther, 1
  Hugh Harold, 1
  J. J., 1
  John F., 1
  Joshua A., 1
  Ruth Maria, 1
ADGY, John, 28
AGNEW, David, 1
  James, 1
  Margaret, 18, 52, 95
  Mary Jane, 1
  Sophia, 53
ALEXANDER, Isabel, 28
  William, 28, 77
ALISON, ---, 78
  Frances, 78
  Francis, 77
  Martha, 78
  Mary Ann, 78
  Ms., 44
ALLEN, James, 28
  Walter, 44
ALLISON, Martha
  Maxwell, 68
  Matilda
  Breckenridge, 10
ALSOP, John, 60
ANGEL, Harriiet, 83
ANGELL, Nathan, 86
ANNAN, Andrew, 1, 70, 71
  Ann, 3
  Charles E., 1
  David Landales, 1
  Elizabeth, 3
  Elizabeth Hawthorn, 3
  Elizabeth Motter, 1, 71
  Emily, 3
  Gertrude, 3
  Helen Francis, 1
  Henry Clay, 3
  Jame Moore, 3
  John M., 1
  Margaret, 2, 3, 18, 95
  Martha Jane, 3
  Mary, 3
  Mary Cochran, 3
  Mary Jane, 1, 3, 78
  Mary Jane McKaleb, 64
  Robert, 2, 3, 9
  Robert L., 22
  Robert Landales, 2, 3
  Robert Lewis, 3
  Sally, 3
  Samuel, 2, 3, 64
  Sarah Jane, 51
  William, 2
  William Howard, 3
  William M., 1
ARBAUGH, Henry, 16
  Matilda, 16
  Rebecca, 16
ARMOUR, Robert, 43
ARMSTRONG, Betsy, 52
  Isaac, 77
  Jane, 18, 95
  Mina, 18, 95
  Nancy, 18, 95
ARTHUR, John, 106
  Samuel, 66
ASHBAUGH, William H., 4
AUGHINBAUGH, Rev., 45

-B-
BACKUS, Rev., 95
BAER, Isabella, 43
BAIRD, Catherine, 16
  Eleanor, 24
  Levi, 16
  Magdelene, 16
  Margaret, 16
  Miram (Hiram), 16
  Rachel Ann, 16
  Samuel, 52
  Sarah, 16
BAKER, Grace, 62
  J. E., 20
  Joseph A., 86
  Susan, 81
BALDEN, Esther, 28
  Rachel, 28
BALDWIN, Daniel, 77
  Elijah, 78
  Elizabeth, 78
  Kizech, 78
  Mary, 78
  Mrs., 37
BARLOW, Alice
  Worthington, 4
  Helen M., 4
  Hester McNaughton Birnie, 8
  Maxwell, 4
  Stephen, 4, 8
BARNETT, Like, 60
  William, 60
BARR, Isabella, 44, 53, 78
  James, 53, 77, 78
  Jane A., 53
  Margaret, 78
  Miss, 52
  Sally, 78
BARRIS, Carolina, 78
BARROCK, James, 60
BARTON, Emma
  Catherine, 4
  Harriet, 4
  Harriet Rebecca, 4
  Isaac D., 4
  Thomas H., 4
  William Henry, 4
BAUER, ---, 14
BAUGHER, Amanda, 36
  Elizabeth, 16
  Frederick, 5
  Isaac, 5, 15, 34, 36
  John Christian Frederick, 5
  Joseph, 5, 15, 16

BAUGHER(BAGER),
   Anna Elizabeth,
   5
   Carl Theodore, 4
   John George, 4, 5
BEALL, Eleanor
   Ogle, 36
   James, 60
   Joseph, 36
   Ninian M., 35
BEAM, Elizabeth, 6
   Geo. P., 6
   George (P. or F.), 5
   George F., 53
   George P., 21
   Harry, 5
   Jane Guthrie, 6, 54
   Robert, 6
   Susan G., 6
BEARD, Adeline, 6
   Athabiad, 6
   Catherine, 6
   David, 6
   Elizabeth, 6
   Frederick, 6, 60
   George, 6
   Jacob, 6
   John, 6
   Joshua, 6
   Louisa, 6
   Lydia Sylvia, 6
   Magdalena, 6
   Margaret, 6
   Mary Jane, 6
   Mary Magdalena, 4
   Melinde, 6
   Napoleon A., 6
   Obed, 6
   Polly, 6
   Samuel, 6
   Sarah, 6
   William, 77
BECK, Ludwick, 7
BECKETT, John
   Maynard, 60
BEGORE, Mr., 52
BENCHOFF, Eva, 89
BENNET, Mrs.
   Richard, 30
BENSILL, William, 7
BENTLY, Nancy, 78
BENTZEL, ---, 14
BERGAW, Mr., 52

BERGSTRESSER,
   Peter, 97
BERKSHIRE, Henry,
   60
BIGGS, Dorothy
   Chapman, 9
BIGHAM, Agnes
   McNair, 66
   Charles, 18, 52, 95
   Kitty, 18, 95
   Margaret, 7, 18, 95
   Miss, 52
   Nancy, 52
   Peggy, 52
   Phebe, 18, 95
   Robert, 7
   Thomas, 66
   William, 7, 18, 53,
      95
BIGLER, Statira C.,
   67
BIRNIE, Amelia, 9
   Amelia Harry, 83
   Ann, 8
   Ann M., 9
   Clotworthy, 4, 7, 8,
      9, 77, 78, 84
   Edward, 8
   Eleanor, 9
   Eliza Roberts, 9
   Ellen, 8
   Frances, 8
   Francis, 7
   Francis Upton, 8
   George Harry, 9
   Harriet
      Worthington, 4
   Henry, 7
   Hester, 8, 78
   Hester
      McNaughton, 4,
      9
   Hester Naughton, 8
   Hugh, 7
   John, 7
   Margaret, 8, 9, 78,
      83
   Margaret Scott, 7
   Mary Worthington,
      8
   Robert Emmit, 8
   Rogers, 8, 9, 83
   Rose, 8, 78

   Samuel Galt, 9
   Upton, 8, 9
BISHOP, Henry, 76,
   86
BLACK, Eliza, 28
   Guy, 12
   James, 77, 78
   Maggie Byers, 12
   Margaret, 96
   Rachel, 28
   Robert, 28
   Weems, 78
BLAIR, Elizabth, 96
   James, 96
   John, 88
   William, 9, 93
BOENS, Ellen, 18, 95
   Nancy, 18, 95
BOLLING, Edith, 44
BOLLINGER,
   Christina
      Overholtzer, 9
   Emma J., 12, 13
   Jacob, 9
BONER, Joseph, 52
BOONE, H.
   Jernongham, 35
BOSSERMAN,
   Solomon, 52
BOSSLER, D., 70
   J., 1
BOWERS, ---, 14
   Catherine Eve, 46
   Elizabeth, 56
BOWLING, James, 40
BOYD, Nathan, 16
BOYER, Paul, 60
BRANNON,
   Margaret, 77
BRAWNER, Edward,
   37
   Elizabeth, 37
   Mr., 43
   Richard, 37
BRAYBLE, Joel, 12
BREASE, John, 60
BRECKENRIDGE,
   James Grier, 9
   Martha, 78
   Mary, 10
   Mary Grier, 9
   Miss, 52
   Polly, 18, 95

R. J., 95
Rebecca McKinney, 10
Rev., 10
Robert, 9, 10, 27
Sally, 18, 95
Sarah M., 10
William, 10, 18, 77, 95
BROCKMAN, Frederick W., 102
BROOKE, Roger, 37
Thomas, 52
BROWN, Alice B., 11
Amos, 11
Annie, 11
David H., 10
Elizabeth Ridgely, 11
Enoch, 10, 27
Isaac, 10
Louise M., 11
Mary E., 11
Ridgely, 10, 11
Sally R., 11
Sarah Ridgely, 11
Sarah Ridgely Griffith, 11
Thomas, 63
William, 47, 58
BRUCE, Normand, 11
BRYANT, James, 60
BUCHANAN, Ann, 2, 3
BUFFINGTON, Ephraim, 11, 76
George H., 76
Luther S., 76
BULLER, James, 60
BURTON, Jacob, 60
Jas., 60
Thomas, 60
William, 60
BUSEY, Samuel, 60
BYER, William, 60
BYERS, Carrie J., 12
Charles Robert, 13
Christian, 11, 12
David, 11, 12
Eleanor, 12
Eleanor Gilbert, 13
Elizabeth, 12

Ethel Grace, 13
Fanny, 12
George, 12
George Gambell, 12
Gilbert G., 12
Harry Bryan, 13
Hazel Marguerite, 13
Jacob, 13
Jacob Krise, 12, 13
Janette, 12
John, 12
Joseph, 12, 13
Luther Gilbert, 13
M. Janette, 12
Mary, 12
Maud Elizabeth, 13
Merle Glenn, 13
Michael, 12
Samuel, 11, 12

-C-
CALDWELL, Francis T. Frank, 13
Frank, 13
John, 13
John W., 13
Martha, 96
Nancy, 52
Peggy, 18, 95
CALVERT, William, 60
CANNON, Patrick, 60
CARPENTER, Samuel, 12
CARR, Elizabeth Krise, 57
CARROLL, Daniel, 23
CARTY, James, 60
CASH, John, 60
William, 60
CHADWICK, Catherine Mary, 71
Mary, 71
CHANDLER, William, 60
CHURCHWELL, John, 60
CLABAUGH, A.J., 23
Amy E., 20, 22, 23
Angeline A., 20
Angeline J., 22

Angeline Shriner, 22
Elizabeth, 57
Emma, 22
George, 9
George W., 4
George Washington, 3
Harry W., 4
Katherine Swope, 4
Mary, 96
Mary C., 81
W.C., 23
William, 21, 22
William C., 20, 22
CLAIRVOUX, Emmeline Dielman, 23
CLANBACH, Sarah, 78
CLARK, Analize, 23
Eliza, 23
Esther, 18, 95
James, 24
Jean Cochran, 24
John, 23, 53
Joseph, 18, 95
Vincent W., 23
CLARKE, Richard, 38
CLAY, John Curtis, 2
CLEMENTS, Caroline, 38
Henry, 60
CLINGAN, Archibald, 27, 77, 78
Elizabeth, 78
Mary Ann, 63
Nancy, 28
Peggy, 27
Polly, 28
Rev., 63
William, 77, 78, 96
COATAM, Thomas, 103
COCHRAN, Andrew, 23
James, 16, 23
Jane, 23
John, 23, 24
Malinda, 23
Margaret, 2
Mary, 2
Sarah, 23, 24
Susan, 16

William, 2, 23, 24
COLESTOCK, ---, 51
COLLIER, Rev., 25
COOPER, Robert, 101
T., 52
CORBEL, Jesse, 77
CORBIN, Margaret Cochran, 24
CORNAL, Thomas, 77
CORNEL, Smith, 77
William, 77
CORNELL, Benjamin, 28
Esther, 78
Jane, 78
Mary, 78
Thomas, 28
CORRELL, A. J., 25
Alice Jane, 25
Alice Virginia, 25
C., 52
Christian, 24, 47
Elizabeth, 24
Harry Taylor, 25
J. S., 25
John, 25
John Q., 24, 25
John Sluss, 25
Lydia, 24
S. O., 25
Susan Elizabeth, 25
William McClellan, 25
COULTER, Elizabeth, 88
John, 28
COURTNEY, D.L., 89
Egbert Hafey, 89
CRABBS, ---, 18
John, 25, 77, 93
CRABSTER, Evalina, 52
John, 77
CRAIG, Margaret, 84
CRAPSTER, Abigail, 25
Basil, 25
Gustavas, 25
John, 25
John H., 25
Peter, 25
Ruliff, 25

Susannah (Klein)Little, 25
William, 25
CREBS, ---, 18
CRETIN, Agnes C., 26
Andrew, 26
Emily Dielman, 30
Emmeline Dielman, 26
James, 26, 30
John H., 26
John Henry, 26, 30
John T., 23, 26
John Thomas, 30
Joseph A., 26
Josephine, 30
Mary, 30
Mary Ann, 26, 30
Mary Dielman, 30
Samon (Simon), 26
CROCKET, James, 18, 95
CROCKETT, Mary, 43, 44
Sarah, 18, 95
CROWL, Henry, 100
CUIN, Andrew, 78
CULBERTSON, Catherine, 26
Hugh, 101
James F., 26
Joseph, 26
Sarah, 26
CUNNINGHAM, James, 52
John, 26
Susan King, 10, 26
CURREN, Jane, 18, 27, 54, 95
Jane J., 27
Lavinia, 18, 95
William, 18, 27, 51, 54, 95
CURRENS, Elijah, 77, 78
William, 77
CUSHING, Joseph, 95
CUSTIS, George Washington Parks, 64
CUTHBERTSON,

John, 24

-D-

DANNER, ---, 18
Mary, 18, 95
Miss, 18, 95
DARBARROW, Isaac, 77
DARBY, Catherine, 78
John, 77, 78
DAVIDSON, Charlotte, 27
Ellen, 61
Jesse, 52
Margaret, 27
Mary, 27
Patrick, 27
DAVIS, ---, 18
John, 63
Mary E. Galt, 43
DAWSON, Emily, 29
Phileman, 28
Philemon, 29
DAY, Polly, 18, 95
DEAN, Joseph, 79, 92
Sarah, 92
DEILMAN, Agnes, 32
Frederick, 32
Henry, 68
Lawrence, 68
Lena, 32
Louis H., 32
DEITRICK, Jacob, 28
Martin, 28
Susan, 28
DELOYVIER, Phoebe, 36
DELOZIER, John, 36
Phebe, 14
Sarah, 14
DENTLER, Eve Margaret, 16
George, 16
Margaret, 16
DETRICK, Jacob, 16
DEUKART, Sophia, 78
DEVINE, Barney, 6
Hetty Maria, 6
DIELMAN, Emily Dawson, 28, 30
Henry, 23, 28, 29,

30, 32
Henry C., 26
John Casper, 32
John Casper
 "Henry", 29
John Casper Henry,
 30, 32
Lawrence, 30, 31
Lawrence L., 26
Louis (Lewis), 32
Mary Cretin, 26, 31
DIETER, Margaret,
 32
DIFFENDERFER,
 Catherine, 12
DINSMORE, Mr., 43
DINWIDDIE, Rose
 Anna, 33
DOBBIN, Alexander,
 101
 Mr., 28
DODENDORF, Anna
 Maria, 16
DONACK, James, 60
DONALDSON,
 Charles, 28
 Fielding, 18, 95
 Kitty, 18, 95
 Margaret, 16
DONWIDDIE, Henry,
 78
DONWODY, Thomas,
 28
DORSEY, Alice T., 44
 Singleton, 22
DOTTERER, Albert,
 32
 Isaac, 102
DRUMMOND, James,
 77
 Sarah, 78
DUCKWALL, Jane
 Maria Maxell, 62
 John W., 62
DULLIS, Charles, 60
DUMFEE, Sophia, 18,
 95
DUNWODDY, Nancy,
 28
DUPHORN, Annie E.,
 33
 Barbara, 33

Emma Barbara, 33
Emma H., 33
Emma R., 33
Franklin Dinwiddie,
 33
Hannah, 33
John, 33
John H., 33
Maria, 33
Mary Hagen, 33
Robert, 33
Robert John, 33
Rosanna, 33
Samuel, 33
Sarah, 33
Sarah Jane, 33
Simon, 33
Thomas W., 33
DUPHORNE, Annie,
 32
 Annie Eliza (Eliza
 Ann), 33
 Calvin F., 33
 Ella M., 1
 Ellie M., 1, 33
 Maria, 1, 32
 Mary Heagen, 33
 Robert Samuel, 33
 Samuel, 1, 32
 Sarah Louisa, 33
DURBORAW, William
 C., 97
DYSERT, Elizabeth
 Galt, 43
 Mary Galt, 43

-E-
ECKENRODE, Mary
 Jane, 67
ECKER, Sally, 52
EDEY, Simmons, 2
EGE, Andrew, 3
 Andrew G., 64
 Margaret Ann
 McKaleb, 64
EGLE, David, 11
 John, 11
 William Henry, 11
EHREHART, C. J.,
 35
 M.E., 34
EICHELBERGER, ---,
 14

Abram J., 34
Anna Margaret, 35
Anna Margaret
 Motter, 35, 71
Charles D., 34, 35
Charles Dick, 35
Columbia Martha,
 35
Elizabeth, 35
Francis M., 34
G. M., 35
George M., 35
Grayson M., 35
Gustavus Milton, 35
Harvey, 35
James, 71
James W., 34, 35, 70
Jane, 18, 35, 95
Leonard, 35
Lillie, 34
Lydia, 35
Marion F., 34, 35
Martin, 34
Mary Elizabeth, 34,
 35
Mary Jane, 35
Mary Magdalene, 35
Miles, 35
Motter, 34
Motter E., 35
Philip Frederick, 35
Samuel, 34
Samuel William, 35
Virginia, 34
EIKER, Lydia, 106
ELDER, Aloysius, 14,
 37
 Ann, 14, 37
 Ann Wheeler, 14, 37
 Anne(or Nancy), 38
 Arnold, 14, 37
 Basil Spalding, 37,
 38
 Basil T., 37
 Catherine, 38
 Charles, 36
 Charles D., 37
 Christiana, 38
 Clementina, 38
 Eleanor, 37
 Elizabeth, 37
 Elizabeth Spalding,
 37

Francis, 37
Francis W., 37
Guy, 36, 37
Ignatius, 37, 38
Jacoba Clementina, 14
Jacoba Clementina Livers, 37, 38
James, 37
James C., 37
Joseph R., 37
Maria M., 38
Mary, 14, 36
Mary Elizabeth, 38
Richard, 14, 36
Teresa, 38
Thomas H., 37, 38
Thomas Richard, 38
Thomas S., 37
William, 14, 23, 36, 38, 58
William Henry, 37
William Pius, 38
ELIS, Benjamin, 66
ELKER, David, 106
ELLIOT, Matilda Reinewald, 80
Wm. J., 80
ELLIOTT, Elizabeth, 38
EMMIT, Mary, 95
Samuel, 87
EMMITT, Abigail, 18, 95
Mary, 18
Sarah, 18, 95
EPPLEY, Adam, 50
Jane G., 50
EREHART, Charles J., 34
Margaret, 34
Thomas, 34
EVANS, Evan, 88
Timothy, 52
EWING, Mr., 43
EYLER, Amelia Ann, 16
Barbara E., 41
Eliza, 16
John, 16
Joseph, 41
Margaret Lucinda, 16

Miss, 52
Sarah, 16
Susanna, 16
William P., 41
EYSTER, Andrew, 40, 66, 99, 100, 101
George T., 40
H.W., 40
Hall Webster, 40
Jacob, 40
John Thomas, 40, 99, 101
Maria Catherine, 40
Mary, 40
Mary Ellen, 40
Mary Margaret Winter, 99
Mary Violet, 40
Mary Winter, 40
Peter, 40
Samuel H., 41
Virginia Scott, 40
EYSTER(EISTER-OYSTER),
Andrew, 39
Anna Maria, 39
Barbara, 39
Catherine, 39
Elisa, 39
Ellen C., 39
Ellen Louisa, 39
George, 39
George T., 39
Hall Webster, 39
Jacob, 39
John Thomas, 39
Madalena, 39
Samuel, 39
Samuel Hueston, 39
Sarah Jane, 39
Sidney, 39

-F-

FARIES, Jane, 18, 95
FARIS, Miss, 52
FEASER, ---, 14
FENDALL, Annie Galt, 44
FENLY, Thomas, 60
FEREE, Marie Warenbuer, 83
FERGUSON, Albert Heck, 62

Ann, 27
Jane, 62
John, 28, 77, 78
Margaret, 18, 95
Miss, 18, 95
Rebecca, 78
William, 18, 77, 95
FERREE, Madam Mary, 104
Maria Warenbuer, 104
FICKES, Margaret, 98
FIELDSTONE, F. H., 19
G.W., 19
FINDLEY, Mary Cochran, 24
William, 24
FISHER, Ann, 53
David, 43
Henry, 60
Isaac, 52
Sarah Row, 82
FITEZ, Ada G., 12, 13
Edna, 62
FLEGEL, Virginia, 49
FLEMING, Ellen Bruce, 41
Jane M., 45
Mary, 41
Miss, 62
Reuben, 41
Robert, 28, 41, 78
FLETCHER, Richard, 60
FLOHR, Ann Eliza, 16
Catherine Ann, 16
Frederick, 81
Phebe Ann, 40
Samuel, 16
FLOOR, Elizabeth, 52
FOOT, Polly, 96
FORNEY, ---, 18
Adam, 41
Christina, 41
Hiram, 76
Johann Adam, 41
John, 41
John A., 41
Louisa, 41
Magdalena, 41

Susanna, 41
FOSTER, Stephen,
  42, 64
FRAILEY, Alice
  Madeline
  Racheal, 42
  Fannie, 32
  Fannie M., 39, 40
  George Clarence, 42
  Oscar D., 42
  Richard E., 42
FRAYLEY, Carson, 42
FREEMAN, Francis,
  60
FUEY, Ann E. Cretin,
  26
  Francis P., 26
FULTON, Jennie, 58
FUSS, John, 73

-G-
GALBRAITH,
  Rebecca, 11
  Robert, 11
GALT, Abner, 43
  Albert Franklin, 44
  Alexander, 44
  Ann Eliza Annan, 3
  Catherine, 43
  Charles, 44
  Elizabeth, 42, 43, 78
  Elizabeth Simpson,
    43, 44, 85
  George Grayson, 44
  George Sterling, 43
  Hannah Mary, 44
  Henry, 3, 44
  Isabella Barr, 44
  James, 43, 44
  James Barr, 44
  James Veitch, 43
  Jane Elizabeth, 44
  John, 42, 43, 44, 77
  John Murray, 43, 44
  John Ross, 44
  Joseph, 43
  Louisa A. Krise, 45
  Louisa Krise, 57
  Lucretia, 43
  Maggie Bell, 44
  Margaret, 42, 78
  Margaret G., 44
  Mary, 9, 42, 43, 44,
    52, 78
  Mary Jane, 43, 44,
    45
  Mathew, 43, 44, 78,
    85
  Matthew, 9, 43, 45,
    77
  Matthew William, 43
  Moses, 43, 77
  Nancy, 44
  Nancy Elizabeth, 43
  Norman, 42, 44
  Peter, 43, 45
  Rebecca, 42, 43, 78
  Robert, 43, 44
  Robert W., 44
  Robert Walter, 44
  Samuel, 42, 43, 44,
    53, 78
  Samuel M., 44
  Sarah, 42, 78
  Sophia, 53
  Sterlin, 78
  Sterling, 42, 43, 44
  Susan, 9, 42, 78
  Susannah, 43, 85
  Thomas, 43, 44
  Washington, 43, 45,
    57
  William, 43, 44
GAMBLE, David, 45
  Emma R., 45
  Joseph, 45
  Margaret Annan, 45
  Samuel, 45
GARDINER, Frances,
  38
  Joseph, 38
GARDNER, William
  P., 45
GAUGH, ---, 18
  Addie E., 46
  C., 45
  Carrie, 45
  Effie Catherine, 46
  Elizabeth, 45
  Elizabeth Catherine,
    46
  George, 45
  Harriet, 45, 46
  Lydia Ann, 98
  Jonathan, 46
  Mary V., 46
  Percival, 45, 46
  Sophia, 4
  W., 45
  William Barton, 46
  Willie B., 45
  Wilson A., 45, 46
GAULT, Matthew, 42
GEHRHART,
  Benjamin, 46
GEHRHART/
  GEARHART,
  Peter, 46
  Sarah, 46
GEIGER, Mary Ann,
  16
GELWICKS, Joseph
  Theophilus, 46
  Martha Isabella, 46
GERVER, Margarite,
  100
  Margreta, 99
GEZELMAN, John,
  18, 95
GIBBS, Harriet, 46
  Sarah, 90
  William, 46
GIBSON, Elizabeth,
  26
  R. G., 26
GILBERT, Adam, 12
  Eleanor, 12
GILILAND, John, 46
GILL, Thomas, 60
GILLAND, Betsy, 24
  Mary (Hays) Smith,
    24
GILLAND/
  GILLELAN,
  Ada S., 49
  Adam Sentman, 49
  Anna Virginia, 49
  Carrie, 49
  Charles E., 49
  Charles Edgar, 49
  David, 49
  David S., 49
  Etta Mae, 48, 49
  George, 49, 73
  George L., 48
  George Lawrence,
    48
  George S., 48, 49
  George Thomas, 48

H. Morris, 49
Hannah S., 48, 49
Harry Morris, 48, 49
Ida S., 48, 49
John 24
John Thomas, 48
Magdalena
  (Hockensmith),
  49
Magdelena, 48, 49
Margaret J., 48, 49
Mary, 48, 78
Rhoda, 48
Rhoda Hannah, 48
Ruth B., 48, 49
Sarah Salome, 49
Virginia, 49
William, 48, 49, 55
William R., 48, 49,
  50
Willy Robert, 49
GILLELAND, Betsy,
  52
John, 47
Mary Hays Smith,
  47
GILLILAND, Agnes
  Shields, 46
Annie M., 47
Jacob, 46
James, 47
Jane, 47
John, 47, 77
John J. F., 47
Margaret, 18, 47, 95
Samuel, 47
GILLILAND
  (GILLEYLEN),
  Agnes, 88
Hester Roome, 88
Jacob, 88
Jane, 88
John, 88
GILLILAND/
  GILLAND/
  GILLELAND,
  Betsy, 47
GILMOUR, William,
  60
GILSON, R., 52
GINGELL, Mary
  Mollie, 40
GORDIN, Mary, 77

GORDON, Elizabeth,
  16
GOSS, Margaret, 83
GRABILL, Elizabeth,
  50
Frederick, 50
Harry George, 50
John, 50
John Stewart, 50
Margaret Ann, 50
Peter, 50
Samuel, 50
Sarah Jones, 50
Sarah Rudisill, 50
GRABILL-GRAYBILL
  Frederick, 50
GRAHAM, Eliza, 50,
  78
Jonas, 28
GRAMBER, Sarah A.,
  25
GRAYBILL, John, 50
GRAYSON, Agnes,
  18, 95
Eliza Ann, 18, 95
Jane, 35
Margaret, 43, 44
N., 52
Nathaniel, 18, 44, 95
William, 18, 95
GREEN, Ann, 26
Clotilda Phoebe, 37
Francis, 37
Nathaniel, 26
Philip, 37
GREENSLEEVES,
  Mrs., 38
GREENWELL,
  Monica, 38
GRIER, A. Margaret
  (Maggie), 51
Elizabeth, 18, 50, 95
James, 10, 51
Jane, 51
John Nathan
  Caldwell, 51
Mary, 10, 27, 51
Nancy, 27
Nathan, 27, 51
R.S., 59
Robert S., 50, 51
Robert Smith, 18,
  42, 51, 53, 79, 95

Sarah Jane, 50
Susan, 51
Susannah Smith, 51
GRIFFITH, Ann
  Ridgely, 11
Nicholas, 11
Zadock, 60
GROBP, Elizabeth, 53
John G., 53
GROFF, Catherine,
  74
GROFT, Caroline
  Louisa, 20
Catherine Louise, 20
GROVE, George H.,
  86
GRUBB, John, 89
GUIN, Andrew, 77
George, 77, 78
GUINN, Esther, 78
Mr., 52
Sally, 28
GUNN, Helen, 9
GUTHRIE, Adam, 5,
  53, 54
George P., 54
Jane, 5, 53
John W., 54
Margaret Wagner, 5,
  54
Mary L., 54
Mary Louisa, 53
Sarah C., 54
Susan C., 54
William, 54

-H-
HAFLEIGH, Jacob,
  16
Mary Ann, 16
Susan, 16
HAGER, Catherine, 5
Christopher, 5
Louisa, 5
HAINTZ, Jacob, 100
HALL, Micheal, 60
HALLER, Frances
  Winter, 99
Harry Francis, 99
Harry Johns, 99
HARBAUGH, Jacob,
  99
John, 99

Jonathan, 52
HARDING, Garah, 60
HARDMAN, Eliza
   Ruth, 16
   Micheal, 16
HARLEY, William, 54
HARPER, Elizabeth
   Witherow, 101
   James, 101
   John, 52, 101
   Margaret, 101
   Sally, 52
   Samuel, 101
   William, 101
HARRIS, Catherine, 78
HARRISON, Thomas, 60
HARRY, Amelia, 9
   Amelia Knod, 9
   George, 9
HARTZELL, Mary Row, 82
HASSLET, Betty, 18, 95
HATCHCRAFT, James, 60
HAUER, Nettie S., 67
HAWTHORNE,
   Elizabeth, 2
   Samuel, 2
HAYDEN, Bernard, 37
   Mary Josephine Green, 37
HAYS, Andrew T., 54
   Annie, 54
   E., 54
   Elizabeth, 54
   Elizabeth Curran, 54
   Elizabeth M., 18, 95
   John, 54
   John Thomas, 54
   Joseph, 54, 77
   T., 54
   Thomas, 52, 54
   Willie Van Lear, 54
HEAGY, Amanda M.K., 55
   Amanda Maria Kitzmiller, 55
   George, 28, 77

   Henry, 54, 55, 90
   Isaac T., 55
   Jacob, 55
   Lewis R., 55
   Margaret R., 55
   Philip, 28, 77, 78
   Polly, 51
   Rachel Shriver, 55
   Sally, 28
   Shriver T., 55
HELMAN, James A., 15, 25
HENERY, Elizabeth, 78
HENKLE, Harriet, 70
HENRY, Catherine Row, 82
HESS, John E. E., 55, 74
HESSON, Abraham, 97
HICKSON, Mary Crapster, 25
HIGBEE, Lucy, 42
HILL, George, 60
   Hannah, 77
   Martha, 34
   Marton, 18, 95
HILLEARY, Thomas, 60
HINCLE, Daniel, 89
HINKLE, Harriet, 71
HIRSCH, Lebright, 70
HITCHAHEW, Ivanna Hockensmith, 56
HITEHASHAW, Margaret Ann, 56
HOCKENSMITH, ---, 18
   Adam Tobias, 56, 89
   Alice Amanda, 56
   Barbara Sluss, 56
   Catherine, 56
   Columbia, 62
   Conrad, 56
   Daniel, 56
   David, 56
   Elizabeth, 56
   George, 55, 56
   Hannah Joanna, 89

   Henry, 56
   Isamiah, 56, 74, 89
   Jacob, 56, 93
   John, 56
   Levi, 89
   Magdalena, 56
   Magdelena, 48
   Mary, 56
   Michael, 56
   Peter, 56
   Robert Eli, 62
   Sarah C., 56
   William, 56
HOFFMAN, Charles, 87
   John, 70, 89
HOKE, Clara, 42
   Eliza, 16
   Frances Ann Rowe, 35, 42
   Michael, 21
   Peter, 35, 42
   Sarah Minnie, 35
   Sarah(Sallie), 81
   William H., 20, 21
HOLLIDAY, George, 60
HOLLINGS, William, 60
HOLMES, Margaret, 18, 95
HOLT, Robert, 52
HOLTZ, Jacob, 60
HOOVER, ---, 14, 18
   Charlotte Singer, 91
   John, 91
   Mary Ann, 16
   Sarah, 18
HOPPER, Dolly, 83
HORNER, A.
   Margaret, 51
   A.M., 50
   Alex, 52
   Alexander, 28, 77, 78, 101
   Amanda, 53
   Andrew, 52, 53, 61, 77, 78
   Ann Elizabeth Annan, 51
   Effie S., 50
   Eli, 52, 53, 78
   Eliza, 52

Elizabeth, 78
James, 78
John, 2, 28, 53, 77, 78
Margaret, 53, 78
Margaret Marshall, 61
O.A., 51
Oliver A., 51
Sarah, 78
Sarah Witherow Marshall, 101
William, 77, 78
HOSACK, Sally, 28
HOSPLEHORN, John T., 85
HOVER, Sarah, 95
HOWELL, John, 38
HUDSON, James, 60
HUNDLY, Lucy, 5
HUNTER, Betsy, 18, 95
Emma Gertrude, 87
John, 28, 78
John J.J., 97
Joseph, 77
Margaret, 78
Margaret Waybright, 98
Miss, 52
Peggy, 96
Susanna, 77, 78
HUTCHESON, Rachel, 102
Samuel, 102
HUTCHISON, Eliza, 16
John, 60
Samuel, 28

-I-
INGLE, Jeanet, 50

-J-
JACKSON, Daniel B., 79
JACOBS, Amelia Selina, 67
William, 60
JAMISON, Grizelda, 84
John, 77
Sally, 78

Susan, 78
Widow, 77
JENKINS, Mrs., 37
JENNINGS, Sophia Crapster, 25
JOHNS, R. J., 95
JOHNSON, E. S., 86
JOHNSTON, E.S., 97
JONES, Catherine, 16
Eli, 16
John, 60, 77
Mary, 78
Mr., 52
William, 43, 52
JORDAN, Elizabeth, 95
JORDON, Elizabeth, 18
JOURDAN, Adelaide Dielman, 30
Charles H., 30
JUNGLING, ---, 14
JUNKIN, Eleanor Cochran, 10, 24, 27, 63
Joseph, 24

-K-
KELAM, James, 60
KELLER, Benjamin, 4, 74, 91
Ezra, 89
KELLY, Emma K. Scott Eyster, 39
George, 60
Mr., 52
KENNEDAY, John, 60
KERR, David, 18, 95
Joseph, 18, 95
Margaret, 6
Polly, 28
KERRIGAN, James M., 21
KEY, Francis Scott, 7, 84
KIME, Allen B., 40
Frederick D., 40
KING, Nancy, 28
Robert, 28
KIRK, Thomas, 60
KIRKHAM, Emma

Reinewald, 80
Joseph, 80
KITZMILLER, Ann Christina, 57
KLEENHOPP, Jane, 59
KLINHOOF, Jean, 28
KNOX, Margaret, 18, 69, 95
Mary, 18, 95
Samuel, 102
KOBER, ---, 14
KONIG, ---, 14
KOONS, Elizabeth, 85, 86
Jacob, 43
William, 85, 86
KRISE, Abraham, 45, 57, 85, 105
Calvin P., 57
Christian, 57
David, 57
George H., 57
Henry, 57
Jacob, 57
John, 57
Louisa, 45
Lydia, 57
Samuel, 57
Sarah, 90
William, 57
KUHN, Elizabeth Margaret, 20, 103
Johannes, 103
KUNKEL, Ada Serena, 69

-L-
LAMBIL, Mary, 73
LANDERS, Carrie, 57
Florence Bruce, 57
Harriet, 52
Mary Grier, 57
Sarah, 57
William Crawford, 57
LANE, Miss., 52
LANTZ, Charles R., 99
Fannie A., 58
Harry H., 99
Vernon, 58

LARRIMOR,
    Elizabeth, 78
LARRIMORE, Betsy,
    78
LAUGHLIN,
    Alexander, 96
LAVERTY, Ann, 50
    Elizabeth, 51
LAW, Hannah, 18, 95
LAWRENCE, Daniel,
    21
LEECH, Mary, 27
    Robert, 77
LEIDY, Pastor, 13
LILLY, Richard, 36
    Samuel, 36
LINAH, Abraham, 78
    Margaret, 78
LINARD, Abraham,
    96
LIND-LYNN-LINN,
    Catherine
    Harper, 58
    Johann Melchoir, 58
    John, 58
    Matthew, 58
LINN, ---, 14
    Ann, 27
    James, 77
    John, 58
    Nancy, 18, 95
    Polly, 6
    Robert, 6
    Sally, 28
    Samuel, 77
    Solomon, 52
LINNER(LINAH),
    Abraham, 27
LITTLE, David, 73
    Hannah, 43
    Susan, 18, 95
    Susanna, 77
    Ursula, 52
LITTLE(KLEIN),
    Peter, 25
    Susannah, 25
LIVERS, Arnold, 14,
    36, 58
    Jacoba Clementina,
    14, 36
    Jacoba Clementine,
    58
LOCKLIN, Mr., 52

LOMER, Mr., 52
LONAL, Abraham, 77
LONG, Margaret, 18,
    95
    Mary, 18, 95
    Philip, 58
    Rosanna Fuss, 19
    William, 18, 95
LONGLEY, Mary D.,
    43
    Thomas, 43
LONGWELL,
    Hamilton, 59
    Howard, 59
    James, 59
    Jane, 59, 78
    Jennie, 59
    John E. McKaleb, 59
    John K., 59, 64
    Joseph Augustus, 59
    Joseph M., 59
    Margaret, 59
    Martha Agnew, 59
    Mathew, 28
    Matthew, 59
    Sallie, 59
    Sarah J., 59
    Sarah McKaleb, 64
    Wilson, 59
LORIMORE, Thomas,
    77
LOUDEN, William, 60
LOVE, Polly, 28
    Robert, 77
    Thomas, 45
LOWMAN, Catherine,
    106
    George, 105
    John, 105, 106
    Mary Zimmerman,
    105
    Rebeca, 106
    Rebecca, 106
LOWTHER, James,
    60

-M-
MCALISTER, Betsy,
    78
    James, 77
    John, 77, 78
    John W., 78
    Mary, 78

MCALLEN, Joseph,
    60
MCALLISTER,
    James, 53
MCCALISTER,
    Alexander, 78
    James, 78
    Lucinda, 78
    Mary, 78
MCCALLEN, Polly,
    27
MCCALLISTER,
    William, 66
MCCANDLESS,
    Elizabeth, 3
MCCELLAND, John,
    63
MCCLANAHAN,
    Ann, 78
    John, 78
MCCLARY, John, 60
MCCLEAF, Polly
    Hockensmith, 56
MCCLEAFE, Mary,
    96
MCCLELLAN, Miss,
    52
MCCLONAHAN,
    John, 27
MCCOLESTER,
    Barbara, 52
MCCOLLUM, Mary,
    88
MCCORD, Mr., 84
MCCORMACK,
    James, 60
MCCOY, James, 60
MCCREA, Ann, 63
    Anna Mary, 63
    Elizabeth, 63, 77, 78
    Jane, 78
    Mary, 63
    Sophia, 63
    Sophia Thomson, 63
    Thomas, 77
    Thompson, 78
    Thomson, 63
MCCREARY, Ann, 78
    Maria, 78
    Nancy, 18, 95
    Robert, 77, 78
    William, 52, 63
MCCRERY, John, 60

MCCULLOUGH,
  Annie, 61
  Archie, 63
MCCUNE, Ann, 27
  John, 27
  Mary, 78
  Thomas, 77, 78
MCCURDY, James,
  28
  Robert, 28
  William, 28
MCDONALD, Betsy,
  88
  George, 60
  Robert, 60
MCDONNEL,
  Catherine, 16
MCDOWELL,
  Alexander, 63
  Andrew, 42, 63
  Andrew Nathan, 64
  James, 63
  Jane Denny, 42, 64
  John, 63
  Margaret, 63
  Mary, 63, 64
  Mary Maxwell
    (Maxell), 64
  Nancy, 63
  Nathan, 63
  Patrick, 63
  Susan, 63
  Susanna Maxwell
    (Maxell), 64
  Thomas, 63
  William, 63, 64
MCELHENNY,
  Nancy, 28
MCGAUGHY, Hugh
  F., 53
  James, 27
MCGINN, Miss, 52
MCGUFFIN,
  Elizabeth, 96
MCGUIGAN,
  Barbary, 18, 95
  Jane, 51
  Robert, 18, 95
MCGURGAN, Robert,
  52
MCHONER, Newton,
  97

MCILHENNY, James,
  77, 78
  John, 77
  Maria, 78
  Sally, 78
MCILLHENNY,
  Margaret, 52
MCILVANE, Moses,
  77
MCINTIRE, John, 6
  Margaret, 6
MCKALEB, John, 3,
  77
  John K., 59
  Margaret Ann, 3
  Mary Ann Clinton, 3
  Mary Jane, 2, 3
  Sarah, 59
  Sarah(Sallie), 59
MCKALEB-
MCKELLIP, Jane, 65
  John, 64
  Joseph, 64, 65
  Joseph Augustus, 64
  Martha, 65
  Mary, 65
MCKALIP, John, 77
MCKAY, William, 60
MCKEAN, Betsy, 52
MCKEE, John, 18, 95
  Miss, 52
  Nancy, 18, 95
  Peggy, 18, 95
  Susanna, 65
  Thomas, 65
MCKEEHAN, Jane,
  18, 95
  Martha, 18, 95
MCKELLIP, Ann, 78
  James, 65
  John, 65, 78
  Mary, 65
  Mary A., 65
  Sarah Jane, 65
MCKELOB, John, 78
MCKINLEY, Sally,
  18, 95
MCKINNEY, Esther,
  78
  Rob., 52
  Robert, 78
  Susanne, 78
MCKINNY, John, 77

MCKINSIE, James,
  60
MCKISSIE, Ann, 88
MCMILLAN, Samuel,
  53
MCNAIR, Agnes, 66
  Agnes(or Ann), 65
  Alexander, 65, 66,
    67
  Ann Jane, 67
  Anne, 66
  Antionette, 67
  Elizabeth, 66
  Ellen, 67
  Eugenia, 66
  Harry, 67
  Hiram, 67
  Jane, 67
  Lavina, 66, 67
  Livinia, 39
  Margaret, 66, 67
  Maria, 66
  Martha, 66
  Robert, 65, 66, 67
  Samuel, 39, 66, 67
  Samuel Newton, 67
  Samuel Scott, 66, 67
  Statira C. Bigler, 67
  Susan, 66
  Susannah, 66
  Watson W., 67
  William, 66
  William Burns, 67
MCNAUGHTON,
  Hester, 8
MCNEALY, ---, 27
MCPHERSON,
  Agnes, 64
MCSHERRY,
  Barnabas, 18, 95,
    96
MAGINLY, James,
  102
  Jane Eliza, 102
MAINS, Sarah, 51
MAJOR, Robert, 77
MAJORS, Jane, 52
  Samuel, 52
MANN, Henry, 40
MANNING, Charles
  Augustus, 60
  H.F., 68

Harry F., 30, 60
MANSON, Anna
    Maria, 60
    Johannan, 60
    Mary Ann, 60
MARING, Geo. G., 86
MARONY, Philip, 60
MARSDEN, John H., 51
MARSHALL, Eliza, 52
    Elizabeth, 61
    James, 61, 101
    John, 60
    S., 28
MARTIN, ---, 19
    Anna Margaret, 61
    George, 19
    Henry, 106
    James, 61
    James P., 61
    John, 61
    Lewis, 61
    Maria Magdalena, 61
    Martin, 61
    Mary Magdalena, 70
    Mathias, 61
    Samuel, 61
MATTHIAS, Anna Margaretha, 61
    John Jacob, 61
MAXELL, Anna Eliza, 81
    Catherine, 67
    Charles Albert, 62
    Ella May, 62
    Francis A., 21
    Jane Ferguson, 94, 105
    Margaret C., 105
    Mary Agnes, 94
    Samuel, 94, 105
    Samuel Robert, 62
    William Fleming, 62
MAXELL (MAXWELL),
    Albert Heck, 62
    Jane Ferguson, 62
    Samuel, 25, 62
MAXWELL, Agnes, 63
    Catherine, 63, 68
    Elizabeth, 63
    Francis Allison, 62
    Henry, 62
    James, 63
    John, 63
    Mary Agnes, 62
    Mary Catherine, 62
    Patrick, 63
    Racheal, 63
    Ruth, 63
    Samuel, 68
    Samuel J., 62
    Susannah, 63
    Thaddeus(Theodore) Augusts, 62
    William, 62, 63, 68
MAXWELL-MAXELL, Samuel, 62
MAYNARD, John, 60
MEADE, General, 4
MEHRING, ---, 14
MERCKLE, ---, 14
MERONEY, Henry, 60
MILES, George, 60
MILLER, Ann Rebecca, 103
    Ephraim, 40
    John, 60
    Martin, 40
    Rachel, 78
    Richard Philip, 28
MILLS, Abner, 67, 68
    Catherine Maxwell (Maxell), 68
    Elizabeth, 37
    Emma M., 67, 68
    Helen Catherine, 67
    Justinian, 37
    Rebecca, 68
    Samuel, 67
    Sarah Jane, 67
MINNICK, W.G., 96
MONTGOMERY, Jane, 88
MOOR, Miss, 52
MOORE, Annie, 44
    Daniel, 52
    Edgar H., 68
    Emma, 68
    Emma Chase, 30
    Georgia, 30, 68
    James, 18, 68, 95
    Jane Scott, 68
    Margaret, 68
    Martha, 28
    Mary J., 3
    Miss, 52
    Rebecca, 68
    Rebecca Delaney, 68
    Rebecca Dielman, 26
    Rebecca Dielman Quinn, 30
    Rob, 52
MORRISON, David, 18, 52, 68, 95
    David A., 68
    Hannah, 18, 95
    Harriet, 18, 68, 95
    Helen E., 68
    John R., 68
    Penninah J., 68
    Reuben, 68, 76
    William B., 68
MORROW, James, 69
    Jeremiah, 69
    John, 69
    John Knox, 69
    Margaret, 69
    Mary Lockhart, 69
    Rebecca, 23
    Sarah, 69
MORT, John, 69
MOTTER, Alice, 71
    Alice C., 3
    Anna Margaret, 34, 70
    Barbary, 70, 92
    Carrie May, 71
    Catherine, 5
    Charlotte, 71
    Elizabeth, 1, 70
    Ellen, 71
    Grace, 71
    Harriet H., 70
    Isaac, 69, 71
    Isaac H., 70
    Isaac M., 69, 71
    Jeanette, 69
    John C., 60
    Joshua, 70, 71
    Joshua S., 21, 69
    Leathy A., 71
    Leathy A.Stokes, 69

Lewis, 1, 5, 34, 61,
  69, 70, 71, 92
Lewis Edwin, 71
Lewis Martin, 3, 69,
  71
Lewis R., 34
Louis Martin, 70
Magdalena, 70
Magdalena Motter,
  71
Mary Josephine, 72
Mary M. Martin, 71
Mary Martin, 1, 69,
  70, 72, 92
Samuel, 30, 70, 71
Valentine, 70, 71
William, 70, 72
william, 71
William Rudisil, 71
MOUTZ, Mary
  Antionette, 67
MUNRO, Isabella, 72
  Robert G., 72
MUNSHOWER, ---,
  18
MURDOCK, Ann, 72
  Mary, 72
  William, 72
MURPHY, Patrick, 60
MUSGROVE,
  Catherine, 78
  Sally, 28
  Samuel, 77
MUSHOWER, Harry,
  75
MUSSELLMAN, A.
  C., 40
  John, 15
MYERS, Jacob, 96
  John, 18, 95, 96
  Martha, 18

-N-
NEALL, Bennett, 60
NEELY, George
  McBeth, 62
  Maude Amelia
  Maxell, 62
NEGRO, Jack, 78
  Kelly, 78
NEIL, Hannah, 96
NICHOLS, Ninion, 60
NOBLE, Capt., 8

Harriet E. Birnie, 8
NOLTON, Peggy, 18,
  95
NUT, N., 52

-O-
OCKER, ---, 18
OGLE, Benjamin, 72,
  104
OGLER, Susannah
  Singer, 91
OHLER, ---, 18
  A.C., 73
  Alice Jane, 75
  Alice Virginia, 74
  Amanda Susannah,
  75
  Andrew Jackson, 73
  Ann E., 75
  Anna C., 74, 75
  Anna Shorb, 75
  Beecher, 74
  Cameron, 74
  Catherine, 11, 68,
  73, 74, 76
  Christena, 73
  Christina, 74
  David, 74
  David S., 73, 75
  David Samuel, 73
  Dorothea, 72, 73, 74
  Edward, 75
  Edward T., 75
  Edwin, 73
  Elizabeth, 72, 75
  Elizabeth (Betsy),
  76
  Elizabeth Catherine,
  74
  Elizabeth(Betsy), 68
  Ellanaro Francis, 75
  Emma Jane, 74
  Emory, 73, 75
  Esther, 76
  Esther Elizabeth, 73
  Ezra Levi, 74
  Fannie V., 73, 75
  Flora Belle, 73
  Frederick, 73
  Gearge Adam, 73
  George, 72, 73, 75
  George A., 76
  George Adam, 73,

  74
  George H., 76
  George W., 75
  Hannah, 74
  Harriet, 73
  Harriet Marenda, 75
  Harry, 75
  Harry B., 75
  Helen, 74
  Helen M., 75
  Helen May, 73
  Hettie, 73
  Ida, 73
  Ida S., 48
  Isaac, 55, 56, 74, 97
  Isaiah James, 74
  Isamiah, 74
  Isamish
    Hockensmith, 97
  Isiamiah
    Hockensmith, 55
  J.T., 73
  Jacob, 74
  Jacob Rowe, 73
  James, 73, 74
  James Henry, 74
  John, 11, 72, 74
  John E., 75
  John George, 75
  John Thomas, 73,
  74, 75, 76
  Joseph, 74, 75
  Katie T., 73
  Levi, 74
  Louisa, 11, 76
  Louise, 75
  Margaret, 73
  Mary (Merry), 76
  Mary Catherine, 75
  Mary E., 75
  Mary Ellen, 74
  Maud, 75
  Maude, 93
  Maude R., 75
  Micheal, 74
  Minnie, 73, 74
  Phillip Jacob, 73, 74
  Phillipp, 72
  Phillipp Jacob, 72
  Rosannah Ott, 73
  Rose, 73
  Sallie Belle, 55, 74
  Samuel, 74, 75

Samuel G., 48, 91
Samuel George, 73
Sarah, 74
Sarah Jane, 73, 74
Thomas, 68, 73, 76
William Daniel, 74
William Morris, 74
Wm. Henry, 75
OISTER, Peter, 39
O'NEAL, Eveline
    Crapster, 25
  Walter, 25
ORENDORF, ---, 14
OTT, Rosanna, 72
  Rosannah, 73
OTTA, Eliza, 57
OVERHOLTZER,
  Jacob, 53
  Lewis, 76
  Lewis A., 76
  Mary Alma, 81
  Mary Jane, 76
  Rebecca Ann, 76
OYSTER, ---, 18
  George, 40
  Jacob, 40, 41
  John, 40
  John H., 40
  Maria, 40
  Mary, 40
  Samuel, 40, 41

-P-

PARKE, Martha
    Jane, 84
PARSON, Mr., 66
PATTERSON, Ann,
    88
  Geo. M., 76
  George, 76
  Hugh, 18, 95
  Isaac M., 79
  James, 101
  Jane, 18, 95
  John, 76
  L., 76
  Lydia, 76
  Mary Lowe, 30
  Matthew, 76
  Milliard, 12
  Molley, 18, 95
  Nellie G., 12
  Robert H., 76
PAXTON, Cassandra,
    18, 95
  Clara E., 77
  E. J., 77
  Emily J., 77
  James, 18, 95
  Jean, 28
  John William, 77
  Margaret, 78
  Mary, 28
  Nathan, 27
  S. C., 77
  Samuel C., 77
  Thomas, 77
  William, 77, 78
PEARCE(PIERCE),
    Joshua, 60
PENN, William, 104
PHILPOT, Warren,
    60
PHILPOY (TAYLOR),
    Charles, 60
PICKING, Esther
    Burns, 103
  John, 103
  Sarah, 103, 104
PORTER, Jane
    Denny, 64
POTTS, Emma, 103
PRATT, Captain, 82
PRICE, John, 60

-Q-

QUINN, Bernard, 30
  Francis, 60
  H. A., 30
  Harry A., 68
  Josephine Mary, 30
  Nina, 30, 60, 68

-R-

RAHAUSER, John,
    70
RANDOLPH, Eliza,
    18, 95
  Joseph, 18, 52, 95
  Nathaniel, 18, 95
  Sally, 18, 52, 95
REA, William, 52
REASER, George B.,
    71
REDFORD, Thomas,
    81
REESE, Catherine, 6,
    16
  Henry, 6
  Violetta, 16
REEVES, Jacob H.,
    80
REID, Francis, 52, 77
  Margaret, 78
  Mary, 78
  Patrick, 18, 95
  Paul, 84
REIFSNIDER, John,
    80
  John I., 80
  Margaret Ellen, 80
REINEWALD,
    Catherine
    Sommer, 80
  Charles, 80
  Henry J.Mat, 80
  Joseph Lewis, 80
  Mary M., 80
REYNOLDS, William,
    63
RHEA, Joseph, 80
  Wm. Crawford, 101
RHINEDOLLAR,
    Amelia, 78
RHODES, Blanche G.
    Byers, 12
  Elisha, 60
  J. Lewis, 12
  Jacob, 60
RICHARDS, Ann, 37
RIDOUT, John, 95
RIFE, Mary Fisher,
    90
RIFFLE, G., 16
  George C., 16
  James Bishop, 16
  Laura J., 16
  Lydia Ann C., 16
  M., 16
  Maria, 16
RITTER, Ernest W.,
    97
ROBERTSON, G. W.,
    81
  Robert, 27
ROBINSON, Betsy,
    52
  Hannah, 18, 95
  Margaret, 96
  Micheal, 81

Robert, 77
RODDY, Frank, 31
ROSS, Eleanor, 18, 95
　James, 77, 78
　William, 52
ROW, Christiana Smith, 92
　Lucy Ann, 82, 92
　Micheal, 92
　Miss., 52
ROW(ROWE), ---, 18
　Abraham, 81
　Andrew, 81, 82
　Arthur, 81
　Barbara, 81
　Elizabeth, 81, 82
　Frederick, 81
　George, 81, 82
　Jacob, 81, 82
　John, 81, 82
　Joseph, 81, 82
　Julian, 81
　Margaret, 82
　Micheal, 81, 82
　Nathaniel, 82
　Sally, 82
　Samuel, 81, 82
　Susan Baker, 82
　William, 82
ROWE, Anna Eliza Maxell, 62
　Anne Mary, 82
　Charles, 62
　Charles F., 81
　Edward Norman Hoke, 81
　Elizabeth, 105
　Eugene L., 35
　Fannie Belle, 81, 99
　Howard M., 81
　Jacob, 90
　James A., 81, 99
　Joseph, 73, 81, 96
　Mary Anna, 100
　Rebecca C., 90
　Sally, 81
　Sarah Ann, 81
　Sarah Hoke, 99
　Sarah Jane, 96
　Susan Adaline, 73
　Susan Baker, 82
　Susan F., 81

Susanna Baker, 96
Susannah Baker, 73
RUDISIL, Alice, 69, 71
RUDISILL, Sarah, 50
　Tobias, 50, 71
RUFF, Hannah, 57
RUPERT, George, 96
RUPP, Margaret, 19
RUSH, Dr., 2
RUTHRAUFF, Rev., 70

-S-

SADLER, ---, 14
SANDOE, Rebecca, 67
SCARBOROUGH,
　Joseph J., 83
　Rogers Birnie, 83
　William, 83
　Wm., 9
SCHENECH, Sue, 9
SCHROETER,
　Johann Daniel, 100
SCHUYLER, Jennett, 2
SCHWAL, Anna Elizabeth, 4
SCOTT, David, 93
　Elizabeth, 84
　Francis, 7, 84
　Hugh, 84
　Jean, 84
　John, 84
　Margaret, 7, 84
　Margaret Craig, 7, 84
　Patrick, 60
　Upton, 84
SEABROOK, Alice, 83, 105
　Alice M., 82
　Catherine Zimmerman, 82
　Elisha A., 82
　Katherine Zimmerman, 83
　William, 105
　William C., 82
　William Chamberlain, 82,

83
SEABROOKE,
　Gideon, 52
SEHOM, Edward, 60
SEITZ, Elizabeth, 6
　Erastus, 6
　Hetty Maria, 6
　Jeremiah, 6
　Joshua, 6
　Louisa, 16
　Louise, 16
　Stewart, 84
SENSS, ---, 14
SENTMAN, Amanda Isabella, 84
　Clara S., 84
　Pearson Peterso, 84
　S., 96
　Sallie A. C., 84
　Solomon, 36, 84, 89, 97
SHANK, John, 60, 106
SHARETS, Lucinda Catherine, 97, 98
SHAW, Elizabeth, 84
　Hugh, 77, 84
　Joseph, 85
　Moses, 84
　Samuel, 85
　Susan E., 84
　Thomas, 84, 85
　William, 43, 85
SHEADS(SHEETS, Maria (Mary), 98
SHEANER,
　Elizabeth, 18, 95
　Melcher, 18, 95
SHEETS, Abraham, 53, 85, 86
　Alfred, 86
　Ann Elizabeth (Ella M.), 86
　Barbara E., 85
　Barbara(Barbary) Ann, 85
　Daniel, 85, 86
　David, 85, 86
　David Myers, 85
　David Sentman, 86
　Florence Virginia, 85
　Frances, 86
　George, 85, 86

Hannah, 86
Hannah Elizabeth, 86
Harriet Ida Isadora, 86
Harriet Virginia, 86
Harry, 85
Harry Pitzer, 86
Isadore M., 85
Jacob, 86
Jacob Sentman, 85
John, 86
Lizzie, 86
Lydia A., 85
Lydia F., 86
Margaret, 86
Mary, 90
Mary Jane, 86
Matilda Ann, 86
Mattie R., 86
Miranda, 86
Peter, 86
Riley, 86
Sarah C., 86
Savilla, 86
Sentman, 85
Susan E., 86
SHEETS(SHEADS),
  Abraham, 85
  Catherine, 85
  Hannah, 85
  Isaac, 85
  Jacob, 85
  Mary (Maria), 90
SHEETZ, Jacob, 85
SHEHAN, Daniel, 60
SHIELDS, Agnes, 88
  Andrew Jackson, 89
  Banner, 88
  David, 88
  Ebenezer, 17, 88, 89
  Eliza Ann, 52
  Henry, 88
  James, 47, 88
  Jane Bentley
    Williams, 17, 46, 47, 88
  Jane Gilliland, 47
  Jefferson, 89
  John, 88
  John Henry, 89
  Margaret, 88
  Mary, 88

  Maxwell, 101
  Patterson, 88
  Robert, 87
  Samuel, 88
  William, 17, 46, 47, 86, 87, 88
  William Vanburren, 89
SHIRK, Maria, 106
SHOCKEY, Eli, 106
SHOEMAKER,
  Abraham, 77, 78
  D. L., 89
  Daniel, 89
  Daniel Lawrence, 89
  Elizabeth, 89
  Herbert, 60
  Jacob, 78
  Jerimiah David, 89
  John M., 89
  John Maxell, 89
  Margaret, 78
  May G., 89
  Walter, 97
  William, 77
  William Bowers, 89
SHORB, Ann, 73, 76
  Anna Catherine, 74
  Tom, 89
SHOWMAKER, Otis, 93
SHRINER, Angeline A., 20
SHRIVER, Andrew, 90
  Anna, 90
  Barbara, 90
  Betsy, 18, 95
  Catherine, 90
  Christian, 90
  Elizabeth, 90
  Ernest R., 97
  Frederick Wm., 90
  George Lewis, 90
  Jacob, 90
  Lewis, 55, 90, 98
  Magdalena, 96
  Mary, 90, 105
  Rachel, 90
  Sally, 52
  Sarah, 90
  Susannah, 90
SHUFF, Charles O.,

  90
  Ella Gillelan, 49
SHUNK, Aberillia, 90
  Benjamin, 43, 90
  Mary, 90
SILVER, Samuel, 60
SIMONTON, Rev., 79
  William, 90
SIMPSON, Sophia, 25
SINGER, Ann
  Elizabeth, 91
  Charlotte, 91
  Eva, 91
  John, 91
  Mary, 91
  Samuel, 91
  Sarah, 91
  Susannah, 73
SINK, George, 77
SITES, Jeremiah, 16
SIX, George, 77
SKAGGS, William, 60
SKILES, H., 91
  Hopkins, 91
  L., 91
  Lettice, 91
  Thomas A., 91
  William E., 91
SLAYBAUGH,
  Elizabeth
  Hockensmith, 56
SLEMMONS, John, 79, 92
SLEMONS, Rebecca, 28
SLUSS, ---, 18
  Alice Jane, 24
  Barbara, 56
  John, 24, 56, 82, 92, 93
  Micheal, 92
SMITH, ---, 18
  Albert, 21
  Barbary Motter, 71
  Charles, 70, 71, 92
  Christian, 60
  Christiana, 56, 93
  Christina, 82
  Elizabeth, 56, 78, 93
  Ella J. R., 92
  Emma Alice, 92
  Frances, 92, 93
  George, 56, 82, 92,

93
Henry, 60
James, 77, 78
James A.M., 53
John, 52, 60, 93
John W., 93
Maria, 93
Mary, 52, 93
Nicholas, 77
Obadiah, 77
Robert, 47
Samuel, 77
Sarah, 78
Stephen, 92, 93
Susan, 92, 93
SNATZELL, Louisa, 52
Miss, 52
SNIDER, ---, 14, 28
SNITZEL, Elizabeth, 76
SNIVELY, Mary Ann, 70, 71
SNODGRASS, James, 7
SNOWDEN, Elizabeth, 37, 38
SNYDER, Margaret, 78
SONNINGER, Bertha, 93
SPALDING, Basil, 37
Catherine, 37
Catherine Green, 37
Elizabeth, 37
Henry, 37
SPANGLER, George, 100
SPENCE, John, 93
SPRENKLE, Christine, 16
Daniel, 16
Elizabeth, 16
Mary, 16
William, 16
SPRINGER, Edwin, 93
Mary M., 93
STAMBAUGH, Anna, 93
Effie B., 75
Frank, 93
Freda, 93

Jacob, 75, 93
Rebecca, 102
Ruth, 93
STANSBURY, Amelia, 62
Anna, 73
Jeminia, 62
Nicholas, 62
STAUFFER, David, 96
STEEL, William, 16
STEVENSON, Isabel McNair, 66
James, 66, 77
Miss, 52
Peggy, 78
William, 27, 77, 78
STEVINSON, Miss, 95
STEWART, Andrew, 52
Elizabeth, 52
John, 18, 95
Margaret, 51
Rosanna, 18, 95
STIER, ---, 14
STINCHCOMB, Nathaniel, 96
STOCKSLAGER, Anna, 104
STOEVER, Rev., 61
STOKES, Helen Margaret, 103
Henry, 21, 93, 94
J. Henry, 21
Margaret, 103
Mary J., 94
Mary Lizzie, 94
STONER, Micheal, 12
STOREY, ---, 95
STOVER, Jacob, 16
John Casper, 4
STREET, Mary, 52
SUMWALT, Isaac, 94
John, 94
John H., 62
Rachel, 94
Runyon, 94
SUTTON, W.B., 95
SWARTZ, Lousia, 97
SWEENEY, Miss, 52
SWENY, Amos T., 94

C., 94
Christina, 94
Columbia Alice, 94
James, 94

-T-
TANNENHILL, James, 60
TARBEE, John, 38
TEST, John, 60
THOMAS, James, 96
THOMPSON, Ann, 78
Eleanor, 78
Elizabeth, 78
Henry, 14
Hugh, 78
John, 78
Mary, 78
Peggy, 28
Polly, 28
Robert, 78
Samuel, 27, 78
Sarah, 78
William, 78
THOMSON, Hugh, 77
Jno., 77
Robert, 77
Samuel, 77
TIERS, Edward, 60
Emily, 60
TIPPER, Cambell, 53
TOMSON, William, 95
TOOT, Mr., 66
TOPPER, Jacob L., 22
TOTT, Jane, 57
TOUNGE, Richard, 60
TRAXEL(TROXEL), 18
TROXELL, Charles, 96
Frederick W., 96
James W., 96, 103
Joanna, 100
John, 96
John W., 20
Peter, 61, 96
Sarah Jane Rowe, 96

-U-
UHLHORN, Rev., 13

-V-
VALENTINE, Elmer, 74
Helen Ohler, 75
Martin V., 73
Milton, 44
VANCE, Eleanor, 47

-W-
WACHTER, Denton D., 75
Mary E. Ohler, 75
WADDELL, Esther, 88
Rachel, 88
WADDLE, ---, 18
Joseph, 97
Sarah, 97
WAGNER, Margaret, 53
WALKER, Andrew, 28, 53, 77, 78
Jane, 53
Mary, 77
William, 78
WANTZ, Robert, 97
WARD, Julia, 36
WARE, Margaret, 88
WARTENBACKER, Louis, 16
WATCHTER, Denton A., 74, 97
WAYBRIGHT, Abraham, 98
Abram, 98
Ann Margaret, 97
Emma Amelia, 97
Franklin Abraham, 97
Franklin Abram, 98
Harriet May, 97
Harriet Rebecca, 98
Jacob, 98
Jacob Fickes, 97, 98
Margaret, 98
Margaret E., 97
Margaret Fickes, 98
Margaret Mary, 97
Micheal, 98
Oliver J., 97

Robert Lewis, 98
Samuel Abraham Lincoln, 98
Sarah E., 97
WAYGAND, William, 98
WEAGLEY,
Catherine, 16
Isaac, 16
Lydia Ann, 16
Malinda, 16
WEANT, Christiana Row, 82
David, 98
Lydia Ann, 98
WEAVER, David, 106
WEEMS, Fanny, 77
Frances, 78
WEIKERT, Mary, 105, 106
Peter, 90, 98
WELLER, Cyrus, 62
Henry Ferguson, 62
Roy Forest, 62
Thaddeus Augustus, 62
WELLS, Richard, 60
WELTY, David, 106
Elizabeth, 106
Harriet, 106
Henry, 106
John Zimmerman, 106
Nancy, 106
Rebecca, 106
WERTS, Elizabeth, 16
Lucinda, 16
WETZEL, Daniel, 52
WHARLEN, James, 28
WHARTON, James, 51, 77
WHEELAN, Christopher, 60
WHEELER, Ann, 36
Samuel, 60
WHILE, Miss, 62
WHITE, John Dinwiddie, 99
Sarah Ann Ruth, 99
Walter W., 81, 99
WHITEHALL,

Hannah, 63
WHITMORE,
Barbara, 19
Benjamin, 19
Catherine E., 102
Christian, 19
David, 102
Elizabeth, 19
Fred., 19
George, 102
John Jacob, 102
Mary, 19
Mary B., 102
Milton, 102
Rebeca, 102
Sarah Cover, 102
Simon, 102
Susan, 102
WICKHAM, Elenor, 36
Nathaniel, 36
Priscilla Tyler, 36
Sabina, 36
WIEART, Jacob, 52
WIERKERT, Joseph, 83
Mary, 83
WILDER, Anna Margaret, 98
Margaret Anna, 98
WILLIAMS, Henry, 99, 101
Jane, 18, 95, 99
Jane Bentley, 87
Jane Bently, 86
Jane Witherow Cooper, 101
John, 86, 87
Washington, 99
WILLIAR, Kattie, 75
WILLSON, Walter D., 22
WILSON, Ann, 28
Betsy, 52
Charles, 77
Edith Bolling Galt, 42
Isabel, 44
Jane, 78
John, 78
Mary, 78
Peggy, 27
Rebecca, 78

Sally, 52
William, 43, 77
Woodrow, 42
WINEGARTEN,
  George, 103
WINGARD, Harriet, 42
WINNICK, W. G., 97
WINTER, Anna B., 99
Catherine, 100
Christian, 100
Columbia, 40, 100, 101
Elizabeth, 99, 100
Frances(Frank), 101
Francis, 100
George, 99, 100
George Jacob Rowe, 100
Harvey C., 99
Henry, 99, 100, 101
J., 100
Jacob, 99, 100
Jacob Rowe, 99
Joanna, 99
Joanna Troxell, 99
John, 70, 100
Joseph, 100
Margaret, 99
Margaret E., 99, 100
Margureite Gerver, 100
Martin, 100
Mary Ann, 100
Mary Ann Rowe, 100, 101
Mary Anne Rowe, 99
Mary Frances, 100
Mary Magdena, 99
Mary Margaret, 39, 100, 101
Susan, 101
Susanna, 100
Tereasa, 99
WITHEROW,
  Bettsey, 101
Eliza, 101
Elizabeth, 101
Jane, 18, 95
John, 18, 61, 95, 101, 102
Margaret, 18, 95, 101, 102
Margaret Barbour, 61, 102
Mary, 102
Moses, 102
Polly, 18, 95
Rachel, 102
Rebecca, 101
S. McClean, 101
Samuel, 18, 95, 101, 102
Samuel D., 102
Sarah, 18, 61, 95, 101
William, 102
WOLF, ---, 14
William, 16
WOODS, Michael, 46
WORK, Dorcas, 96
WRIGHT, John B., 38

-Y-
YINGLING, Urian, 91
YOUNG, John, 81

-Z-
ZACHARIAS, Anna
  Elizabeth, 104
Anna Stockslager, 103
Christian, 19, 20, 103, 104
Christian Thomas, 103
Esther Ann, 103
Helen, 104
Henry, 103
Hettie, 103
Horace E., 103
John, 104
John L., 104
Maria Elizabeth
  Catherine, 104
Mary, 91
Mary E., 96
Mary Elizabeth, 20, 103
Mathias, 19, 20, 91, 103, 104
Mathias Picking, 103
Maurice C., 103
Ralph L., 104
Richard M., 104
Sarah, 19
Sarah Adelaide, 103
Sarah Picking, 20
William Jackson, 104
ZACHARIS, Anna, 20
Anna Z., 20
Elizabeth Margaret
  Kuhn, 103
John, 20
Mary, 20
Mathias P., 20
Mathias S., 20
ZACHARIUS, John
  Flavius, 103
ZAHN, ---, 14
ZECK, Detrick, 96
Mary Ann Rowe, 96
ZIMMERMAN, Ann, 83
Anna, 105, 106
Annie, 57
Barbara, 106
Catherine, 105
Charles Francis, 105
Edna Mae, 105
Elizabeth, 106
Esther, 106
Ezra Rowe, 62, 105
Fanny Catherine, 83
Hans, 83, 106
Joseph, 105, 106
Judith, 106
Luther Maxell, 105
Margaret C. Maxell, 62
Maria Shirk, 83
Mary, 105, 106
Mary Shriver, 105
Mary Weikert, 105
Nancy Ann, 106
Peter, 83, 104, 105, 106
Samuel, 106
Susanna, 106
Thaddeus Elmer, 105
ZOLICKOFFER,
  Elizabeth, 9
ZOLLINGER,
  Elizabeth Row, 82

www.ingramcontent.com/pod-product-compliance
Lightning Source LLC
Chambersburg PA
CBHW070458090426
42735CB00012B/2603